Forbidden Psychology

&

Manipulation, NLP and Body Language Stoicism

Secrets of the Dark to Penetrate and Bend
Vulnerable Minds to Your Will

Blake Reyes

TABLE OF CONTENTS

Forbidden Psychology

Manipulation, NLP and Body Language Stoicism

FORBIDDEN PSYCHOLOGY

Beyond Mind Games - The Complete Guide to Discover Techniques of Mass Manipulation and Subdue Anyone's Mind through Subliminal Persuasion and Dark NLP

by

Blake Reyes

INTRODUCTION

The aura that covers the forbidden is irresistible. Seduced people are not satisfied until they fulfill the desires that the unallowed situations awaken. If they fail to achieve them, they fall into the eternal question: "What if I had done it?" Living forever in these illusions.

According to psychology, it is natural that people want to stop curiosity and, mainly, try new things because freedom, security, and independence are the most delicious. Just like the biblical story that says that Eve did not resist temptation and tasted the forbidden fruit, we also always have many forbidden fruits that arouse will. We constantly imagine the pleasure they can provide us.

This happens right from birth where, at each moment, the human being is in constant learning about the moral, ethical, and social limits, each one with its values and rules. Thus, the child is always learning what is right or wrong, and the first people who will dictate this path are parents and, soon after, society, which continues to inject limits and points that cannot be overcome.

Consequently, our condition and prohibition lead us to experiment, and attract us to what is denied; after all, the forbidden is better. This is because we always need to know more and test how far we can go, get to know new airs, to venture out, even if later we will face the consequences.

Want to be more lovable, valued, admired, cherished, and worshiped? Do you feel like people are manipulating you, and making you do things you don't want to do?

Are you sick and tired of having someone taking

advantage? Do you want to stand up, be in control, and never feel disrespected?

What if I told you I could make you a master persuader who can almost easily and most importantly... unknowingly get everything you want?

Here's a preview of the important techniques that you'll learn from this book:

Convince even the world's most stubborn guy, and make him almost blindly obey your commands!

Make friends everywhere you go – it's easy to learn some "mind-tricks" that you will enjoy anywhere.

Make anyone follow your orders so quietly that they won't even know what's going on.

"The Secrets of Manipulation" will teach you tested techniques to win every debate!

Methods of Persuasion.

Gain control of ANY social circle Instantly.

How to get the truth out of someone at any time.

How to say thrilling and attentive stories.

How to turn yourself into a super positive person and make others appealing to you!

The technique to convince and PERSUADE effectively.

Be irresistibly attractive and interesting to others.

CHAPTER 1

FORBIDDEN PSYCHOLOGY

Psychology is a study of mental processes and human comportment, according to the American Psychological Association (APA). Therefore, psychology refers to the study of the mind, how it functions, and how it influences human actions.

The study of psychology encompasses all facets of human life, from brain functions to countries' behavior, from child growth to caring for the elderly, and from scientific research centers to mental health programs, "understanding behavior" is the role of psychologists in the most varied contexts. (APA)

Psychologists and psychiatrists work together to support people with mental health problems, but they are not the same. While the psychologist treats a patient through psychotherapy, helping to relieve symptoms through behavioral changes, the psychiatrist, who is a doctor specializing in psychiatry, focuses more on prescribing medications and other interventions to manage mental health conditions.

Psychology is now considered to be the science that studies the human "mind" and behavior. Being both an area of activity (applied science) and a field of research (academic science), psychology studies human behavior and the functioning of the human mind, that is, how conscious, and unconscious cognitive processes influence how we make decisions and behave.

As a multifaceted discipline, psychology includes many

sub-fields of study such as human development, sport, mental health, clinical, social, community behavior, and cognitive processes, to name a few.

The researchers of psychology aim to understand and explain how thoughts, behaviors, and emotions work.

Now, what is forbidden psychology?

Forbidden psychology is a term for explaining Psychology's dark side. It revolves around all of the things culture is warning us not to do. Those are things the UN and Genova organisations regulate and prohibit.

If someone has the mandate to understand how and why we humans are doing what we are doing, they may use it against others. Here are some of the other things you can do if you are aware of forbidden psychology:

- Manipulation
- Mind control
- Emotional Seduction
- Mental abuse
- Deception
- Brainwashing
- Torture

Now all of the above things look negative and cruel to someone. The truth is that life is harsh too, and someone can know about this stuff, and then use it against you. Learning about forbidden psychology is important because people use it to trick the mind. That's a good way to think about studying or reading this. You may get a sense of when someone wants to exploit you or abuses you emotionally or uses brainwashing to seduce you. People also use the methods to prosecute and torment people across the globe.

History Of Dark Psychology And How It Applies In Real Life

Dark Psychology is Human Condition Research. It applies to people's psychological nature of preying on other people driven by criminal and deviant drives that lack intent, general theories of instinctual drives and the theory of social science. All humanity can hurt other human beings and living creatures. Although this urge is restrained or sublimated by others, some act upon such impulses.

Dark Psychology attempts to explain certain emotions, feelings, beliefs, and mechanisms of subjective thinking that contribute to aggressive actions and are antithetical to contemporary human behavioral understandings. Dark Psychology believes that violent, deviant, and abusive activities are purposive, and 99.99 percent have some logical, goal-oriented motivation. It is the remaining sections of .01 percent that make up Dark Psychology from Adlerian theory and Teleology. There is an area within the human psyche that Dark Psychology postulates, causing certain individuals to perform atrocious actions without intent. In this hypothesis, the Dark Singularity was coined.

Dark Psychology posits that all humankind has a reservoir of malevolent intent toward others ranging from minimally obtrusive and fleeting thoughts to utter psychopathic deviant behavior without any clear cause. This is called the Dark Spectrum. It is mitigating influences that serve as accelerators and attractants to reach the Dark Singularity. The heinous acts of an individual that fall into the Dark Spectrum is what Dark Psychology calls Dark Cause. Below is a brief introduction to certain definitions.

Dark Psychology is not only our moon's dark side but the

combination of all moons' dark side.

Dark Psychology includes all that makes us who we are, linked to our dark side. This proverbial cancer is present in all cultures, all religions, and all of humanity. From the moment we come into being, until the time of death, inside us, there is a side lurking that some have called evil, and others have described as criminal, deviant and pathological. Dark Psychology presents a third philosophical construct that takes a different view of these behaviors from religious dogmas and theories of contemporary social science.

It is the one who is not interested in his fellow men who has the greatest difficulties in life and who gives others the greatest injury. It is from these men that all human weaknesses spring up.

Some people commit these same actions in dark psychology positing and doing so for power, money, sex, revenge, or other known purposes. Without a target, they commit those horrid acts. Simplified, the end doesn't justify the means. There are people who, for the sake of doing so, abuse and harm others. The capacity lies inside all of us. The field examined here is the potential to damage others without intent, reason, or intention. Dark Psychology believes that this dark potentiality is extremely elusive and much harder to describe.

Dark Psychology believes that we all have the capacity for predator behaviors, and the capacity has access to our emotions, feelings, and beliefs. We all have this ability as you can read in this text, but only a handful of us act upon them. At one time or another, we all had thoughts and emotions about having to act harshly. We have always had thoughts that we want to harm others without mercy seriously. If you're frank with yourself, you'll have to admit that you've had thoughts and felt like you want to commit evil deeds.

Because of the truth, we consider ourselves to be a kind of benign species; one would like to think that such thoughts and feelings do not exist. Unfortunately, all of us have these ideas, and fortunately, never act upon them. Dark Psychology suggests that there are people who have the same ideas, emotions, and experiences but act upon them deliberately or impulsively. The apparent difference is that they act upon them when others have merely vague thoughts and emotions.

Dark Psychology claims that this type of predator is purposive and has some logical, purpose-oriented motivation. Religion, philosophy, psychology, and other dogmas have been convincing in their attempts to describe Dark Psychology. It is true that most human behavior, linked to evil acts, is purposeful and purpose-oriented, but Dark Psychology suggests an environment where purposeful behavior and purpose-oriented motivation tend to become nebulous. There is a continuum of victimization of dark psychology, ranging from thoughts to pure psychopathic deviance, with no apparent rationality or purpose. This spectrum, Dark Spectrum, allows the Dark Psychology theory to be conceptualized.

Dark Psychology discusses the aspect of the human psyche or universal human condition that enables sexual behavior and can even animate it. Many of the behavioral patterns' features are its lack of apparent moral purpose, its universality, and its lack of predictability in certain cases. This basic human condition is believed by Dark Psychology to be special or an extension of evolution. Let's look at some very simple evolutionary tenets. Next, remember that we evolved from other animals and are the perfection of all animal life. Our frontal lobe allowed us to become the creature at the apex. Now let us presume that being alpha predators doesn't exempt us from our animal instincts and predatory behavior.

When animals hunt, the smallest, weakest, or females in the group are always stalked and killed. While this fact sounds psychopathic, it is because of their chosen victims that their own risk of injury or death is subdued. All animal life act and behave in that way. All of their barbaric, aggressive, and bloody acts contribute to evolutionary theory, natural selection, and survival and reproductive instinct. There are no aspects of Dark Psychology for the rest of life on our planet. We, human beings, are the ones who embody what Dark Psychology is seeking to discover.

When we look at the human experience, theories of evolution, natural selection, and animal behavior, their abstract tenets appear to disappear. We are the only beings on the planet's face to prey on one another for the species' survival without the excuse of procreation. Human beings are the only species that prey unexplained desires upon others. Dark Psychology discusses the aspect of the human psyche or universal human condition that enables sexual behavior and can even compel it. Dark Psychology believes that there is something intrapsychic that drives and is anti-evolutionary to our behavior. Humans are the only species to murder each other for reasons other than life, food, land, or procreation.

Dark Psychology also believes that this dark side is unpredictable. Unpredictable in understanding who is acting on these dangerous impulses, and even more unpredictable in the lengths some will go completely negated with their sense of mercy. Some people rape, assassinate, torture, and violate without cause or intent. Dark Psychology speaks of behaving like a predator, pursuing human prey without clearly specified reasons for such acts. We are extremely dangerous to ourselves as human beings and to any other living being. The reasons for this are numerous and Dark Psychology attempts to investigate certain dangerous elements.

Important Concepts Of Dark Psychology

The more readers can understand Dark Psychology, the more prepared they are to their chances of being victimized by human predators. It is necessary to have at least a minimum understanding of Dark Psychology before proceeding. Six tenets are required to understand Dark Psychology thoroughly, as follows:

1. Dark Psychology is a part of the human experience as a whole. This build has exerted historical influence. All cultures, communities, and the people who live in them maintain this aspect of human nature. According to the most compassionate men, they have this evil domain, but never act upon it and have lower levels of violent feelings and thoughts.

2. Dark Psychology is Human Condition Research, as it relates to the emotions, feelings, and beliefs of people linked to this inherent capacity to prey on others without simple definable motives. As all action is purposeful, goal-oriented, and conceptualized by modus operandi, Dark Psychology puts forth the notion that the closer a person comes to the "black hole" of pure evil, the less likely he/she has a motivational purpose. While some believe that pure evil is never achieved, Dark Psychology claims that some are coming close since it is infinite.

3. In its latent form, Dark Psychology may be

underestimated due to its potential for misinterpretation as aberrant psychopathy. History is full of examples of this latent propensity to manifest itself as aggressive, destructive behavior. Current psychiatry and psychology describe the psychopath as an unrepentant abuser for his actions. There is a spectrum of intensity Dark Psychology posits, ranging from thoughts and feelings of violence to extreme victimization and abuse without rational intent or motivation.

4. In this spectrum, Dark Psychology's intensity is not judged less or more horrific by victimization behavior but maps out a variety of inhumanity. Comparing Ted Bundy and Jeffrey Dahmer will be an easy example. Both psychopaths were serious, and their acts were heinous. The difference is that Dahmer committed his atrocious assassinations for his misguided desire for companionship while Ted Bundy was assassinated and sadistically caused suffering from pure psychopathic cruelty. On the Dark Spectrum, both will be higher, but Jeffrey Dahmer can be best understood by his desperate psychotic desire to be accepted.

5. Dark Psychology believes that every human being has a capacity for aggression. This ability is innate in all humans, and multiple internal and external influences increase the risk of development of this ability through unpredictable behaviors. Such actions are fundamentally aggressive, and may often act without purpose. Dark Psychology claims individual interpretations of the predator-prey relationship. Dark Psychology is simply a human phenomenon and no other living being experiences it. In other living organisms, aggression and mayhem occur, but humans are the only species that can do so without intent.

6. An awareness of Dark Psychology's underlying causes

and triggers would help enable society to identify, treat, and potentially minimize the dangers inherent in its impact. Learning Dark Psychology concepts serves a twofold purpose, which is beneficial. First, recognizing that we all have the capacity for bad, those with this information will reduce the risk of it erupting. Second, understanding Dark Psychology's tenets ties in with our original evolutionary intent of striving to survive.

CHAPTER 2
FUNDAMENTALS IN PERSUASION

In this chapter, we introduce the notion of persuasion, whose field of study, history, and the scope of the disciplines and concepts involved are much larger than this chapter's subject, namely technological persuasion. On the other hand, it is the essential starting point for any study on the subject. First to understand the role played by technology, that of the persuader (i.e., what should be its characteristics?). Then to understand the action that exercises this technology on the user, namely the persuasion process (i.e., what are the persuasion techniques?). Finally to understand the impact of this action on the user and the mechanisms at work in the latter, the persuaded (i.e., understanding these mechanisms to optimize the action of persuasive technology).

First, we briefly recall the history of the concept of persuasion over the centuries, then we define the main terms related to this activity. Finally, we recall the main theories developed in the context of psychology to account for human activity.

Historical roots

Persuasion has a long history in the West, which is rooted in Greek and Roman antiquity. Under the name of rhetoric, it was an integral part of the education of the children of the elite of the Greek cities. Knowing how to influence crowds, inspire emotions, change opinions, or motivate to act, was an art deployed during speeches within the agora or the forum. The mastery of eloquence was even seen as the key to maintaining a healthy democracy.

In antiquity, persuasion was closely linked to philosophy. If the debate, dear to Plato, aims at establishing knowledge through dialogue or the examination of distinct positions, rhetoric focuses less on the discovery of truth than on the ability to influence by the speech. Aristotle, the disciple of Plato and tutor of Alexander the Great, devotes three books to rhetoric. He then defines it as "the faculty of considering, for each question, what can be persuasive." Later, Schopenhauer will say in the art of being always right, that "we can indeed be objectively right about the debate itself while being wrong in the eyes of those present, and sometimes even in our own eyes."

In ancient Rome, Cicero was the main theorist of rhetoric and argumentation. He devotes many treatises to the art of oratory based in particular on his experience as a lawyer and politician. For Cicero, a speech must fulfill three functions: to instruct, please, and move.

These works of ancient philosophers will be a reference for many centuries to come. It was not until the 17th century, notably with Francis Bacon, René Des-Cartes, or John Locke, to distance itself from Aristotelian concepts. If this is not strictly speaking rhetoric, Descartes' rationalism and the empiricism of Bacon and Locke will profoundly change the way of understanding knowledge and of arguing. By defining reason and experience respectively as the source of knowledge, they will allow the sciences to develop outside the fields of theology and metaphysics and open the way to modern sciences.

It is one of those sciences, psychology, which from the beginning of the 20th century, will produce most of our knowledge on behavior, attitude, and how to influence them. As in antiquity, interest in persuasion is not uncorrelated from public life. For example, ambitious research programs have been implemented in social psychology to determine the causes of changes in attitude and behavior to meet the American government's need to convince its citizens to support the war effort. Hovland and the Yale school thus discovered several decisive results in persuasions, such as the importance of the source's credibility, the content of the argument, or the channel conveying the persuasive message. The results obtained in psychology also find concrete applications in marketing, advertising, or even education, areas where the ability to influence can be decisive. These disciplines have managed to appropriate this knowledge and go beyond it by developing theories and models dedicated to their fields of action.

Definitions

In this section, we study the definitions of persuasion, and the two main concepts it manipulates are behavior and attitude.

Persuasion

The first difficulty in defining persuasion is identifying its purpose. If the most common acceptance sees persuasion as a means of influencing others, its actions, beliefs, and desires, some limit its field of action to attitudes. The change in behavior is then seen only as a consequence of the change of perspective about the object of attitude, just as can be the emotions. Thus, Petty and Cacioppo define persuasion as "a change in beliefs and attitudes resulting from exposure to communication."

If there is a difference of finality in the definitions of persuasion, there is also a difference in the processes implemented to achieve this finality. In its broadest sense, all means are good for managing to influence others. Romma thus indicates that it can be "linguistic, argumentative or psychological processes such as seduction or manipulation, up to body language, images, etc." She adds that persuasion can "be direct and explicit or, conversely, implicit conveying meaning in a disguised manner." On the other hand, in a more restricted view, the change of attitude or behavior must be voluntary and conscious. In this view, persuasion can be compared to communication. An author communicates a message, via a channel, to a target that processes this message to possibly modify his beliefs or actions. Each element in this chain of communication is important to the success of persuasion. Lasswell sums it up by the question "Who says what, by which channel, to whom, in what channel and with what effect?", called in English the 5W (Who says What to Whom in What channel with What effect?). Perlo thus defines persuasion as "a symbolic process in which communicators try to convince people to change their attitudes or behaviors about a subject by transmitting a message in an atmosphere of free choice." Petty and Cacioppo's definition also corresponds to this restricted vision of persuasion, even if it limits finality to attitudes.

By adopting this strict perspective, persuasion is not the only way to change attitude and behavior. For Girandola, the two main methods studied in psychology to influence others' attitudes or behavior are persuasion and commitment. If persuasion, in the strict sense, influences behavior through attitude, engagement does the opposite. It is based on the need for coherence in individuals between thought and action by encouraging them to make their attitudes conform to specific behaviors. Kiesler defines engagement as "a bond that unites the individual to his behavioral acts." We will detail a little more in the chapter engagement dedicated to the theory of cognitive dissonance to which it is attached. Note that persuasion in the broad sense includes engagement.

Other methods of influencing behavior exist. Through an analysis of nineteen frameworks dedicated to behavior change, Michie et al., for example, identified nine behavioral influence methods, which they grouped under the term behavior change wheel. Beyond persuasion and commitment, this behavior change wheel identifies:

- Education: "increasing knowledge and understanding."
- The incentive: "to create an expectation of reward."
- Coercion: "create an expectation of punishment or cost."
- Training: "transmitting skills."
- The restriction: "using rules to reduce the opportunities to practice the behavior."
- Restructuring of the environment: "to modify the physical or social context."
- Modeling: "provide an example that inspires, that people imitate."
- Facilitation: "increase resources and reduce barriers to the practice of behavior."

Many of these techniques can be thought of like persuasion, in its broadest definition. For example, Fogg, a precursor of technological persuasion, integrates them all into this discipline except coercion, because for him, even if coercion can lead to a change in behavior through the use of force (or at least threat), it cannot be assimilated to persuasion which implies a framework of freedom. He thus defines persuasion as "an attempt to change attitudes, behavior, or both simultaneously, without the use of coercion or deception."

Behavior

The definition of the concept of behavior seems to elicit little debate in the literature. The great dictionary of psychology defines it, for example, as "the set of objectively observable reactions that an organism, generally provided with a nervous system, executes in response to the environment's stimuli, themselves objectively observable."

Attitude

As early as 1935, Allport made an attitude "the most distinctive and indispensable concept of contemporary social psychology." At the beginning of the 20th century, it is first apprehended as "emotion or a thought comprising a motor (or behavioral) component." The link between attitude and behavior is therefore identified very early on as fundamental. Subsequently, two other dimensions complete the definition of attitude: the cognitive component which makes the attitude a knowledge or a belief towards an object of attitude (i.e., a person, a physical object, a concept, a behavior, ...), and the affective component which makes the attitude an evaluation, positive or negative of the object of attitude. For Rosenberg and Hovland, "attitudes can be conceptualized as cognitive, affective, and behavioral components consistent with one another. For a given object, beliefs and knowledge about the object, the evaluation of this object, and the behaviors resulting from it are consistent in the same individual.

Others prefer to retain only the attitude component, the cognitive and behavioral components being the only secondary in their eyes. The attitude is then above all an evaluation towards an object, a concept, an action, or an individual. These different points of view are explained by the fact that an attitude is not directly observable. It is by his way of acting, expressing himself, or expressing an emotion that we can assess an individual's attitude.

However, in its effective component, the link between behavior and attitude is not always as obvious as the definition of Rosenberg and Hov-land might suggest, as Wicker showed. Several explanations for this divergence are then considered: a difficulty in measuring behaviors and attitudes in the experiments studied, the influence of external factors in the choice of behaviors, the competition of several attitudes, or again the need to introduce a notion of strength of attitudes. Fishbein and Ajzen thus propose introducing new factors such as social norms or the perception of control, in competition with attitude to determine behavior. We will study their theory of planned activities in a dedicated chapter.

Another track studied is that of the strength of an attitude. The stronger an attitude, the more resistant it is to change, the more stable it is over time, and the more it influences behavior and cognition. If the cognitive, affective, and behavioral dimensions make it possible to assess the direction of attitude (positive or negative), Krosnick et al. propose ten dimensions to assess their strength:

- Accessibility: "the ease with which an evaluation comes to mind when encountering an object of attitude."
- The extremity: the more important the evaluation of the attitude (towards the negative or towards the positive), the more extreme it is.
- Intensity: identical at the end but for the

emotional reaction elicited.

- Certainty: "the degree of confidence given to an attitude."
- Importance: "the subjective perception of interest in an attitude."
- Interest: "the extent to which an object of attitude is hedonically relevant for the holder of the attitude."
- Direct experience: "the more frequently a behavior is expressed, the more accessible the attitude is specific to it."
- Knowledge: the sum of knowledge which supports the attitude
- A structural consistency: "a close relationship between the feeling towards the object and the beliefs about its attributes."
- The latitude of rejection and non-engagement: "the more an individual opposes or rejects the arguments put forward in a message, the clearer his initial attitude."

Theories and models of behavior

In this section, we wish to study human behavior, particularly how each individual determines his actions and is likely to be influenced by a persuasive attempt. For this purpose, psychology is an unavoidable discipline. For more than a century now, human beings in general have been studied, and their mental processes, notably those at work in the development of human behavior. Many models and multiple theories have been proposed, which allow us to anticipate better and grasp human action and its constraints. Even if we cannot be exhaustive, these models and these theories that we wish to explain here, focus on those cited in the section on technological persuasion. We describe the processes it exhibits for each of them, and we illustrate it with a common example: selective sorting of waste.

Operational conditioning

Principle

Conditioning is a learning theory, developed at the beginning of the 20th century by Pavlov. It is built around the link between an environmental stimulus and the reaction it causes in a living being (in a dog in the case of Pavlov's work). This theory is particularly interested in stimuli, classifying them into three categories:

- Neutral stimulus: does not cause behavior.
- Unconditional stimulus: systematically provokes the behavior without prior learning.
- Conditional stimulus: initially neutral, this stimulus causes behavior after the learning phase.

Learning takes place by combining a neutral stimulus with an unconditional stimulus, then suppressing the unconditional stimulus to make the neutral stimulus a conditional stimulus. Pavlov thus associated different sounds (neutral stimulus) with the action of feeding his dogs (unconditional stimulus) and measured their salivation (behavior). Once conditioned, the sound alone (conditional stimulus) created salivation (behavior) without bringing food.

Skinner then introduces the notion of operant conditioning, which differs from Pavlovian conditioning by taking into consideration the consequences of behavior. The probability of reproducing the behavior is greater if the consequences of it are perceived as positive by the individual: he anticipates the consequences of the behavior before deciding to adopt it. There are four types of operant conditioning:

- Positive reinforcement: Increases the probability of appearance of behavior following the addition of an appetitive stimulus.
- Negative reinforcement: Increases the probability of the appearance of behavior following the withdrawal of an aversive stimulus.
- Positive punishment: Decreases the probability of a behavior appearing by adding an aversive stimulus.
- Negative punishment: Decreases the probability of the appearance of behavior by the withdrawal of an appetitive stimulus.

As a result of operative conditioning, individuals, subject to a new situation, would learn by series of "trial and error" to establish a map of the consequences and better choose the behavior appropriate to the situation (i.e., the stimulus).

Illustration on selective sorting

An individual can decide whether or not to sort his waste by anticipating the consequences of this behavior. The ecological consequences will favor the sorting of waste, while the anticipation of the additional efforts required by this behavior can curb it.

It is possible to influence the individual by adding positive or negative consequences to the behavior. For example, some municipalities have implemented a tax linked to the weight of unsorted waste (negative reinforcement associated with non-sporting behavior). This incentive could be seen as a positive reinforcement associated with sorting behavior if it took the form of a bonus linked to the sorted waste weight.

Social cognitive theory

Principles

Cognitive, social theory is, in part, a reaction to the behaviorist current of which operant conditioning is a part. It first offers an alternative to learning by trial and error, judging it uneconomical, long and dangerous. Indeed, trying different behaviors in a new situation requires effort, time, and risks in the absence of knowledge about these tested behaviors' consequences.

For Bandura, the preferred learning method for individuals would be observed, which he calls vicarious learning or modeling. However, this observation does not lead to mere mimicry. It is an active observation where the observer filters, interprets, and symbolizes the information he perceives. He assimilates behavior patterns and skills and modifies his motivation to adopt the behavior by interpreting its consequences in the model individual. The characteristics of the model, such as its similarity or its effective proximity to the observer, favor vicarious learning.

Bandura also redefines the place of human beings in action in their environment. The individual is not an automaton reacting to environmental stimuli, as behaviorist theories might lead us to believe. He is an actor in his own life, able to direct the course of his actions. This is what he calls the human agency.

Environmental stimuli undergo the effect of the cognitive processes. They are filtered, analyzed, interpreted before they can have any effect on behavior. The individual anticipates the results of his actions, sets goals, and evaluates his activity in self-regulation of his activity and motivation. Self-regulatory processes act in anticipation and feedback on behavior. The individual develops an objective according to the result he wishes to obtain (anticipated consequences) and his confidence in his capacity to obtain this result (called self-efficiency by Bandura). He self-assesses throughout the activity, comparing his performance to the target. If the goal is achieved, the self-assessment will provide satisfaction to the individual.

Conversely, if the objective is not reached, the individual will feel dissatisfaction. The more ambitious the objective, the greater the satisfaction obtained by achieving the objective. The development of an objective is a source of motivation by the anticipation of the result of the behavior and the anticipation of the satisfaction provided by the self-evaluation. Self-assessment can also provide motivation. In the event of failure to achieve the goal, if the individual maintains their goal, then they will wish to continue or even strengthen their efforts (a manifestation of motivation) to achieve the goal. Maintaining the goal will greatly depend on the individual's confidence in their abilities (self-efficacy). But failure can also lead the individual to discouragement, which will manifest itself in a downward revision of his goal, or even complete abandonment.

Bandura argues that the interactions between behavior, environment, and personal factors form a reciprocal triadic causality. Each of these three elements influences the other two with an intensity that varies according to the situation and according to the activity in progress.

As we have just seen, personal factors influence behavior, in particular, through self-regulatory processes. In return, the behavior can influence personal factors such as effects or cognitions, for example, if the behavior fails.

Interactions between the environment and personal factors can, in one sense, take the form of persuasion or vicarious learning and, in the other, the influence of the individual on his environment outside of his action. Physical characteristics (age, height, gender...) for example, can create reactions and, therefore, modifications in the social environment.

Finally, through his behavior, an individual can affect his environment (for example, moving an object, interacting with someone). In return, the environment can act on behavior (sometimes indirectly, because cognitions mediate it), show the behaviorist theories.

Illustration on selective sorting

If an individual can see another person apply selective sorting to their waste, can observe how he implements it (for example, the use of containers dedicated to recyclable waste, the installation of a composter in the garden,...), and can perceive the benefits that he derives from this behavior (for example, the satisfaction of being more ecological, the reduction of tax on household waste,...), he will be encouraged to adopt the same behavior.

An individual will set the goal of sorting his waste in anticipation of this behavior (for example, more ecological, fewer taxes...). And because he feels capable of sorting (for example, he knows recyclable waste, he knows how to send his waste for recycling...). Subsequently, he self-evaluates his action about the goal he has set for himself. If he considers that he has achieved his goal, he derives satisfaction from it and strengthens his esteem to sort his waste. If he considers that he has not reached his objective, he may abandon it, revise it or, on the contrary, redouble his efforts to achieve it, according to his level of confidence in his capacity to achieve this objective.

Theories of a link between attitude and behavior

Principles

To better understand the link between attitude and behavior, Fishbein and Ajzen propose the theory of reasoned action. This model integrates an intermediate cognition between attitude and behavior, intention, which they identify with motivational factors in favor of behavior. For Ajzen, intention denotes the effort that the individual is willing to put into adopting the behavior.

We find an attitude as one of the two determinants of intention, the second being the social norm. Fishbein and Ajzen define attitude as a personal positive or negative feeling against behavior. This attitude is itself formed from beliefs about the consequences of carrying out the behavior, balanced by the importance of the individual attaching to each of these consequences. The other determinant of intention to act, the social norm, reflects the opinion of the individual's social environment on the adoption of the behavior by the latter. The importance also balances that the individual attaches to it. We then speak of subjective standards.

This model has shown a good ability to predict human behavior in many areas (marketing, management, social psychology, health...). However, it ignores certain antecedents of behavior, those who escape the individual's control, such as the resources, skills, or opportunities necessary for certain behaviors.

To answer this problem, Ajzen proposes a new model, called the theory of planned behavior. She takes up the theory of reasoned action, which she enriches with a new antecedent for intention: the perception of control over behavior.

Perceived control represents the degree of ease or difficulty associated with adopting the behavior. It depends both on the resources available to the individual, his skills, and the environment's opportunities. These are the internal and external constraints to the individual, or more precisely, the individual's perception and importance given to these constraints.

Illustration on selective sorting

It is possible to persuade a person to sort their waste (i.e., get them to intend to sort their waste):

- by making them perceive the advantages of sorting their waste (i.e., changing their attitude towards sorting behavior)
- by encouraging his social environment to put pressure on him to sort his waste
- by making it easier for them to sort their waste by providing suitable containers, for example, or by reassuring them about their ability to adopt this behavior.

Cognitive dissonance

Principles

The theory of reasoned action presents a rational vision of the individual. He would act according to his attitudes. With the theory of cognitive dissonance, Festinger shows that the human being is also a rationalizing being, granting his opinions and beliefs to his actions after the fact. This theory postulates that the dissonance between two cognitions of the individual — in the case that interests us here, his behavior and attitude towards this behavior — creates an emotional discomfort that prompts the individual to reduce the dissonance by modifying the least resistant cognition.

One of the experiments conducted by Festinger to illustrate his theory consists of having an essay written in favor of an attitude contrary to the beliefs of the individual. The evaluation of the attitude after the experience shows an evolution of beliefs in the direction of the opinion defended in the dissertation. Attitude changes afterward to be in line with behavior.

To change behavior or attitude using cognitive dissonance, three phases are necessary:

- The awakening of dissonance: when two cognitions of the same individual become contradictory.
- Emotional discomfort: The awakening of dissonance generates a need for change to return to a state of well-being.
- The reduction of dissonance: can take the form of a change in attitude, a change in behavior, and the identification of an external justification ("I didn't want, I was forced") or in relativizing the behavior, to the point of forgetting it.

Illustration on selective sorting

Asking an individual who is not in favor of selective sorting to sort their waste for some time for an experiment can lead them to revise their opinion and thus become more favorable to selective sorting.

Skills, Motivations and Opportunities

Principles

According to the Motivation - Opportunity - Ability or MOA model, the adoption of behavior by an individual is directly influenced by the individual's motivation to adopt it, moderated by his capacities and the opportunity offered by the environment.

Unlike the other theories cited here, the MOA theory is derived from marketing. It has been implemented to explain, more specifically, the behavior of consumers in the face of advertisements. However, it has since been used in many fields to explain different behaviors, notably technological persuasion.

McKinnis sees motivation as an extension of the notion of consumer involvement. It is "goal-oriented excitement." Ability represents the skills necessary to adopt the behavior. More than ability, Bandura has shown that it is the confidence that individuals have in their skills that truly influences behavior. Finally, the opportunity represents the circumstances favorable to the execution of the behavior, brought to the user's attention. It depends above all on the execution environment of the behavior.

Illustration on selective sorting

The probability that an individual will sort their waste depends on:

- his motivation: does he want to sort his waste?
- his skill: does he have the skills and knowledge to sort his waste?
- opportunities offered by the environment: does his physical and social environment allow him to sort his waste?

Information processing

Principle

The model of the probability of elaboration and the model of systematic heuristic information processing are two theories, very close to each other, which study the analysis of persuasive messages by individuals and their impact on their attitudes. According to these two models, two modes of information processing would be used:

- The systematic or "main" mode is characterized by an analysis of the message's semantic content. The resulting judgment will, therefore, depend on the quality of the arguments.
- The heuristic or "peripheral" mode is based on rules, patterns that allow the individual to develop an attitude while minimizing the effort of message analysis. It is not the content of the message and its analyzed arguments, but indices peripheral to the message and information related to the transmission context. For a heuristic to be used by the individual, it must be available in memory, and the index that activates it must appear during the transmission of the message. A typical example of heuristics is "if the message is from an expert, then it is true." The source's expertise index could be a title or a particular outfit, for example. Peripheral indices generally relate to:
- *The characteristics of the source of the message: identity, credibility, physical appeal, emotional state. . .*
- *The behaviors and opinions of the social environment about the object of attitude to which the message relates: opinion of an individual, spontaneous reaction of an audience, and a survey.*
- *The properties, non-semantic characteristics of the message: its length, number of arguments, speech speed, medium, and typography.*

Individuals process information according to the principle of least cognitive effort (for better optimization of cognitive resources) and suspense (i.e., sufficient confidence in the judgment resulting from the processing of information about the goal pursued). The more the individual has the capacities and the motivation to process the message, the more he is willing to provide efforts for this processing. Therefore, the more he favors the systematic mode.

However, heuristic and systematic processing are not exclusive. An individual generally uses two types of processing, favoring one type rather than another depending on his cognitive abilities, motivation to process the message, and the availability in memory of the heuristics and knowledge that apply to the message and the context. It gradually incorporates the results of the various treatments and assesses the opinion it builds on the attitude object (from evaluating each treatment). If the confidence in this opinion is not sufficient, he seeks to enrich it with new heuristic or systematic treatments until he obtains sufficient confidence in his evaluation of the object of attitude. The level of confidence that he considers necessary will depend on his motivation, which characterizes the importance he attaches to the attitude he builds.

Illustration on selective sorting

An individual can change their opinion to favor selective sorting if they believe the arguments presented to them are relevant, but other factors can modify their judgment. For example:

- Is his interlocutor credible?
- Does he feel close, similar to his interlocutor?
- Did the individuals present to adopt the opinion of

    their interlocutors?
-    Is the number of arguments presented important?

Therefore, the history of persuasion spans more than 2000 years, calling on a wide spectrum of disciplines and presenting multiple fields of application. Because of this richness, the definitions of the concept of persuasion are numerous. As part of the study of persuasive technologies, we adopt that proposed by the precursor of this discipline, namely BJ Fogg. Persuasion is then "an attempt to change attitudes, behavior, or both at the same time, without the use of coercion or deception. This definition has the advantage of targeting both attitude and behavior (not limited to attitude), and of including a large number of means to achieve this (all except coercion and deception for ethical reasons), leaving by extension a wide spectrum of fields of application and a wide choice of implementation available to persuasive technologies.

In technological persuasion, this preliminary passage through persuasion, and a fortiori through psychology and its many theories on human behavior, is rich in lessons. This lighting influences our way of apprehending the user and conceiving the interaction between him and the persuasive system. Thus, it seems important to us to avoid two pitfalls. The first is to see the user as submissive to his environment, be it physical, social, and technological. It, therefore, seems illusory to aim for a total efficiency of a persuasive device which does not know how to take into account the particularities of each of these users, and the singularity of the situation in which he finds himself (in the same way as traditional persuasion is not always a successful activity either).

Likewise, the user should not be seen as a rational being, who would only practice the behaviors he wishes to practice, and all the behaviors he wishes to practice. The reasons which explain the non-adoption of a behavior can be numerous (low motivation, little confidence in its capacity to adapt it, the influence of the social environment, insufficient resources and opportunities, ...), and do not show a hostile attitude towards the behavior or an absence of interest in its adoption. It is not a binary situation where the user completely rejects the behavior, in thought as in act, or conversely adopts it. More generally, the study of models and theories relating to human behavior has shown us that the factors influencing behavior are numerous and that persuasive situations are complex. Therefore, it seems important for us to take this complexity into account in the design and implementation of persuasive technology to optimize its efficiency.

CHAPTER 3

THE PSYCHOLOGY OF PERSUASION

In general, persuasion can be understood as a form of strategic communication that aims to convince other people. Through persuasion, it is possible to induce someone to assume a certain position, perform a specific task, or accept an idea.

This communication includes an adequate posture, emotional appeals, and, mainly, a strong and logical argument. In this way, it is easy to see that the psychology of persuasion is associated with basic topics such as knowledge, rhetoric, and image.

This competence is important for everyone, regardless of profession or industry, but it becomes even more essential for leadership positions, sales professionals, and those who work on projects. And, like most behavioral skills, it can be assimilated and improved.

The Psychology Of Persuasion

In the book "The psychology of persuasion," author Robert Cialdini states that the individual can develop this communication capacity to persuade others' actions and decisions.

Based on his studies, Robert Cialdini created the persuasive communication theory, which is based on the concept of taking advantage of some patterns of conduct internalized collectively, to suggest behaviors. This theory lists the six principles of the psychology of persuasion, which can be taught, learned, and applied:

- **Reciprocity:**

The theory determines that people are more likely to respond to an offer when they have already received something in exchange. Social norms encourage us to respond positively to those who have done us a favor or helped us at some other time.

- **Consistency:**

The individual is also more likely to follow a pattern if he thinks that this model is consistent with his ideals and values.

- **Authority:**

According to this principle, the authority and seniority transmitted by the communicator determine factors for others to feel predisposed to approve or validate something. At this point, the communicator's reasoning and stance have special prominence.

- **Social Validation**:

According to Cialdini, the greater the common sense about behavior, the greater the likelihood that someone will adopt attitudes that fit this pattern.

- **Scarcity:**

In this principle, the author reiterates that the charm generated by a product, service, or situation is inversely proportional to its availability. That is, the scarcer, the more relevant.

- **Friendship/friendliness:**

Finally, the sixth principle indicates that people are more inclined to collaborate or agree with others when there is an identification, a friendship relationship, or some attraction.

It is worth remembering that the principles of Robert Cialdini's influence should not be used autonomously, but combined, as part of more efficient and provocative communication.

The Importance Of Empathy

It is worth mentioning that the power of persuasion can only be improved through an additional skill: listening with the sincere intention of understanding the other. Thus, the speech of the broadcaster deserves full attention. It is necessary to understand the message and the lines and everything behind each comment, such as concerns, expectations, and feelings.

Therefore, it is essential to be prepared to listen and, at the same time, collect information, emotions, and impressions.

It is also important to emphasize that knowing how to listen includes rational and emotional aspects, but does not imply agreeing with the other. Differences may remain, but with effective communication, they are better understood.

The Strength Of The Argument

The argument, in turn, is based on coherence and uses real facts to consolidate a thesis. A good argument is full of examples, data, technical studies, research, and comparisons, to prove the truth of a statement or the feasibility of a proposal.

Thus, the communicator can involve others, making everyone start following the same line of reasoning until they are persuaded.

This power of persuasion is significantly increased when the argument is joined with empathy. In this case, it is possible to create a communication that mixes reason and emotion, reaching the main centers of convincing.

Persuasion In The Corporate Universe

It is easy to see that relationships have become increasingly virtual and, often, less productive. This movement is caused not only by the advancement of technology but also by the underutilization of important skills.

Among these skills are empathy and the ability to argue, which can ensure healthier and more collaborative relationships, especially in the corporate environment - where peaceful coexistence between professionals with the most diverse profiles is a basic need.

Individualism has become a major problem, hampering teamwork and collectivity. Therefore, it is necessary to be careful with the virtualization of communication and the almost exclusive use of e-mails, messaging applications, and social networks.

It is also important to consider that dialogue is an efficient way to perceive fears, motivations, and needs, normally hidden in fully digital communication. Personal contact creates ideal conditions for feedback, negotiation, guidance, advice, and convincing.

Also, the correct application of the psychology of persuasion is one of the main characteristics of true leaders, who manage to inspire and engage their teams. Therefore, this issue must be present in the leadership preparation program. With a powerful argument, it is possible to induce critical thinking — a fundamental ingredient for the formation of high-performance teams. The results will be even better if the communicator is recognized for the positive reference that inspires others.

Aspects That Impact The Power Of Persuasion

Some simple aspects can impact the individual's power of persuasion. Therefore, you need to pay attention to the following tips:

- **Posture, gesture, and tone of voice:**

Posture, gestures, and tone of voice are points that generate trust and credibility. Thus, it is necessary to understand these characteristics and adapt to the model imposed by your interlocutor. Eye contact is part of this same tactic, as it ensures greater proximity. With a few attempts, a connection emerges.

- **Language:**

The language must also be adapted to the model of the interlocutor so that the conversation flows naturally. Also, it is important to reach people's emotions through stimuli aligned with personal desires and goals. These are excellent ways to persuade.

- **Interruptions:**

To be persuasive, it is essential to avoid interruptions. Harsh cuts and conclusions are signs of anxiety and unpreparedness. A productive dialogue demands time, tranquility, and attention.

- **Converging questions:**

The questions help the communicator to keep the conversation focused on their main goal. This attitude contributes to a more dynamic conversation, because, through structured questions, the interlocutor is also invited to rethink his opinions and evaluate new alternatives.

- **Knowledge:**

The sound argument depends on knowledge. Therefore, it is essential to be up to date, have clear answers, understand the events, and interpret data to establish communication strategies.

The principles of the psychology of persuasion are important skills that can be acquired through specific training, discipline, and focus. Adjustments in one's behavior are fundamental in this improvement process, which will reward the achievement of more productive interpersonal relationships — indispensable for a successful career.

CHAPTER 4

WHAT IS SUBLIMINAL PERSUASION?

The term subliminal means under consciousness.

Subliminal manipulation affects people below their conscious consciousness. It affects more people than just words. It's the force behind or beneath the words. It uses the plain word's normal message in combination with a lower level of conscious cognition to influence a person's decision-making or line of thinking effectively.

Why use subliminal persuasion?

The truth is, you can't use it.

You send other messages non-verbally, whether or not you know them, any time you communicate with words. So why not relay both verbally and non-verbally an important sales message?

Yes, subliminal methods of persuasion are your weapons in this modern world. This helps you gain a lead in a competitive market and keeps you ahead of the game. Dave Lakhani, who wrote many books concerning persuasion and power, said:

"It's no longer convincing to persuade that looks like conviction."

If you feel confident about the decision to buy, you buy a chance.

The moral consciousness of your prospects often provides an unconscious dimension of persuasion to start any successful selling interactions.

As salespeople, you give your unconscious mind feelings of ease and excitement about buying while at the same time offering justification to rationalize this choice.

Your prospects must be open to discussion and trust. Doubts are the adversary of persuasion. Since at the beginning of a sales call, your primary function is to help a prospect speak to you and to believe what you are saying, you have to establish relationships and trust.

Subliminal persuasion is the most powerful form of report construction.

Other factors that are subliminal affect credibility.

For example, you have to know what works for you and, in particular, you have to connect your sales, the industry in which you work to optimize your impact on people.

The appropriately dressed salesperson displays an appreciation for the customers that they are meeting and gives the illusion that they take care of how they look and act.

During the sales call, your prospects assess your trust, skill, and motives.

You might be the best salesman on earth, but if your viewpoint is assumed that you're only going to make money off them, it's doubtful that you'll make a sale. Also, if you don't know well what your product is, your prospect is likely to doubt any of what you are saying.

For example, a salesperson standing before him saying in a weak voice that it would be useful for the future, somewhat meekly and with a questioning tone, is not convincing. The message is not congruent.

There are important lessons for salespeople in the above

paragraphs: be aware of your product, learn the benefits it offers to its users, and be seen subliminally in your sales presentation. Your intentions can also come through readily when you deliver the bid.

There is an Australian seller who is the leading seller in her industry. She dresses impeccably, always fast and efficient, and none of her business counterparts are familiar with her industry, industry players, regulations, and goods. Therefore, she is the most popular seller in Australia, highly paid, and constantly pursued abroad in this industry.

You can improve your chances by making the viewer feel good. Some it call the law of association.

The saying "It isn't what you say, it's how you say it," is a lot of truth.

In your language, the way you use intonation and inflammation is important for what you say.

Here's an example:

In reality, though, inflection is much of the actual meaning. Look at each sentence below, each with a different word highlighted, and followed by the implicated meaning.

> The phrase "I can't promise you that value" has only one meaning.
- (but perhaps someone can.)
- I can't promise you.
- (There's no way.)
- I can't promise that price to you.
- (Perhaps you will get it.)
- I can't PROMISE that price.
- I can't assure you of the price. (But I can promise somebody else.)

51

- (Perhaps a reasonable price.)
- I can't give you the amount.
- (but I can promise something.)
- I can't promise you the Amount.

What we emphasize is the significance of our statements, and it is a subtle process.

We have three options. When we say it, we will end the sentence with: The intonation we use when saying a sentence.

An intonation with:

- An upward expression
- Unaltered intonation of the voice
- A high/low intonation of the accent

Pick a word and say, "You want to buy this," for you. Do this for yourself.

When you repeat this phrase and say the last two words in a higher-pitched voice, it sounds like you are asking. There are languages (e.g., Italian) where, through the intonation of a sentence, you indicate you are asking questions.

Then say the sentence that holds the tone of your voice consistent. It's not different. The tone is a statement you make.

Speak the same sentence again, but say it more and more loudly, the last two words. This is command tonality, which hypnotics use well and can also be used in hypnotic sales techniques.

How is this useful in selling?

Well, when you comment, "This product is the one you want," it has very little positive impact if you utter it with a question type tonality. It sounds like you are asking a question and are not sure if it's a good product or the best one to use.

You should construct phrases carefully with a commanding tonality that defines what you want people to do. Those are called Embedded Commands and are a highly powerful method of subliminal persuasion.

For instance:

"When customers contract my business, John, all we do is to achieve results."

"Hire my company, John ... get results... now," hears your unconscious mind.

Put together enough of these sentences in a sales presentation, and the performance will significantly improve.

To subliminally carry out your bids, you can use presuppositions.

What are the premises?

The budgets are the linguistic equivalent of the assumptions which most people name.

They are already what must be considered valid for the statement to be valid or meaningful. Budgets are supposed to be taken for granted instead of clearly defined making it much harder to avoid presuppositions.

Think of what you want to recognize as a fact to use assumptions, and then create a term that assumes this.

The strength of assumptions can be immense.

Let me give you a case in point.

The discrepancy is the use of premises, "Did you find anything in our product interesting?"

And what about:

"What do you think is most interesting about our commodity?"

The first sentence above presupposes almost nothing of value. At the same time, the second sentence presupposes several things, and the reader must choose.

Persuasive Writing Techniques

Some things do not change over time, and although we have advanced a lot in technology, there are things that, as human beings, will continue to function.

In this section, I am going to talk about persuasion techniques that are highly known and that it does not matter why they will continue to work for you whenever you use them.

Do you want to convince your readers to do something or agree with your point of view?

Well, I know this is a silly question. Of course, yes.

Persuasion is generally an exercise where a win-win situation is created. You present a case that others find beneficial. They are made an offer that they cannot refuse.

It is simply a good deal or a position that makes sense to that particular person.

However, some techniques can facilitate this work and make your case a more convincing case. While this list is by no means exhaustive, these strategies are widely used as they work!

Persuasive Writing Technique 1: Repetition

Talk to someone well versed in the psychology of learning, and they will tell you that "repetition is the mother of learning." It is also essential in persuasive writing since a person cannot agree with you if he cannot follow what you are saying.

Of course, there are good and bad repetitions. To stay on the bright side, deliver your message in different ways: directly, through an example, with a story, a quote from a famous person, and once again, in the recap.

Persuasive Writing Technique 2: Why

Note the power of the word. Psychological tests have shown that people are more likely to react to an application simply because they give them a 'why' explanation ... Even if this isn't important.

When you think about it, the plan itself makes sense. Without fair justification, we do not like to be told or asked to behave. Often offer reasons to people who you want to be open to your thinking.

Persuasive Writing Technique 3: Consistency

It has been called the "troll of small minds," but consistency in our thoughts and actions is a trait of social value. We don't want it to seem inconsistent, since, rightly or wrongly, that characteristic is associated with instability and frivolity, while consistency is related to integrity and rational behavior.

Use this in your writing, getting the reader to agree with something in advance (something easy, that almost nobody can disagree with). Then rigorously assemble your case, with lots of supporting evidence, at the same time relate your endpoint to the opening stage that has already been accepted, and there you have it!

Persuasive Writing Technique 4: Social Proof

Seeking guidance from others about what to do and what to accept is one of the most powerful psychological forces in our lives. We are social beings, and we continually look at ourselves when acting, especially when we are in a new setting where we have no previous experience (imagine sitting at a very traditional banquet with ten different types of forks on one side and knives on the other — what would you do? I'm sure you would look at the closest person to see which cutlery you choose to start with.)

Persuasion techniques: The six principles of a winning speech.

The six principles of a winning speech that every manager should know.

1. Don't be in a position of authority when you speak. Be an authority.

The difference is that they will see the first one (because of who he is). The second, they will listen to him (for what he provokes). The first speaks from the pride of the position and not from the humility of the perpetual apprentice. The second makes attendees feel first and reason later, and vibrate with each articulated gesture, with each uttered word. They follow him because they see him as credible. After all, his messages spark sparks of illusion, attention, or interest.

And that is what we have to achieve when we sit down to write a speech and when we rehearse its declamation. Provoke emotional and sensory impacts that make them draw what they hear on their mental staff, and that you feel those vibrations in the depths of their hearts because depending on how we make them feel, this will motivate them to accompany us, vote for us, applaud us... remember us.

One of the most important aspects is the brevity of

sentences: short, slow, patterned. As if they were headlines for the news. Because if you save your words, you save their attention. A long message is only enunciated if this is a quote or requires a literary figure.

Remember: whoever talks a lot and with an archaic language does so to hide their ignorance or confuse the audience. Avoid both purposes, or your credibility will be affected. Only if your words create value, what you say is worth it.

2. Don't be a wrapper, but a caramel. The content gives value to the continent.

A good example is the well-known sensation that we have all experienced when we see a speaker standing on a podium, and before he utters the first word, we observe how many have already bought his message (product). Like when we buy a new detergent for the suggestiveness of the messages or a juice from a striking package and attractive colors. We do not know if we will like what is inside since we have not yet tried it. But what we do know is that its exterior has already seduced us.

As with a product, it also happens to speakers. What is the reason for that sudden success, that unrepeatable salesperson aura, that intoxicating spell that makes him win our love with his mere presence? To the charism, to the pure and simple charism. They are those types of people who want to make good the phrase that AnetteBenning receives from her lover in the movie American Beauty: "To be successful, you have to project a sense of success."

Well, you must, dear manager, be that type of person. But beware because the initial perfume can start to evaporate if you do not meet a series of unwritten requirements. The listener can never perceive that behind that seductive, different, luminous, and charismatic packaging, there is something worse than a bad product: nothing — the intellectual or personal emptiness of the person speaking to them.

It turns out that they will have spent their time listening to someone who has convinced them that their product is the best when there is simply no product. Now I ask you: What are you doing at that time? How many times have you felt like this being a listener and not a speaker? How many times have you resisted the captive urge to get up and go home? How often have you waited to sing forty to the trickster of the word, to the falsifier of consciences?

How to avoid that the one who is there, in front of you, ends with that feeling, with that void (of content)? It is easy. Don't talk like you take a flower out of your jacket. Speak as if the heart were drawing that flower on your face. Speaker, not actor. This game is not about communicating much but about communicating what is correct. Words that create added value to your listeners' knowledge, interests, and motivations. That's what they were for. Don't waste their time with cliches and platitudes. Offer them techniques, methods, tools, ways, and advice that improve their professional and personal activity.

At the beginning of your speech, say who you are, what you have done and what you are going to do, and then be consistent with your words. Do not be who you are not, do not appear as what they do not expect from you; do not promise what you know that you will not fulfill. You commit yourself to future suicide for a few moments of present illusory recognition. Think about it.

Remember: when we do not shine (sincerity and

knowledge) on the counterpart but only try to dazzle it (rhetorical flash), in the end, the communication space becomes a twilight zone (no credibility).

3. If you submit to the papers, in the end, you will end up losing them.

Remember this maxim when you have a public appearance, private intervention, or keynote speech. If you read, you do not connect the same, and you are not so natural or spontaneous. If you submit to the dictatorship of the folio, the base of every tree, you will end up like this: subject to its roots, immovable, insecure, and accommodated in a fictional comfort zone that, little by little, will take you away from the listener.

Paper is a good stick, perhaps the best to support your momentary imbalances with your speech presentation. It helps you find yourself, it helps you locate yourself, but it makes you walk on your own. Therefore, I advise the following system: once you have written your speech, underline in each paragraph the opening phrase and the most important concept of that paragraph, the one that gives it value. Memorize them, only that part, only that phrase, and that concept, and dedicate yourself to reading the rest over and over again.

When the time comes for the speech, your naturalness will rest because you have what you want in your mind. You can express the rest with your words without losing what you want to say. In this way, you do not force yourself to make an impossible memory effort or force the audience to see how well you read, but how little you transmit.

Reading is not easy, and not even being a good speaker makes it easy to be a good reader. And accommodating yourself in reading (before in sheets and today even in teleprompters) also accommodates your brain, memory, and therefore your ability to respect yourself. Your self-esteem will be higher if you find that you can count, relate, and communicate without the magic stick's continuous help. Use it, but never abuse it. Or you will end up losing the papers.

Remember: paper is speech. But what makes that oratory is you. If you star in the role, they will end up asking you to mail it to them, and each time you will communicate to more empty audiences. Your positioning begins by assuming that you, and no one but you, are the protagonist.

4. Your history will make History.

Dare to tell stories (personal, plausible) since the public feels identified with them, either because they sound close, or because they sound credible since they will listen more and be more in agreement with your ideas. Today good storytellers succeed. We have to look for conflict, and it builds the story. Make it simple and easy to transmit from one to the other, because therein lies the key to its virality and diffusion.

Tell something that causes or has caused you pain, laughter, guilt, something perfectly adaptable to your listeners' soul and heart. We are used to listening to stories from a young age. They are interesting, visual, let the imagination run wild, and foster powerful narrative communication. In short, they are very powerful. But they must see it (and feel it). Because if they see it, they will tell it.

5. Break patterns. Change paradigms. It provokes. Be flamboyant.

Before writing your speech, think about how you want your conclusion to be seen. As a nice, outgoing, reference speaker in his field, close, educational, entertaining, all of this at the same time. How? This panoramic HD (High Definition) will define your intervention. And if you fill it with continuous stimuli, the better. That they see something that they have never seen before, that they hear a phrase never before constructed. That they leave with the feeling that there must be a second part in their agendas to listen to you again.

Seek originality, but stay away from geeks. Innovate, but always remain attached to creativity and talent and not to spontaneous improvisation. Encourage them to emulate you. And for this, help yourself with the community symbology, that is, with those references, examples, that link, unite or bring you closer to those present so that they see you as close, accessible, and even as one of their own.

6. Tactical wins win the strategy.

Tactical victory comes when you master every part of your speech; when you know by heart the structure that will guide your steps with a firm word. That electrifying start, that 20-second connection that will make you begin to earn the respect of those present. The right moment to introduce the story, example, or anecdote is the timing domain (now I stop, now I accelerate) using the full-stop technique.

That end that is approaching and for which people were already warned by creating prior expectations. Small continuous points achieve the game, and many games allow you to win the set. In the speech, it is key to balance and control the rhythm and voice of the words, their correct intonation and speed, their exact location, and their relationship to the context you speak. There may be good arguments, sound ideas, irrefutable examples that if we do not control the rhythmic and musical pentagram, we will not convince.

We must know how to locate and identify the important idea of each paragraph of each part of our speech. And just before getting to that important idea or concepts, the corresponding pause, proper silence. With this, we will generate what I call communicative tension: create expectations with your messages. People have to perceive that what comes next in your speech exceeds what they have already heard. The speaker should be the thermostat of the speech: controlling the rhythm to pause and guide your messages and regulating the voice to define them.

Remember: Never scream or speak too loud. Where ideas do not reach, your voice should not reach because the tone of the message is the spirit of the idea.

CHAPTER 5

METHODS OF MASS MEDIA INFLUENCE ON THE SUBCONSCIOUS

Mass media is the most effective weapon for mass exploitation used by the capitalist class. They form and describe natural, reasonable attitudes and opinions. This chapter explores the activities of mass media to explain their true position in society through the ideas of the main thinkers, the mechanism of power and strategies they employ.

Some of the theories in this chapter speak about the supernatural symmetry found in popular culture objects. Many valid questions emerge from such a theory about the meaning of such symbols and the people who put them here. But without considering many other items, I cannot provide satisfactory answers to these questions.

Programming Via Mass Media

Mass media are forms of media designed to reach the widest possible audience. These include TV, film, radio, magazines, books, songs, games, the internet, and video games. In the past century, numerous studies have been carried out to measure the impact of mass media on the population to identify the best techniques for influencing them. From these studies emerged the science of communications used in marketing, public relations, and politics: mass communication is a necessary tool for the functioning of a vast democracy; it is also a necessary tool for a dictatorship. It all depends on its use.

In the preface to his 1958 Best of the Worlds, Aldous

Huxley paints a rather somber portrait of society. He believes that an "impersonal force controls it," a ruling elite that manipulates the population through various methods.

The impersonal forces over which we had almost no control seem to all push us towards the Best-worldly nightmare; and this impersonal push is being knowingly accelerated by representatives of political and commercial organizations which have developed several techniques to manipulate, in the interest of a certain minority, the thoughts and feelings of the masses.

His dark perspective is not just a mere hypothesis or an illusion of paranoia. It is a certified fact, present in the most important world studies on mass media. Here are a few:

ELITE THINKERS

WALTER LIPPMANN

The American intellectual Walter Lippmann was one of the first works on mass media use and was awarded the Pulitzer Prize two times. Lippmann compares mass in public opinion (1922) with a "big beast" and a "perplexed flock," which was to be led by a ruling class. He described the governing elite as a "specialized class with a vast diversity of interests beyond the local community." According to Lippmann, the experts who often have called themselves "the Elite" will soon be a system of intelligence that circumvents the key democratic shortcomings, representing the impossible dream of an "all-powerful citizen." "Puzzled herd" has its function to roar and trample, to be "the disinterested spectator of the event," not a participant. The "responsible person," who is not an ordinary citizen, is obliged to participate.

Thus, mass media and propaganda are instruments which must be used without physical correction by the elite to direct the public. The 'fabrication of consent,' in other words, manipulating the public opinion to embrace the elite's plan is an important idea put forth in Lippmann. The general public can not reason and determine important issues in Lippmann's view. So the elite will decide "for their own sake," and then sell the decisions to the masses.

I think no one denies that this manufacture of consent can make major improvements. The mechanism by which public opinion is formed is certainly no less nuanced than its pages and the possibilities for exploitation, which are fairly obvious for anyone who understands the method... The practice of democracy has changed as a result of psychological research combined with modern communication means. The influence of propaganda, not necessarily in the pejorative sense of the term, has made the old conservatives of our thought unpredictable. The change takes place that is more important than all the variations in the economy... For example, the original democracy dogma cannot be taken for granted; the human heart naturally derives the intelligence required to handle human affairs. If you act on this theory, you expose yourself to frustration and forms of belief that you can not verify. We are proving to do nothing to deal with the world beyond our grasp with intuition, awareness, or accidents of hasty opinion.

It is worth noting that Lippmann is one of the founding fathers of the CFR, the world's most influential think tank for foreign policy. It must give you some insight into the elite's state of mind in the use of the media.

In the United States, political and economic influence is centralized within a "ruling class," which is in the hands of the majority of foreign businesses, the mass media, the most powerful foundations, private universities, and most public services in the United States. The Foreign Relations Board was established in 1921 and is the key connection between large companies and the federal administration. This was called the 'school of state people' and something like an organ of what C. Wright Mills called the Power Elite — a group of people who have the same interests and the same ways of thinking that shape events from the background the invulnerable.

The new CFR Members include David Rockefeller, Dick Cheney, Barack Obama, Hilary Clinton, Rick Warren, and leading companies, including CBS, Nike, Coca-Cola, and Visa. Other new CFR members include:

CARL JUNG

Carl Jung is the pioneer of analytical psychology and discusses the mind's comprehension through vision, poetry, mythology, religion, symbolism, and philosophy. At the root of many psychological concepts, such as archetype, complexity, individual, introvert/extravert, and synchronicity, is the Swiss therapist. The hidden environment of his family greatly influenced him. A fervent Freemason, his grandfather, Carl Gustav, was the great Master, and the Rosicrucians were found out by Jung himself. It could explain the great interest he had in the philosophy of the West and the East, Alchemy, Astrology, and Symbolism.

There is a second psychological structure of a collective, universal and impersonal type, identical with all individuals, as well as our immediate, truly personal consciousness, which we believe is the only empirical psyche (even if we insert the personal unconscious in the appendix). We do not grow this collective unconscious individually but by heritage. It consists of pre-existing forms, the archetypes that can only be secondarily recognized, and offer that psychic material a defined form.

In various civilizations, the collective unconscious emerges by the presence of identical images and mythological characters. The archetylistic symbols seem to have been integrated into our collective subconscious, and we exhibit a natural curiosity and appeal when we are exposed. Therefore, occult symbols may have a significant impact on people, even if many people never directly are confronted with the mystical meaning of the symbol. This concept has been found by mass media thinkers like Edward D. Bernays to manipulate the public's collective and personal subconscious.

EDWARD BERNAYS

The "Public Relations man," Edward Bernays, uses techniques that his uncle Sigmund Freud invented to influence public opinion using the Unconscious. He shared the dream of Walter Lippmann for the population as irrational and subject to the "herd revolution."

Conscious and intelligent manipulation of organized mass habits and views is a key element in a democratic society. An invisible government that powers the country is the one who manipulates this invisible system of society.

We are governed, our minds are created, our preferences are influenced, and our ideas are suggested, mostly by people we never heard of. The way our democratic society is structured is a logical result. Many people have to work together this way if they want to stay together again in a trouble-free community.

In certain cases, our unseen rulers are unaware of their colleagues' presence in the closed circle.

The way American society works has dramatically changed creative marketing strategies by Barneys. He generated "consumerism" literally by developing a society where Americans shop for pleasure rather than survive. That's why Life Magazine is considered one of the Top 100 of 20th-century prominent Americans.

HAROLD LASSWELL

In 1939-1940, the University of Chicago hosted a series of secret communications seminars. These think tanks were funded by the Rockefeller Foundation and included the most important researchers in communication and sociological studies. One of his scholars was Harold Lasswell, a leading political scientist and communications theorist specializing in the analysis of propaganda. He also shared that democracy, a people-led government, could not be sustained without a specialized elite that shaped public opinion through propaganda.

In his Encyclopedia of Social Sciences, Lasswell explains that when the elites lack the strength required for forced obedience, social managers must turn to "a whole new technique of control, largely through propaganda." He added the conventional justification to it: "ignorance and stupidity [of] ... the masses and not succumb to democratic dogmatisms that men are the best judges of their interests."

Lasswell has studied the area of content analysis extensively to understand the effectiveness of different types of propaganda. In his essay, The Contents of Communication, Lasswell explains that, to understand the meaning of a message (i.e., a book, a speech, a film, etc.), the frequency of use of such symbols in the message, the way these symbols serve to influence the viewers' views and the strength of the symbols used must be considered.

Lasswell was famous for his media analysis based on this:

"Who (says) What (to) Who (through) What Means (with) What Effect."

Using this model, Lasswell indicates that to analyze a media product properly, we need to look at who produced it (the people who ordered it), for whom it is intended (the target audience) and what are the desired effects of the product (inform, convince, sell, etc.) on the audience.

Here's the review of a Rihanna video: WHO PRODUCED: Vivendi Universal; Whom: Rihanna's pop artist; TO WHOM: consumers aged 9-25; WHAT MEANS: the clip; and WHAT EFFECT: the seller: its music, its image, and its message.

The study of films and videos on The Vigilant Citizen gives the message that has been conveyed to the considerable public significance. The word "Illuminati" is sometimes used to describe a select group of leaders who secretly rule the masses. Though the word may sound very caricatured and conspiratory, it accurately represents the elite closeness of secret societies and occult knowledge. Yet I refuse to explain what is happening in the mass media using the word "conspiracy theory." Could we still call this "conspiracy theory" because all the details about the industry's elitist character are publicly available?

Throughout popular culture, there were many different beliefs, thoughts, and opinions. But the convergence of media companies has culminated in the entertainment sector being consolidated. Have you ever wondered why all new music sounds the same, and all new movies look the same? In the following section, the answer can be found:

Media Ownership

A list of properties managed with AOL Time Warner is contained in ten pages listing 292 separate companies and subsidiaries. Twenty-two of them are joint ventures with different stages of media operations. These partners include 3Com, E-Bay (American Express, Homestore, Sony, Viva, Bertelsmann, and Polygram), and Hewlett-Packard (Cities Group, Citygroup). AOL Time Warner's most familiar properties: Book of the Monday Club: Little Brown Publishers, HBO and its seven networks, CNN, seven international and specialty networks, Beep beep, vil coyote studios, Popular science, and 52 other record labels. -- "New Media Monopoly," Ben Bagdikan.

Warner's AOL Time:

-- 64 ratings, among them TIME, LIFE, People, MAD, DC comics.

-- Film features for Warner Bros, New Line, and Fine Line.

-- More than 40 labels, with Warner Bros, Atlantic and Electra included.

-- Various networks of television, such as Network AB, HBO, Cinemax, TNT, Cartoon Network, CNN.

Viacom has the following:

CBS, MTV, MTV2, UPN, VH1, Showtime, Nickelodeon, Central Comedy, TNN, CMT, BET

-- Nickelodeon films, MTV films, Paramount images

-- Videos from Blockbuster

-- 1800 film displays by famous players

Disney has a hockey team called the Anaheim Mighty Ducks, which is no longer adequate to reflect the Empire's vastness. Hollywood continues to be the icon and has eight production studios and dealers: Walt Disney Pictures, Hollywood Pictures, and Caravan Pictures.

ABC Television Network with its ten networks, in the Top five of its activities on the market; 30 radio stations, including all the largest on the market; 11 cable outlets, including Disney and ESPN (jointly), A&E and the history channel; 13 internal outlets, including Disney and ESPN (jointly) CASS, manages eight publishing houses of Walt Disney and ABC Publishing Books.

-- Ibid.-Ibid.

The corporation owns Walt Disney:

-- ABC, ESPN, A&E, ESPN, Web of History.

-- Walt Disney Images, Hollywood Pictures, and Aspect of the Miramax Film Corp.

-- Hannah Montana, Miley Cyrus, and Jonas Brothers. Montana and Selena Gomez.

Universal Vivendi has the following:

-- 27% of the US sales of music, including Interscope, Geffen, A&M, Island, Def Jam, MCA, Mercury, Motown, and Universal

-- Universal Studios, Channel studio, Polygram Films.

-- A lot of Internet and telecommunications companies,

-- Lady Gaga, Lil Wayne, Mariah Spears, Mariah Carey, Lil Gaga, The Black Eyed Peas.

Sony controls the following:

-- Columbia photos, gems, classical Sony photos

-- 15% of music sales in the US: Columbia, Epic, Sony, Arista, Jive and RCA Records

-- Michael Jackson, Alicia Keys, Christina Aguilera, Beyonce, Shakira,

A few cultural actors represent a limited number of views and ideas that are open to the public.

It means, too, that an idea can quickly saturate all media platforms to agree (such as "mass destruction weapons in Iraq").

The Standardization Of Human Thought

A global oligarchy of media conglomerates has been formed through the merger of media companies in recent decades. FIVE companies are making the TV shows, the songs that we listen to, the films we watch, and the newspapers that we read. The members of these organizations are closely linked to the global elite and are the elite in several respects. Such conglomerates have the power to build a common and consistent view of the future that promotes "standardization of the human imagination" by providing all those channels that can touch the masses.

Even the movements and styles considered marginal are, in fact, extensions of the main thought. The mass media produce their rebels who seem to be part of it and continue to be part of the established order and challenge it. Artists, creations, and ideas that do not correspond to the main way of thinking are forgotten and mercilessly rejected by the conglomerates, making them virtually disappear from society itself. However, ideas that are considered valid and desirable to be accepted by society are skillfully marketed to the masses to turn them into self-evident standards.

In 1928, Edward Barneys had already seen the immense potential of cinema to standardize thoughts:

American cinema is the largest subconscious carrier of propaganda in the world today. It is a great distributor of ideas and opinions. The cinema can standardize the ideas and habits of a nation. Because images are made to meet market demands, they reflect, emphasize, and even exaggerate popular trends, rather than stimulating new ideas and opinions. The cinema uses ideas and facts that are in vogue. While the newspapers seek to provide the facts, it [the cinema] seeks to provide entertainment.

In the 1930s, Frankfurt school thinkers like Theodor Adorno and Herbert Marcuse marked these facts as a threat to human freedom. Three key issues with the cultural industry were identified. Branching can:

1. Reduce people to "population status" by hindering the creation of self-employed persons who can determine rationally.

2. Replace the valid dynamism of individuality and self-visibility with the tranquility of conformism and passivity.

3. Validate the belief that people are trying to escape the insane and cruel world they live in by hypnotically losing themselves.

The notion of escape is even more relevant today with the advent of online video games, 3D movies, and home theaters. The masses, seeking state-of-the-art entertainment, will resort to big-budget products that can only be produced by the world's largest media corporations. These products contain deliberately placed messages and symbols that are nothing more than entertaining propaganda. The public has been trained to LIKE this propaganda, to the point of spending their hard-earned money to be exposed to it.

About propaganda, the early defenders of universal

literacy and the free press considered two possibilities: propaganda may be true, or it may be false. They did not foresee what happened, especially in our western capitalist democracies — the development of a vast mass consumer industry, concerned in absolute terms neither with the true nor with the false, but more or less irrelevant with the unreal. In a term, the almost limitless human appetite for diversion was not taken into consideration.

A single medium also has no enduring impact on the psychology of humans. However, the mass media creates a living environment in which we evolve every day because of their omnipresent nature. The norm is defined, and the unwanted excluded. Likewise, when wearing the blinds, the masses can only see where they are supposed to see so that they can only see what is before them.

The emergence of the mass media makes the use of propaganda techniques on a societal scale. The orchestration of the press, radio, and television to create a continuous, lasting, and total environment makes the influence of propaganda virtually unsuspected precisely because it creates a constant environment. Mass media provides the essential link between the individual and the demands of the technological society.

One of the reasons why the mass media successfully influences industrial society is due to the considerable amount of research on cognitive sciences and human nature that has been applied to it...

Handling techniques

Advertising is a deliberate attempt to control the public's perception of a subject. Advertising topics include people (for example politicians or playing artists), goods and services, organizations of all types, works of art and entertainment.

The effort to sell products and ideas to the masses has led to an unprecedented amount of research on human behavior and the human psyche. Cognitive science, psychology, sociology, semiotics, linguistics, and other related fields were still greatly sought after by well-funded studies.

No group of sociologists can approach advertising teams about the collection and processing of social data. Advertising teams have billions per year to spend on research and reaction testing, and their products are magnificent accumulations of substance regarding the feelings and experiences of the entire community.

These studies' results are applied to advertisements, films, clips, and other media to make them as influential as possible. The art of marketing is highly scientific and calculated because it must reach both the collective and the individual unconscious. As far as the big-budget goods are concerned, a video is never "just a video." To achieve the desired effect, images, symbols, and meanings are put strategically.

It is also with the knowledge of the human being, his tendencies, desires, needs, psychic mechanism, and automatisms as that of social psychology and analytical psychology that propaganda can refine his techniques.

Propaganda today hardly ever uses logical or rational arguments. It will directly draw on the most basic human needs and instincts to generate an emotional and irrational response. If we thought rationally, likely, we would not buy 50% of what we have.

Sex is ubiquitous in mass media since it attracts and keeps the viewer's attention. This immediately puts itself in communication with our instinct to perpetuate the species, to reproduce us. When it is triggered, this instinct can overshadow any other rational thought in our brain.

Subliminal Perception

What if the messages mentioned above could reach the audience without even knowing what is happening? What if? This is the purpose of subliminal perception. In 1957 US market researcher James Vicary coined the word 'subliminal advertising,' which claimed that anyone who went to the films could drink 'Coca-Cola' and 'eat popcorn.' The presentation of these messages is brief enough for the spectator to be unaware of.

Subliminal awareness is a deliberate process produced by communication technicians that allows you to receive and address information and instructions without understanding it.

This technique is frequently used in commercialization, and we all know that sex sells.

Although some sources claim that subliminal publicity is ineffective or even an urban legend, the documented application of this technique in mass media shows that its designers believe in its power. The efficacy of recent studies has also been demonstrated, particularly when the message is negative.

"To instill negative thinking, a team at University College London, funded by the Wellcome Trust, found that it was especially good." "There has been a lot of speculation about whether people can interact with emotional information, including pictures, faces, and words in a subconscious way," said Professor Nill Lavie. "We have demonstrated that people can understand the emotional meaning of subliminal messages and have shown that people are much more in line with bad words.

Desensitization

In the past, when people were subject to changes, they took to the streets, protested, even triggered riots. The main reason for these clashes was because the changes were clearly announced by the leaders and understood by the population. It was sudden, and the effects could be analyzed and assessed. Today, when the elite needs the public to understand part of their plan, they do so through desensitization. The program, which may go against the best interests of the public, is slowly, gradually and repeatedly presented to the world through films (by involving it in the plot) clips (which make it cool and sexy) or the news (which presents it as a solution to current problems). After several years of mass exposure to a particular program, the elite openly exposes its project to the world. Because of mental programming, it is greeted with general indifference and passively accepted. This technique comes from psychotherapy.

These psychotherapy techniques, widely practiced and accepted as a means of curing psychological disorders, are also methods of controlling people. They can be systematically used to influence attitudes and behaviors. Systematic desensitization is used to alleviate anxiousness to ensure that a specific fear of violence, for example, no longer perturbs the patient (the public). [...] If they are exposed to them enough, people respond to terrifying circumstances.

You can often find predictive programming in the science fiction genre. It represents a specific image of the future — the one desired by the elite — which ultimately becomes inevitable in men's minds. Ten years ago, the public was desensitized to the war against the Arab world.

Today, the public is gradually exposed to the existence of mind control, transhumanism, and the existence of an Illuminati elite. Emerging from the shadows, these concepts are now everywhere in popular culture. This is what Alice Bailey describes under the name "outsourcing of the hierarchy": those who lead in the shadows reveal themselves slowly ...

Occult Symbolism In Popular Culture

Metropolis - An elite film for the elite?

Documentation on occult symbolism is rather difficult to find. This should not be surprising since the term "occult" literally means "hidden." It also means "reserved for those who know" since it is only communicated to those who are considered worthy of this knowledge. It is neither taught in schools nor discussed by the media. It is therefore considered marginal or even ridiculous by the general population.

Occult knowledge in occult circles, however, is NOT seen as absurd. It's considered eternal and sacred. There is a long history of hermeneutic and supernatural knowledge, taught by secret societies from Ancient Egypt, the Mystics of Eastern Europe, the Templar kings, and modern Freemasons. Even if nature and the extent of this knowledge have most probably been modified, altered through the centuries, the schools of the occult have kept their main characteristics, which are highly symbolic, ceremonial, and metaphysical. These characteristics, which were a complex part of ancient civilizations, have been completely removed from modern society to be replaced by a materialist pragmatism. Thus, there is a large gap in understanding between the average person and the ritualist institution.

If this esoteric doctrine has always been hidden from the masses, for whom a simpler code has been partitioned, is it not highly probable that the representatives of every aspect of modern civilization — philosophical, ethical and scientific — are ignorant of the true meaning of these very theories and principles on which their beliefs are based? That hiding behind their beautiful façade are the arts and sciences which the race has inherited from older nations, a mystery that only the most enlightened intellectuals can understand? Surely that's the case.

The "simpler code" partitioned for the masses used to be organized religions. It has become the Temple of Mass Media and daily preaches extreme materialism, spiritual emptiness, and an individualistic, self-directed existence. It is exactly the opposite of the attributes required to become a truly free man, as taught by the great schools of thought. Is a stupid population easier to deceive and manipulate?

These blind slaves are told that they are "free" and "well educated," even when they walk behind the signs that would make them flee from panicking and shouting any peasant of the Middle Ages. The sign on the sign will be similar to the symbols that Modern Man accepts in the naive faith of a child: "Direct your death and slavery," as a peasant of antiquity would understand.

This chapter examines the leading thinkers in mass media, the structure of media influence, and the techniques employed for mass manipulation. I think it is important to consider "why" in matters on The Vigilant Citizen that are discussed. The dichotomy that is portrayed in many articles between the "population base" and "ruling class" is not a "construction theory," but is a fact that has been accurately articulated in the work of some of the most important men of the twentieth century.

Lippmann, Lasswell, and Bernays all said that it is difficult for the public to determine its fate, which is the goal of democracy. Their thoughts continue to apply to societies. It is becoming increasingly clear that an ignorant population is not an obstacle that the leaders have to face; it's something DESIRABLE, and indeed necessary to ensure complete leadership. Their idea is always being applied to society, but a hidden regime, a ruling class in charge of the puzzle. An ignorant community is not searching for its rights, and it is not trying to obtain a better understanding and authority of the problems. It just goes along with the pattern. Popular culture provides and nurtures ignorance by constantly serving as entertainment for the brain and bringing degenerate celebrities to worship.

This hopes for what has never been and will never be if it wishes to be naive and free.

CHAPTER 6

PSYCHOLOGICAL METHODS OF MANIPULATING THE MENTAL CONSCIOUSNESS OF MAN AND THE MASSES

Consider the psychological techniques of manipulating the mental consciousness of man and the masses. For convenience, we divide the proposed methods into eight blocks, effective both individually and together.

The life of any person is multifaceted by the life experience that this person has, by the level of education, by the genetic component, by many other factors that must be taken into account for the psychological impact on the person. Specialists in manipulating the psyche (psychotherapists, hypnologists, criminal hypnotists, fraudsters, government officials, etc.) use different technologies to control people. It is necessary to know such methods, including and to counter this kind of manipulation. Knowledge is power. It is knowledge about the mechanisms of manipulation of the human psyche that allows you to resist illegal intrusions into the psyche (into the subconscious of a person) and, therefore, protect yourself.

It should be noted that there are a large number of methods of psychological impact (manipulation). Some of them are available for mastering only after a long practice (for example, NLP), some are freely used by most people in life, sometimes without even noticing it; it is enough to have ideas about some methods of manipulative influence to defend oneself already; to counteract others, you need to have a good command of such techniques (for example, gypsy psychological hypnosis), etc. To the extent that such a step is permissible, we will reveal the secrets of controlling the mental consciousness of a person and the masses (collective, assembly, audience, crowd, etc.).

It is worth noting that only recently has the opportunity appeared to talk about early secret techniques openly. At the same time, such tacit permission from the oversight bodies is quite justified, since we are convinced that a certain part of the truth is revealed to a person only at a certain stage. Collecting such material bit by bit — a person is formed into the desired person. If for some reason, a person is still ready to comprehend the truth, fate itself will lead him aside. And if such a person even finds out about some secret techniques, then he will not be able to realize their significance. That is, this kind of information will not find the necessary response in his soul, and in his psyche, a stupor will turn on, thanks to which such information will simply not be perceived by the brain, i.e., will not be remembered by such a person.

Below we will consider the manipulation techniques outlined by blocks of equivalent ineffectiveness. Even though its inherent name precedes each block, nevertheless, it should be noted that the specifics of methods of influencing the subconscious are very effective for all, without exception, regardless of the specific target audience or typical personality characteristics of a person. This is explained by the fact that the human psyche has common components and differs only in insignificant details, hence the increased efficiency of the developed manipulation techniques in the world.

- The first block of manipulation techniques

Methods Of Manipulating The Human Mental

Consciousness

1. False interrogation, or deceptive clarifications

In this case, the manipulative effect is achieved because the manipulator pretends that he wants to better understand something for himself, asks you again, but repeats your words only at the beginning and then only partially, introducing a different meaning into the meaning of what you said earlier, thereby changing the general meaning of what was said to please yourself.

In this case, you should be extremely careful, always listen to what you are being told about, and noticing a catch — clarify what you said earlier; moreover, to clarify even if the manipulator, pretending not to notice your desire for clarification, tries to move on to another topic.

2. Deliberate haste, or leaping to a new topic

The manipulator in this case, after voicing any information, seeks to quickly switch to another topic, realizing that your attention will immediately be redirected to new information, which increases the likelihood that previous information that has not been "protested" will reach the subconscious listener; if the information reaches the subconscious, it is known that after any information is in the unconscious (subconscious), after a while, it is realized by a person, i.e., passes into consciousness. Moreover, if the manipulator additionally strengthened his information with an emotional load, or even introduced it into the subconscious by the encoding method, then such information will appear at the moment necessary for the manipulator, which he will provoke (for example, using the principle of "anchoring" from NLP, or, in other words, by activating the code).

Also, as a result of haste and skipping topics, it becomes

possible for a relatively short period to "voice" a large number of topics; which means that censorship of the psyche will not have time to let everything through it, and the likelihood that a certain part of the information will penetrate the subconscious mind will increase. From there, it will affect the manipulated object's consciousness in a way that is beneficial to the manipulator.

3. The desire to show their indifference or pseudo-carelessness

In this case, the manipulator tries to perceive both the interlocutor and the information received as indifferently as possible, thereby unconsciously making the person try to convince the manipulator of its significance for him at all costs. Thus, the manipulator can only control the information emanating from the object of its manipulations, obtaining those facts that the object was not going to spread before. A similar circumstance on the part of the person to whom the manipulation is directed is laid down in the laws of the psyche, forcing any person to strive at all costs to prove his case by convincing the manipulator (not suspecting that he is a manipulator), and using the existing arsenal of logical controllability of thoughts — that is, the presentation of new circumstances of the case, facts that, in his opinion, can help him in this.

In this case, it is recommended to strengthen their voluntary control and not succumb to provocations as a counteraction.

4. False inferiority, or imaginary weakness

This principle of manipulation is aimed at the desire on the part of the manipulator to show his weakness to the object of manipulation, and thereby achieve the desired result because if someone is weaker, the indulgence effect is turned on, which means that censorship of the human psyche begins to function in a relaxed mode, as if not perceiving what is coming from manipulator information in earnest. Thus, the information coming from the manipulator passes immediately to the subconscious, is stored there in the form of attitudes and behavior patterns, which means that the manipulator reaches his goal, because the manipulation object itself, without suspecting it, will begin to execute the settings laid down in the subconscious, or, in other words, to execute the secret will of the manipulator.

The main method of confrontation is the complete control of information coming from any person, i.e., any person is an adversary, and he must be taken seriously.

5. False love, or the euthanasia of vigilance

Because one individual (manipulator) plays love, excessive respect, reverence, etc. in front of another (manipulation object) (i.e., expresses his feelings in a similar vein), he achieves incomparably more than if he openly asked for something.

In order not to succumb to such provocations, you should have a "cold mind."

6. Violent pressure, or exorbitant anger

In this case, manipulation becomes possible as a result of unmotivated rage on the part of the manipulator. The person to whom this kind of manipulation is directed will have a desire to calm someone angry with him. Why is he subconsciously ready to make concessions to the manipulator?

Countermeasures can be different, depending on the skills of the object of manipulation. For example, as a result of "tuning" (the so-called calibration in NLP), one can first stage a state of mind similar to a manipulator, and after calming down, calm the manipulator as well. Or, for example, you can show your calmness and absolute indifference to the anger of the manipulator, thereby confusing him, which means depriving him of his manipulative advantage. You can sharply speed up your aggressiveness with speech techniques at the same time as a light touch of the manipulator (his hand, shoulder, arm...), and additional visual impact. That is, in this case, we seize the initiative, and with the help of the simultaneous impact on the manipulator with the help of visual, auditory and kinesthetic stimuli — we introduce him into a state of trance. This means he depends on you, because in this state the manipulator himself becomes the object of our influence, and we can introduce certain settings into his subconscious because it is known that in a state of anger, any person is subject to coding (psychoprogramming). You can use other methods of counteraction. It should be remembered that in a state of anger, a person is easier to make laugh. You should know about this feature of the psyche and use it in time.

7. Fast pace, or unjustified rush

In this case, we should talk about the manipulator's desire due to the imposed excessively fast pace of speech to push some ideas, having achieved approval by their object of manipulation. This becomes possible even when the manipulator, hiding behind the alleged lack of time, achieves an incomparably greater amount from the manipulation object than if this happened over a long period, during which the manipulation object would have time to ponder his answer, and therefore not become a victim of deception (manipulation).

In this case, you should take a timeout (refer to an urgent phone call, etc.) to bring down the manipulator at a given tempo. To do this, you can play the misunderstanding of some questions and "stupid" interrogation, etc.

8. Excessive suspicion, or evoking forced excuses

A similar type of manipulation occurs when the manipulator plays suspicion in any issue. As a response to suspicion, the object of manipulation follows a desire to justify himself. Thus, his psyche's protective barrier is weakening, which means that the manipulator is achieving his goal, "pushing" the necessary psychological attitudes into his subconscious.

A defense option is to recognize yourself as a person and to resist any attempt at any manipulative influence on your psyche (i.e., you must demonstrate your self-confidence and show that if the manipulator is suddenly offended, then let him be offended, and if he wants to leave, you don't run after him; this should be adopted by "lovers": do not let yourself be manipulated.)

9. Imaginary fatigue, or a game of consolation

With all his appearance, the manipulator shows fatigue and the inability to prove something and listen to any objections. Thus, the object of manipulation tries to quickly agree with the words given by the manipulator, so as not to bore him with his objections. Well, agreeing, he thereby goes on about the manipulator, who only needs it.

One way to counter this is to not succumb to provocations.

10. The credibility of the manipulator, or deception of power

This manipulation proceeds from such specifics of the individual psyche as the worship of authorities in any field.

87

Most often, it turns out that the very area in which such an "authority" has achieved a result lies in a completely different sphere than its imaginary "request" now. Still, the object of manipulation cannot do anything about it, since in the soul, most people believe that there is always someone who has achieved more than them.

A variant of the confrontation is faith in one's exclusiveness, super personality, the development in yourself of the belief in your chosenness, that you are a super-person.

11. Courtesy, or help fee

The manipulator informs the object of manipulation conspiratorially about something as if advising him to decide in a friendly manner. At the same time, hiding behind an imaginary friendship (in fact, they may be familiar for the first time), as a tip, inclines the object of manipulation to the variant of solution that is primarily needed by the manipulator.

You need to believe in yourself and remember that you have to pay for everything. And it's better to pay right away, i.e., before you are required to pay a fee in the form of gratitude for the service provided.

12. Resistance, or protest

In some words, a manipulator excites feelings in the soul of the object of manipulation, aimed at overcoming the barrier (censorship of the psyche) that has arisen, to achieve his goal. It is known that the psyche is structured in such a way that a person wants to a greater extent what is forbidden to him or what efforts must be made to achieve.

Whereas that which may be better and more important,

but lies on the surface, is often overlooked.

Confidence and will, i.e., you should always rely only on yourself, and not give in to weaknesses.

13. Factor particular, or from details to error

The manipulator forces the object of manipulation to pay attention to only one specific detail, not allowing him to notice the main thing. Based on this, he draws the appropriate conclusions, accepted by the consciousness of it as an uncontested basis of the meaning of what was said. It should be noted that this is very common in life when most people allow themselves to make their own opinions about a subject, without actually having any facts or more detailed information, and often without having their own opinions about what they judge using the opinions of others. Therefore, such an opinion is possible to impose on them, which means manipulating them to achieve their goal.

To counter, it is necessary to constantly work on yourself to increase your knowledge and education level.

14. The irony, or the manipulation of a grin

Manipulation is achieved because the manipulator chooses an initially ironic tone as if unconsciously calling into question any words of the object of manipulation. In this case, the object of manipulation is much faster "losing his temper"; and since anger makes critical thinking more difficult, a person enters into ASCs (altered states of consciousness), in which consciousness easily passes early forbidden information through it.

For effective protection, you should show your complete indifference to the manipulator. The feeling of being a super-person, "chosen," will help you to be condescending to the attempt to manipulate you — as to children's fun. The manipulator will immediately feel this condition intuitively, because the manipulators usually have well-developed sense organs, which, we note, allows them to feel the right moment for carrying out their manipulative techniques.

15. Interruption, or departure of thoughts

The manipulator achieves his goal by constantly interrupting the thought of the object of manipulation, directing the topic of conversation necessary for the manipulator.

As a counteraction, you can ignore the interruptions of the manipulator, or use special speech psychotechnics to make fun of him among the audience. If you laugh at a person, all his subsequent words are no longer taken seriously.

16. Provoking imaginary, or far-fetched accusations

Such manipulations become possible as a result of communicating to the object of manipulation the information that can cause him anger, and therefore reduce the criticality in assessing the alleged information. After this, such a person is broken for a certain period, during which the manipulator achieves the imposition of his will.

Protection - believe in yourself and not pay attention to others.

17. Trapping, or imaginary recognition of the opponent's gain

In this case, the manipulator, while carrying out the act of manipulation, hints at more favorable conditions in which the opponent (the object of manipulation) is supposedly located, thereby forcing the latter to make excuses in every possible way, and become open to manipulations that usually follow the manipulator.

Protection is self-awareness as a super-personality, which means a completely reasonable "elevation" over the manipulator, especially if he considers himself "insignificant." Therefore, faith in yourself and faith in your exceptionalism will help overcome any traps on the way to your consciousness from the side of manipulators.

18. Cheating in the palm of your hand, or imitation of bias

The manipulator intends to place the object of manipulation in certain predetermined conditions. The person selected as the object of manipulation, trying to avert his suspicion of excessive bias towards the manipulator, allows manipulation to take place due to the unconscious conviction of the good intentions of the manipulator. That is, he seems to be giving himself the option not to react critically to the manipulator's words, thereby unconsciously allowing the words of the manipulator to pass into his consciousness.

19. Intentional misconception, or specific terminology

In this case, the manipulation is carried out through the use of the manipulator of specific terms that are not clear to the object of manipulation. The latter, because of the danger of seeming illiterate, lacks the courage to clarify what these terms mean.

The way to counter this is to ask and clarify something incomprehensible to you.

20. The imposition of false stupidity, or through humiliation to victory

The manipulator seeks in every way to reduce the role of the object of manipulation, hinting at his stupidity and illiteracy, to thus destabilize the positive mindset of the object of manipulation, plunge his psyche into a state of chaos and temporary confusion, and thus achieve his will over him through verbal manipulation and (or) coding the psyche.

Protection - do not pay attention. It is generally recommended to pay less attention to the meaning of the words of the manipulator, and more to the details around, gestures and facial expressions, or even pretend that you are listening, and think "about your own," especially if you have an experienced fraudster or criminal hypnotist.

21. Repeatability of phrases, or the imposition of thoughts

In this type of manipulation, due to repeated phrases, the manipulator accustoms the object of manipulation to any information that is going to convey to him.

Protective installation - do not fix attention on the words of the manipulator, listen to it "in the ear," or use special speech techniques to transfer the conversation to another topic, or seize the initiative and enter the settings you need into the subconscious of the interlocutor-manipulator yourself, or many other options.

22. Erroneous speculation, or lack of understanding involuntarily

In this case, the manipulations achieve their effect due to:

- Deliberate lack of understanding by the manipulator.
- Erroneous speculation of the object of

manipulation.

Moreover, even if a fraud is detected, the object of manipulation gives the impression of his guilt because he did not understand it or did not hear something.

Protection - exceptional self-confidence, the education of super-will, the formation of "chosenness" and super-personality.

23. Imaginary inattention

In this situation, the object of manipulation falls into the trap of the manipulator, playing on his own supposed inattention, so that, having achieved his own, refers to the fact that he allegedly did not notice (hear) the protest from the opponent. As a result, a manipulator puts the object of manipulation before the fact of the perfect.

Protection - clearly clarify the meaning of "agreements reached."

24. Say yes, or the path to agreement

Manipulations of this kind are carried out because the manipulator seeks to build a dialogue with the object of manipulation to always agree with his words. Thus, the manipulator skillfully brings the object of manipulation to pushing his idea, and therefore the implementation of manipulation on him.

Protection - to bring down the direction of the conversation.

25. Unexpected quotation, or the words of the opponent as evidence

In this case, the manipulative effect is achieved by unexpected quoting by the manipulator, the previously spoken words of the opponent. Such a technique acts discouragingly on the selected object of manipulation, helping the manipulator to achieve a result. Moreover, in most cases, the words themselves can be partially invented, i.e., to have a different meaning than the object of manipulation said earlier on this issue. Because the words of the object of manipulation can be simply invented, or have an only slight similarity.

Protection - also apply the method of false citation, choosing, in this case, the allegedly spoken words of the manipulator.

26. The effect of observation, or the search for similarities

As a result of preliminary observation of the manipulation object (including during the dialogue), the manipulator finds or invents any similarities between himself and the object, gently draws the attention of the object to this similarity, and thereby partially weakens the protective functions of the psyche of the manipulated object, after which he pushes his idea.

Protection - sharply emphasize in words your dissimilarity to the interlocutor-manipulator.

27. The imposition of choice, or initially the right decision

In this case, the manipulator asks the question in such a way that he does not leave the object of manipulation the possibility of making a choice other than the one voiced by the manipulator. (For example, would you like to do this or this? In this case, the keyword is "do," while initially the object of manipulation probably was not going to do anything. But he was not left with the right to choose but to choose between the first and second.)

Protection - do not pay attention, take control of any situation.

28. Unexpected revelation, or sudden honesty

This manipulation consists of the fact that after a short conversation, the manipulator suddenly confidentially tells the object he has chosen to manipulate that he intends to communicate something secret and important, which is intended only for him because he liked this person. He feels that he can trust him with the truth. At the same time, the object of manipulation unconsciously arises confidence in this kind of revelation, which means that we can already talk about the weakening of the protective mechanisms of the psyche, which, through the weakening of censorship (criticality barrier), passes the lies of the manipulator into the subconscious mind.

Protection - do not succumb to provocations, and remember that you can always rely only on yourself. Another person can always fail (consciously, unconsciously, under duress, under the influence of hypnosis, etc.)

29. A sudden counterargument, or insidious lie

The manipulator, unexpectedly for the object of manipulation, refers to words supposedly spoken earlier, according to which the manipulator simply develops the theme further, starting from them. After such "revelations," the object of manipulation has a feeling of guilt. The barriers put forward in the way of those words of the manipulator that he previously perceived with a certain degree of criticality should finally break down in his psyche. This is also possible because the majority of those targeted by manipulation are internally unstable, have increased criticality about themselves, and therefore, such a lie on the part of the manipulator turns, in their consciousness, into one or another piece of truth, which, as a result, helps the manipulator to get things done.

Protection - the development of willpower, exceptional confidence and self-respect.

30. The accusation of theory, or imaginary lack of practice

As an unexpected counterargument, the manipulator puts forward a demand according to which the words of the object of manipulation chosen by him are kind of good only in theory, while in practice, the situation will supposedly be different. Thus, unconsciously making it clear to the object of manipulation that all the words just heard by the manipulator are nothing and are good only on paper, but in the real situation, everything will turn out differently, which means that you cannot rely on such words.

Protection - do not pay attention to the speculations and assumptions of other people and believe only in your mind's power.

- The second block of manipulation techniques

Ways To Influence The Media Audience Through Manipulation

1. The principle of priority

This method's essence is based on the specifics of the psyche, which is structured in such a way that it takes for granted the information that was first received by the consciousness. It is also no longer necessary that we get more accurate information later.

In this case, perceiving primary information as truth is triggered, especially since it is impossible to understand its contradictory nature immediately. And after that, it is already difficult enough to change the formed opinion.

A similar principle is quite successfully used in political

technologies when some accusatory material (compromising material) is sent to a competitor (through the media), thereby:

- Forming voters with a negative opinion about him.
- Forcing to make excuses.

(In this case, there is an impact on the masses through widespread stereotypes that if someone makes excuses, it means to blame).

2. "Witnesses" of events

Ostensibly there are eyewitnesses of events who, with the necessary sincerity, report information transmitted in advance by manipulators, passing it off as their own. The name of such "eyewitnesses" is often hidden ostensibly for the conspiracy, or a false name is called, which, along with falsified information, nevertheless achieves an effect in the audience, since it affects the unconscious psyche of a person, causing the intensity of feelings and emotions in him. As a result, the censorship of the mind is weakened and can pass information from the manipulator without identifying its false essence.

3. The image of the enemy

By artificially creating a threat and, as a result of this, passions, the masses are plunged into states similar to ASC (altered states of consciousness). As a result, such weights are easier to control.

4. The shift in emphasis

In this case, a deliberate shift in emphasis occurs in the material presented, and something not quite desirable for the manipulators is shown in the background, but the opposite is highlighted — what they need.

5. Use of "opinion leaders"

In this case, the manipulations of the mass consciousness proceed on the basis that when specific actions are taken, individuals are guided by opinion leaders. Various figures may become leaders of opinions that have become authoritative in a particular category of the population.

6. Reorienting attention

In this case, almost any material can be generated without fear of its unwanted (dangerous) portion. This becomes possible based on the rule of reorienting attention when the information necessary for hiding seems to recede into the shadow of seemingly randomly displayed events that serve to distract attention.

7. Emotional charging

This technology of manipulation is based on such a property of the human psyche as emotional infectivity. In the process of life, a person builds specific protective barriers to obtaining undesirable information for him. To circumvent such a restriction (censorship of the psyche), the manipulative effect must be directed to the senses. Thus, by "charging" the necessary information with the underlying emotions, the obstacle to the mind can be surmounted. A person's emotions will erupt, forcing him to worry at some point about the information he has heard. Then comes the effect of emotional charge, which is most prevalent in the crowd, where, as you know, the criticality threshold is lower.

(Example. A similar effect of manipulation is used during a series of reality shows when participants speak in elevated tones and sometimes show significant emotional excitement, which makes them watch the events they demonstrate and empathize with the main characters. Or, for example, when speaking on television, especially ambitious politicians who impulsively shout out their ways out of crises, due to which information affects the feelings of individuals, and emotional contagion occurs in the audience, which means that the ability of such manipulators to force attention to the material presented is increased.)

8. The ostentatious issues

Depending on the presentation of the same materials, different, sometimes opposing, opinions can be obtained from the audience. That is, some event can be artificially "not noticed," but on the contrary, be paid increased attention, and even on different television channels. At the same time, truth itself seems to fade into the background. And it depends on the desire (or lack of desire) of the manipulators to highlight it. (For example, it is known that many events take place in the country every day. Naturally, coverage of all of them is physical impossible. However, it often happens that some events are shown often, frequently, and on various channels, while something else, which probably also deserves attention is as if deliberately not seen.)

It is worth noting that the flow of information through such a manipulative technique leads to the artificial inflation of non-existent problems. Something important is not noticed that can cause the anger of the people.

9. Inaccessibility of information

This principle of manipulative technologies is called information blockade. This becomes possible when a particular piece of information, undesirable for manipulators, is deliberately not allowed.

10. Strike ahead of the curve

A type of manipulation based on the early release of negative information for the main category of people. Moreover, this information causes maximum resonance. And by the time of the subsequent receipt of information and the need for an unpopular decision, the audience will already be tired of the protest and will not react too negatively. Using a similar method in political technologies, they first sacrifice some incriminating evidence. Then, when new incriminating evidence appears on the politician they are promoting, the masses no longer react. (Tired of responding.)

11. Dishonorable passions

A way of manipulating the mass media audience when using false passions by presenting allegedly sensational material, as a result of which the human psyche does not have time to react appropriately, creates unnecessary excitement, and the information presented later does not have such an effect, because the criticality decreases due to the censorship of the psyche. (In other words, a false time limit is created for which the information received must be estimated, which often leads to the fact that it almost without cuts from the side of consciousness falls into the unconscious individual; after which it affects the knowledge, distorting the very meaning of the information received, and also taking the place to gain and appraise the information more truthful.

12. The likelihood effect

In this case, the basis for possible manipulation consists of such a component of the psyche when a person is inclined to believe information that does not contradict his previously available information or ideas on the subject under discussion.

(In other words, if through the media we come across information that we do not internally agree with, then we consciously block such a channel for obtaining information. And if we encounter information that does not contradict our understanding of such a question, we continue to absorb such information that reinforces the earlier shaped patterns of behavior, and the installation in the subconscious mind. Also, by a similar principle of manipulation, it is possible to initially supply information that is unfavorable for the manipulator (supposedly criticizing himself), thereby increasing the audience's confidence that this mass media source is relatively honest and truthful. Well, later on, the information necessary for the manipulators is interspersed in the supplied information.)

13. The effect of "information assault"

In this case, it should be said that a flurry of useless information collapses on a person, in which truth is lost.

(People who have undergone this form of manipulation just get tired of the flow of information, which means that analyzing such information becomes difficult and manipulators can hide the information they need, but undesirable for a demonstration to the masses.)

14. The opposite effect

In the case of such a fact of manipulation, such an amount of negative information is released to some person that this information achieves the exact opposite effect. Instead of the expected conviction, such a person begins to cause pity. (An example of the Perestroika years with B.N. Yeltsin, who fell into the river from a bridge.)

15. The everyday story, or evil with a human face

Information that may cause an undesirable effect is pronounced in the usual tone as if nothing terrible was happening. This way of delivering knowledge loses its importance when it comes to audience consciousness— any important facts. Thus, the criticality of the human psyche of negative information disappears, and addiction to it occurs.

16. One-sided coverage of events

This manipulation method is aimed at one-sided coverage of events, when it is possible to speak only on one side of the process, as a result of which a false semantic effect of the information obtained is achieved.

17. The principle of contrast

This manipulation becomes possible when the necessary information is presented against the background of another, initially harmful, and negatively perceived by the majority of the audience. (In other words, against the black background, there will always be noticeable white. And against the backdrop of bad people, you can still show the right person by talking about his good deeds. A similar principle is universal in political technologies when, at first, a possible crisis in the rival camp is examined in detail. Then the true nature of the actions needed by the manipulators of a candidate who does not and cannot have such a crisis is demonstrated.)

18. Endorsement of the imaginary majority

The application of this mass manipulation technique is based on such a specific component of the human psyche as the permissibility of performing any action, after the initial approval by other people. As a result of this manipulation method in the human mind, the criticality barrier is erased after other people have approved such information. Let us recall Lebon, Freud, Ankylosing spondylitis, and other classics of the masses' psychology — the principles of imitation and infectivity are actively operating among the masses. Therefore, what one does — pick up the rest.

19. Emotional punch

When implemented, this principle should produce the effect of psychological shock, when manipulators achieve the desired result by intentionally broadcasting the horrors of modern life, which causes the first reaction of protest (because of the fast development of the psyche emotion), and the desire to punish the guilty at all costs. At the same time, they do not notice that the emphasis in the presentation of the material can be deliberately shifted towards competitors that are unnecessary for manipulators or against information that seems undesirable.

20. False analogies, or sabotage against logic

This manipulation removes the exact cause in a question, replacing it with a false analogy. (For example, there is an incorrect comparison of various and mutually exclusive consequences, which in this case are presented as one. For example, many young athletes were selected in the State Duma of the last convocation. In this case, the merits in sports in the minds of the masses replaced the opinion that the 20-year-olds athletes can rule the country, but remember that every State Duma deputy has the rank of federal minister).

21. Artificial "miscalculation" of the situation

A lot of different information is deliberately thrown onto the market, thereby tracking public interest in this information, and knowledge that has not gained relevance is subsequently excluded.

22. Manipulative commenting

Through the accent necessary for the manipulators, an event is highlighted. In this case, any event undesirable for manipulators when using such technology can take the opposite color. It all depends on how the manipulators present this or that material, with which comments.

23. The effect of presence

The link to the presence at any event allows you to direct the manipulative technique to the maximum achievement of the desired result. By type — an eyewitness is always right.

24. Admission (approximation) to power

This manipulation is based on such a property of the psyche of most individuals as a radical change in their views if such a person is endowed with the necessary authority. (A rather striking example is D.O. Rogozin, who was in opposition to the authorities. We recall the statement of Rogozin in connection with the ban of the CEC on the registration of V. Gerashchenko as a presidential candidate. We remember the hunger strike in the State Duma with the demands for the resignation of the ministers of the socio-economic block of the government. We recall other statements by Rogozin, including about the party in power and the president of the country, and remember Rogozin's speeches after he is appointed permanent representative of Russia to the North Atlantic Treaty Organization (NATO) in Brussels, i.e., nickname representing Russia in an enemy organization.)

25. Repetition

A similar method of manipulation is quite simple. It is only necessary to repeatedly give any information so that such information is deposited in the mass media audience's memory and is subsequently used. Simultaneously, manipulators should simplify the text as much as possible and achieve its susceptibility in the calculation of a low-intellectual public. Oddly enough, practically only in this case you can be sure that the necessary information will not only be conveyed to the mass viewer, reader, or listener but also will be correctly perceived by them. And this effect can be achieved by consistent repetition of simple phrases. In this case, the information is first firmly entrenched in the subconscious mind of the listeners. Then it will affect their consciousness, and therefore the performance of actions, the semantic connotation of which is secretly laid down in the information for the mass media audience.

26. The truth is half

In this method of manipulation, only part of the reliable information is presented to the public. In contrast, the other section, explaining the possibility of the existence of the first part, is hidden by the manipulators. (An example of the times of Perestroika, when rumors were first circulated that the Union republics allegedly contained the RSFSR. At the same time, they forgot about Russian subsidies. As a result of deceiving the republics' population that are friendly to us, these republics first left the USSR. Afterward, part of their community began to come to earnings to Russia.)

- The third block of manipulation techniques

Speech Psychotechnics

In the event of such an impact, it is forbidden to use direct information impact methods, spoken in an orderly manner, replacing the latter with a request or proposal, and at the same time using the following verbal tricks:

1) Truisms

In this case, the manipulator pronounces what is in reality, but in fact, in his words, a fraudulent strategy is hidden. For example, a manipulator wants to sell goods in a beautiful package in a deserted place. He does not say: "buy"! Instead he says: "Well, the cold! These are great, very cheap sweaters! Everyone buys, you won't find such cheap sweaters anywhere!" and twirls packets of sweaters in his hands.

As noted by Academician V.M. Kandyba, such an unobtrusive purchase offer, is more focused on the subconscious, works better, as it corresponds to the truth and passes the critical barrier of consciousness. It is really "cold" (this is one unconscious "yes"), indeed the package and pattern of the sweater are beautiful (the second "yes"), and really very cheap (the third "yes"). Therefore, without any use of the word, "Buy!" it seems to him that an object of manipulation is born an independent decision made by him to buy at a cheap price and on the occasion an excellent thing, often without even unrolling the package, but only asking for the size.

2) The illusion of choice

In this case, as if in a usual phrase of the manipulator about the presence of any product or phenomenon, some hidden statement is interspersed, which flawlessly acts on the subconscious, forcing to fulfill the will of the manipulator. For example, they do not ask you whether you will buy or not, but say: "How pretty you are! This suits you, and it looks great! Which one will you take, this or this?" and the manipulator looks at you with sympathy, as if the question that you are buying this thing has already been resolved. Indeed, the last phrase of the manipulator contains a trap for consciousness that imitates your right to choose. But in fact, you are being deceived, since the choice "buy - do not buy" has been replaced by the choice "buy this or buy that."

3) Teams hidden in questions

In this case, the manipulator hides his installation command under the guise of a request. For example, you need to close the door. You can say to someone: "Go and close the door!" But it will be worse than if your order was issued with a request in the question: "Could you kindly close the door?" The second option works better, and the person does not feel cheated.

4) The moral impasse

This case is a hoax of consciousness; the manipulator, asking for an opinion on a product, after receiving an answer, asks the next question, which contains the statement on the execution of the action required by the manipulator. For example, the seller-manipulator persuades not to buy, but "just try" his goods. In this case, we have a trap for consciousness, since it seems that nothing dangerous or bad is offered to him and it seems that complete freedom of any decision is preserved, but in fact it's enough to try, as the seller asks another tricky question right away: "Well, did you like it? Did you like it?" And although it seems to be about tastes, but in fact the question is: "Will you buy or not?" And since the thing is objectively tasty, you can't say to the seller's question that you didn't like it, and answer that you "liked", thereby giving involuntary consent to the purchase. Moreover, as soon as you answer the seller that you liked it, he, without waiting for your other words, already weighs the goods and it's as if it's inconvenient for you to refuse the purchase, especially since the seller selects and imposes the best that he has (from that which is visible). Conclusion - you need to think a hundred times before accepting a seemingly innocuous offer.

5) Speech reception: "than ... - so ..."

The essence of this speech psychotechnology is that the manipulator connects what is happening with what he needs. For example, the seller of hats, seeing that the buyer turns the hat in his hands for a long time, deciding to buy or not to buy, says that the customer is lucky, because he found exactly the hat that suits him best. Like, "The more I look at you, the more I am convinced that this is so."

6) Coding

After the manipulation has worked, the manipulators encode their victim into amnesia (forgetting) of everything that happens. For example, if a gypsy (as an extra-class specialist in waking hypnosis, street manipulation) took the ring or chain from the victim, then she will definitely say the phrase: "You do not know me and you have never seen them! These things — the ring and the chain — are strangers! You have never seen them!" In this case, if the hypnosis was not deep, the charm ("charm" - as an essential part of waking suggestion) disappears in a few minutes. With deep hypnosis, coding can persist for years.

7) The Stirlitz method

Since a person in any conversation better remembers the beginning and the end, it is necessary not only to enter the conversation correctly, but also that the necessary words that the manipulation object must remember are put at the end of the conversation.

8) The speech trick "three stories"

In the case of such a technique, the next method of programming the human psyche is carried out. You are told some three stories. But in an unusual way. First, they begin to tell you story No. 1. In the middle, they interrupt it and begin to tell story No. 2. In the middle they interrupt it, and they begin to tell story No. 3, which they tell completely. Then the manipulator completes story No. 2, and then completes story No. 1. As a result of this method of programming the psyche, history No. 1 and No. 2 are recognized and remembered. And story No. 3 is quickly forgotten and unrecognized, which means that, being squeezed out of consciousness, it is placed in the subconscious. But the bottom line is that manipulators laid instructions and commands for the subconscious of the manipulation object in the story No. 3, which means you can be sure that after a while this person (manipulation object) will begin to fulfill the psychological settings introduced into his subconscious, and at the same time he will assume that they come from him. The introduction of information into the subconscious is a reliable way of programming a person to perform the settings necessary for manipulators.

9) Allegory

As a result of such an impact of the processing of consciousness, the information needed by the manipulator is hidden among the history, which the manipulator sets out allegorically and metaphorically. The bottom line is that just the hidden meaning is the thought that the manipulator decided to put into your consciousness. Moreover, the brighter and more picturesque the story is told, the easier it is for such information to go around the criticality barrier and introduce information into the subconscious. Later, such information "begins to work" often just at the moment, the onset of which was originally laid down; or a code was laid down, activated by the manipulator each time to achieve the necessary effect.

10) The method "as soon as ... then ..."

Very interesting method. This speech technique-trick is one that a gypsy, for example, foreseeing some likely future action of a client, says, for example: "As soon as you see your line life, immediately understand me!" Here, by the subconscious logic of the client's view of her palm (the "lifeline"), the gypsy logically connects building confidence in herself and everything that she does. At the same time, the gypsy cleverly inserts a trap for consciousness at the end of the phrase "immediately understand me", the intonation of which means a different meaning, hidden from consciousness, "immediately agree with everything that I do."

11) Dispersion

The method is quite interesting and effective. It consists in the fact that the manipulator, telling you a story, selects its settings in some way that violates the monotony of speech, including the so-called "anchors" (the "anchoring" technique refers to neurolinguistic programming techniques). It is possible to distinguish speech by intonation, volume, touch, gestures, etc. Thus, such attitudes seem to be scattered among the other words that make up the information flow of a given story. And later, the subconscious of the object of manipulation will only respond to these words, intonations, gestures and so on. In addition, as Academician V.M. Kandyba notes, hidden teams scattered among the entire conversation turn out to be very effective and work much better than those expressed otherwise.

The following methods of manipulative influences on the subconscious are distinguished in order to program human behavior (object of manipulation):

- Kinesthetic methods (the most effective): touching the hand, touching the head, any stroking, patting on the shoulder, shaking hands, touching the fingers, applying brushes on the client's hands from above, taking the client's brush in both hands, etc.
- Emotional ways: raising emotions at the right time, lowering emotions, emotional exclamations or gestures.
- Speech methods: change the volume of speech (louder, quieter); change in the pace of speech (faster, slower, pause); change in intonation (increase-decrease); related sounds (tapping, snapping fingers); change the localization of the sound source (right, left, top, bottom, front, back); change in the tone of voice (imperative, command, hard, soft, insinuating, lingering).
- Visual methods: facial expressions, eye expansion, hand gestures, finger movements, changing body position (tilting, turning), changing the position of the head (turning, tilting, lifting), a characteristic sequence of gestures (pantomime), rubbing your own chin.
- Written ways. In any written text, using the dispersion technique, you can insert hidden information, while the necessary words are distinguished: font size, different font, different color, indentation, new line, etc.

12) The "old reaction" method

According to this method, it is necessary to remember that if in a situation a person reacts strongly to a stimulus, then after a while you can expose that person to the action of such a stimulus, and the old reaction will automatically work, although the conditions and situation may vary significantly from the one in which the reaction manifested itself for the first time. A classic example of an "old reaction" is when a dog suddenly attacks a child walking in a park. The child was very frightened and subsequently in any situation, even with the safest and most harmless, when he sees a dog, automatically and unconsciously, the "old reaction" arises: fear.

Such reactions can result from pain, temperature, kinesthetic (touch), taste, auditory, olfactory, etc., therefore, according to the mechanism of the "old reaction" it is necessary to fulfill a number of basic conditions:

I.   The reflexive reaction should be fixed as many times as possible.
II.   The applied stimulus should in its characteristics match the irritant used for the first time.
III.   The best and most reliable is a complex stimulus that uses the reaction of several senses slmultaneously.

If you need to establish the dependence of another person on you (the object of manipulation), you must:

- Cause in the process of questioning the object a reaction of joy.
- Fix a similar reaction by any of the signaling methods (the so-called "anchors" in NLP).
- If necessary, encode the psyche of the object - "activate" the "anchor" at the right time. In this

case, in response to your information, which, in your opinion, should be deposited in the memory of the object, the person selected for the role of the object will have a positive associative series, which means that the criticality barrier of the psyche will be broken, and such a person (object) will be "programmed" for implementation, conceived by you after the encoding you entered. It is recommended to check yourself several times before fixing the "anchor", so that by facial expressions, gestures, changed intonation, etc. remember the reflex reaction of the object to words positive for its psyche (for example, pleasant memories of the object), and pick up a reliable key (tilting the head, voice, touch, etc.).

- The fourth block of manipulations

Manipulation Through Television

1) Fabrication of facts

In this case, manipulation occurs as a result of small deviations used in the supply of material but always acting in the same direction. Manipulators tell the truth only when the truth can be easily verified. In other cases, they try to present the material in the way they need it. Moreover, a lie becomes most effective when it is based on a stereotype embedded in the subconscious.

2) Selection for reality events material

In this case, an effective condition for programming thinking is the control of the media to supply unified information, but in different words. At the same time, the activities of opposition media are allowed. But their activities should be controlled and not go beyond the scope of broadcasting that they allow. Also, the media use the so-called principle of democracy of noise, when a message unnecessary by a manipulator, has to die under a powerful surge of versatile information.

3) Gray and black information

In the second half of the 20th century, the media began to use psychological warfare technology. The American Military Dictionary of 1948 gives the following definition to psychological warfare: "These are systematic propaganda events that influence the views, emotions, attitudes, and behavior of the enemy, neutral or friendly foreign groups to support national politics." The manual (1964) states that the purpose of such a war is "to undermine the country's political and social structure ... to such a degree of degradation of national consciousness that the state becomes incapable of resistance."

4) Big psychoses

The secret tasks of the media are to turn the citizens of a country into a single mass (crowd), with the goal of the general regulation of the distribution of the flow of information, which processes the consciousness and subconscious of people. As a result, such a crowd is easier to manage, and the average layman unquestioningly believes the ridiculous statements.

5) Approval and repetition

In this case, the information is supplied in the form of ready-made templates that actively use the stereotypes available in the subconscious. Affirmation in any speech means refusal to discuss, because the power of the idea, which can be discussed, loses all credibility. In human thinking, notes Kara-Murza, is the so-called mosaic type of culture. Media are a factor in strengthening this type of thinking, teaching a person to think in stereotypes, and not include intelligence when analyzing media materials. G. Lebon noted that with the help of repetition, information is introduced into the subconscious' depths, where motives of subsequent actions of a person arise. Excessive repetition dulls the mind, causing any information to be deposited in the subconscious mind with virtually no change.

6) Crushing and urgency

In this technique of manipulating the media used, integral information is divided into fragments, so that a person could not combine them into a single whole and comprehend the problem. (For example, articles in a newspaper are divided into parts and placed on different pages; text or a telecast is broken by advertising.) Professor G. Schiller explains the effectiveness of this technique: "When the integral nature of a social problem is intentionally bypassed, and fragmentary information about it is offered as reliable "Information," the results of this approach are always the same: misunderstanding... apathy and, as a rule, indifference." Tearing pieces of information about an important event, it is possible to drastically reduce the impact of the message or completely deprive it of meaning.

7) Simplification, stereotyping

This type of manipulation is based on the fact that a person is a product of a mosaic culture. The media create his mind. Media, in contrast to high culture, is designed specifically for the masses. Therefore, they imposed strict restrictions on the complexity and originality of messages. The justification for this is the rule that the representative of the mass can adequately absorb only simple information, so any new information is adapted to the stereotype so that a person perceives information without effort and internal analysis.

8) Sensationalism

In this case, the principle of such a presentation of information is retained when it is impossible or very difficult to form a single whole from separate parts. In this case, any pseudo-sensation is highlighted. And already under cover of it, the really important news is hushed up (if this news is dangerous for some reason to the circles that control the media).

The continuous bombardment of consciousness, especially by the "bad news," performs an important function of maintaining the necessary level of "nervousness" in society, according to prof. S.G. Kara-Murza. Such nervousness, a feeling of continuous crisis, dramatically increases the suggestibility of people and reduces the ability to critical perception.

9) Change the meaning of words and concepts

Manipulators from the media, in this case, freely interpret the words of any person. In this case, the context changes, often taking the form directly opposite or at least distorted. Prof S.G. Kara-Murza gives a vivid example, telling that when the Pope during a visit to one of the countries was asked how he relates to houses of tolerance, was surprised that they supposedly exist. After that, an emergency message appeared in the newspapers: "The first thing my dad asked when he stepped on our land was, 'Is there tolerance at home?'"

- The fifth block of manipulations

Manipulations Of Consciousness

1. Provocation of suspicion

116

The manipulator initially puts the subject in critical condition when he confidently puts forward a statement like: "Do you think I will persuade you?" suggesting the implied. The opposite effect, when the one over whom the manipulations are carried out, begins to convince the manipulator of the opposite, and thereby, saying the installation several times, unconsciously inclines to the opinion of honesty in something convincing him. Whereas under all conditions, this honesty is false. But under certain conditions, he would understand that the line between the lie and the receptivity of truth is erased in this situation. So the manipulator is achieving his goal.

Protection - do not pay attention, believe in yourself.

2. False advantage of the enemy

The manipulator, in his own specific words, as if initially, casts doubt on his arguments, referring to the supposedly more favorable conditions in which his opponent is. This, in turn, makes this opponent make excuses for wanting to convince a partner and remove suspicion. Thus, the one over whom the manipulation took place unconsciously relieves himself of any attitude towards censorship of the psyche, to defense, allowing him to penetrate his defenseless psyche attacks from the manipulator. The words of the manipulator, possible in a similar situation: "You say so because now your position requires it ..."

Protection - such words as: "Yes, I say that because I have such a position, I'm right, and you must obey me."

3. Aggressive conversation

Using this technique, the manipulator takes an initially high and aggressive pace of speech, which unconsciously denies the opponent's will. Also, the opponent, in this case, cannot properly process all the information received.

What forces him to agree with the information from the manipulator, unconsciously also wanting to stop all this as soon as possible.

Protection - make an artificial pause, interrupt the fast pace, reduce the aggressive intensity of the conversation, and dialogue in a calm direction. If necessary, you can retire for a while, i.e., interrupt the conversation and then — when the manipulator calms down — continue the conversation.

4. Imaginary misunderstanding

In this case, a certain trick is achieved as follows. The manipulator, referring to clarifying the correctness of what you just heard, repeats the words you said, but making your sense in them. Spoken words can be like: "Sorry, if I understand you correctly, you say that ..." and then he repeats 60-70% of what he heard from you, but distorts the final meaning by entering other information — information necessary for him.

Protection - a clear clarification, returning and re-explaining to the manipulator what you had in mind when you said, so-and-so.

5. False agreement

In this case, the manipulator seems to agree with the information received from you but immediately makes his adjustments. According to the principle: "Yes, yes, everything is correct, but ...".

Protection - believe in yourself and do not pay attention to manipulative techniques in a conversation with you.

6. Provocation to scandal

In time with the said offensive words, the manipulator

tries to provoke anger, rage, misunderstanding, resentment, etc., with his ridicule to get you crazy and achieve the intended result.

Protection is a firm character, a strong will, a cold mind.

7. Specific terminology

In this way, the manipulator makes you unconsciously lower your status, as well as develop a feeling of inconvenience, as a result of which you are embarrassed to ask the meaning of a term out of false modesty or self-doubt, which allows the manipulator to turn the situation into the right direction, citing the need for your alleged approval of the words he said earlier. Lowering the interlocutor's status in the conversation allows you to find yourself in an initially winning position and eventually achieve the necessary.

Protection - ask again, clarify, pause, and go back if necessary, referring to the desire to understand better what is required of you.

8. Using the effect of false suspicion in your words

Applying a similar position of psycho-influence, the manipulator, as it were, initially puts the interlocutor in the position of the defender. An example of the monologue used: "Do you think I will convince you of something...", which, as it were, makes the object want to convince the manipulator that it's not so, that you are well located to it (to the manipulator), etc. Thus, as it were, the subject reveals himself for unconscious agreement with the words of the manipulator that follow after this.

Protection - words such as: "Yes. I think that you should try to convince me of this. Otherwise, I won't believe you, and further conversation will not work. "

9. Reference to the "greats"

The manipulator operates with quotes from the speeches of famous and significant people, the specifics of the principles adopted in society, and so on. Thus, the manipulator unknowingly lowers your status. They say; look, all respected and well-known people say so. You think very differently, who you are, who they are, etc. Approximately the same associative chain should unconsciously appear at the object of manipulation, after which the person becomes such an object.

Protection - faith in one's exclusivity and "chosenness."

10. The formation of false stupidity and failure

Sayings like - this is corny, it is complete bad taste and so on - must form the manipulation object's initial unconscious diminution of his role and form his artificial dependence on others' opinions, which prepares the dependence of the person on the manipulator. This means that the manipulator can practically safely advance his ideas through the manipulation object, moving the object to solve the problems needed by the manipulator. In other words, the ground for manipulation has already been prepared by the manipulations themselves.

Protection - do not succumb to provocations and believe in your mind, knowledge, experience, education, etc.

11. The imposition of thoughts

In this case, through constantly or periodically repeated phrases, the manipulator accustoms the object to any information conveyed to him.

The principle of advertising is built on such manipulation. When at first, some information appears before a person (moreover, regardless of his conscious approval or denial of it), or when a person is faced with the need to choose a product, he unconsciously selects one of several types of goods of unknown brands that are already heard somewhere. Moreover, based on the fact that through advertising, an exclusively positive opinion is heard about a product, it is much more likely that an exclusively positive opinion about this product is formed in an unconscious person.

Protection - the initial critical analysis of any information received.

12. Proof, with hints of some special circumstances

This is a way of manipulation through a special kind of an understatement, which forms false confidence in what has been said in the object of manipulation using the unconscious thought of one or another situation by it. And when in the end it turns out that he "misunderstood," such a person practically does not have any component of the protest, because unconsciously he remains sure that he is guilty. After all, he did not understand it. Thus, the object of manipulation is forced (unconsciously) to accept the rules of the game imposed on him.

In the context of such a circumstance, it most likely makes sense to divide it into manipulation, taking into account both unexpected for the object and forced, when the subject eventually realizes that he has become a victim of manipulations. But he is forced to accept them because of the impossibility of conflict with his conscience embedded into his psyche by attitudes in the form of norms of behavior based on certain principles of society that prevent such a person (object) from reversing. Moreover, the agreement on his part can be dictated by a falsely evoked sense of guilt in him, and a kind of moral masochism, which forces him to punish himself unconsciously.

13. Imaginary inattention

In this situation, the manipulation object falls into the trap of the manipulator, playing on his own supposedly inattention, so that after having achieved his own, he refers to the fact that he allegedly did not notice (listen to) the protest from the opponent. At the same time, he actually puts the object of manipulation before the fact of the perfect.

Protection - to clarify and ask again what you misunderstood.

14. The humiliation of irony

As a result of the thoughts spoken at the right time about the insignificance of one's status, the manipulator seems to force the object to assert the opposite and, in every way, elevate the manipulator. Thus, subsequent manipulative actions of the manipulator become invisible to the object of manipulation.

Protection - if the manipulator believes that it is "insignificant" - it is necessary to continue to give his will, reinforcing that feeling in him so that he no longer has thoughts to manipulate you. When you see the manipulator, there is a desire to obey you or to bypass you.

15. Focus on the pros

In this case, the manipulator concentrates the conversation only on the pluses, thereby promoting his idea and ultimately manipulating the psyche of another person.

Defense - to make several conflicting statements, to be able to say no, etc.

- Sixth block of manipulations

Manipulation Of Personality

1. "Labeling"

This technique consists of choosing offensive epithets, metaphors, names, etc. ("labels") to denote a person, organization, idea, or social phenomenon. Such "labels" cause an emotionally negative attitude of others, they associate with low (dishonest and socially disapproving) actions (behavior) and, thus, are used to discredit a person, expressed ideas and suggestions, organization, social group or subject of discussion in the eyes of the audience.

2. "Shining generalizations"

This technique consists of replacing the name or designation of a particular social phenomenon, idea, organization, social group, or specific person with a more general name that has a positive emotional connotation and causes others' friendly attitude. This technique is based on the exploitation of positive feelings and emotions of people towards certain concepts and words, for example, such as "freedom," "patriotism," "peace," "happiness," "love," "success," "victory," etc. Such words, bearing a positive psycho-emotional impact, are used to drag decisions beneficial to a particular person, group, or organization.

3. "Transfer" or "Switch"

The essence of this technique consists in skillfully, unobtrusively, and invisibly to most people, spreading the authority and prestige of what they value and respect for what the source of communication presents to them. Using the "transfer," associative relations of the presented object are formed with someone or something with value and significance, among others. A negative "transfer" is also used to create associations with negative and socially unapproved events, actions, facts, people, etc., which is necessary to discredit specific individuals, ideas, situations, social groups, or organizations.

4. "Link to authorities"

The content of this technique is to cite individuals with high authority or vice versa, which causes a negative reaction in the category of people who are being manipulated. The statements used usually contain value judgments about people, ideas, events, etc., and express their condemnation or approval. Thus, as an object of manipulative influence, a person initiates the formation of the corresponding relationship — positive or negative.

5. "The game of common people"

The purpose of this technique is to establish trusting relationships with the audience, as with similar-minded people, that both the manipulator and the ideas are correct, as they are oriented to the common person. This technique is actively used in advertising and informational promotion and various propaganda for the formation of the chosen image — "a person from the people" — to build trust in him from the people.

6. "Shuffle" or "juggling cards"

The content of this technique consists in the selection and intentional presentation of only positive or only negative facts and arguments, while at the same time ignoring the opposite. Its main goal — using one-sided selection and presentation of facts — shows the attractiveness, or vice versa, the unacceptability of any point of view, program, or idea.

7. "General carriage"

When using this technique, judgments, statements, phrases are required that require uniformity in behavior, creating the impression that everyone does it. For example, a message can begin with the words: "All normal people understand that ..." or "No sane person will object that ...", etc. Through the "common platform," a person is convinced that the majority of members of a certain social community with whom he identifies himself or whose opinion is significant for him, accept similar values, ideas, or programs.

8. Crushing information, redundancy, high pace

Often, such tricks are used on television. As a result of such a massive shelling of people's consciousness (for example, cruelty on TV), they cease to critically perceive what is happening and perceive it as meaningless incidents. The viewer, following the quick speech of the announcer or presenter, misses links to the source of information and, in his imagination, already connects and agrees with all the inconsistent parts of the perceived programs.

9. "Mockery"

When using this technique, both specific individuals, views, ideas, programs, organizations, and their activities or various associations of people who are being fought can be ridiculed. The choice of the object of ridicule is carried out depending on the goals and the specific information and communication situation. The effect of this technique is based on the fact that when ridiculing individual statements and elements of human behavior, a humorous and frivolous attitude is initiated towards the person, which automatically applies to his other statements and views. With the skillful use of such a technique, it is possible to form the image of a "frivolous" person, whose statements are not credible, for a particular person.

10. "The method of negative reference groups"

In this case, it is argued that any set of views is the only correct one. All who share these views are better than those who do not (but share others, often opposed). For example, pioneers or Komsomol members are better than informal youth. Pioneers and Komsomol members are honest, responsive, and if Komsomol members are called up for military service, they are excellent students in military and political training. And informal youth — punks, hippies, and so on — are not good youth. Thus one group is opposed to another. Accordingly, various accents of perception are highlighted.

11. "Repeating slogans" or "repeating template phrases"

The main condition for the effective use of this technique is the correct slogan. A slogan is a short statement, formulated in such a way as to attract attention and influence the imagination and feelings of the reader or listener. The slogan should be adapted to the characteristics of the target audience (i.e., groups of people who need to be affected). Using the technique of "repeating slogans" implies that the listener or reader will not think about the meaning of individual words used in the slogan, nor about the correctness of the whole wording. We can add to the definition of G. Grachev and I. Melnik that the brevity of the slogan allows information to penetrate the subconscious freely, thereby programming the psyche, and giving rise to psychological attitudes and patterns of behavior.

12. "Emotional adjustment"

This technique can be defined as a way of creating a mood while transmitting certain information. The mood is caused by various means (external environment, a certain time of day, lighting, light stimulants, music, songs, etc.). Against this background, the relevant information is transmitted, but strives to ensure that it is not too much. This technique is often used in theatrical performances, game and show programs, religious (cult) events, etc.

13. "Promotion through mediators"

This technique is based on the fact that the process of perceiving relevant information, certain values, views, ideas, and evaluations has a two-stage nature. This means that an effective informational impact on a person is often carried out not through the media, but through people that are authoritative for him. This phenomenon is reflected in the two-stage communication flow model developed by Paul Lazarsfeld in the mid-1950s. In the model he proposed, the distinguished two-step process of the mass communication process is taken into account, firstly, as the interaction between the communicator and the "opinion leaders," and secondly, as the interaction of opinion leaders with members of micro-social groups. "Leaders of opinions" may include informal leaders, political figures, representatives of religious faiths, cultural, scientific, and artistic figures, athletes, military, etc. In the practice of the informational and psychological impact of the media, this has led to the fact that outreach and advertising messages have become more focused on people whose opinions are significant for others. (i.e., ratings and advertising promotion of goods are carried out by "movie stars" and other popular persons). The manipulative effect is enhanced by interspersing with entertainment programs, interviews, direct or indirect assessments of such leaders of any ongoing events, and contributing to the desired impact on the subconscious level of the human psyche.

14. "Imaginary choice"

The essence of this technique lies in the fact that listeners or readers are informed of several different points of view on a particular issue, but in such a way that they gradually present in the most favorable light the one that they want to be accepted by the audience. For this, several additional tricks are usually used:

a) Include in the propaganda materials the so-called "two-way messages," which contain arguments for and against a certain position. The opponent's arguments preempt, such as "two-way communication".

b) Positive and negative elements are dosed. For a positive assessment to look more plausible, a little criticism needs to be added to the characterization of the described point of view, and the effectiveness of a condemning position increases if there are elements of praise.

c) Selection of facts of strengthening or weakening of statements is carried out. Conclusions are not included in the text of the above messages. They should be made by those for whom the information is intended.

d) There is an operation with comparative materials to enhance the importance, demonstrate the trends and scale of events, and phenomena. In this case, all the actual data used are selected so that the necessary conclusion is sufficiently obvious.

15. "Initiation of the information wave"

An effective technique of informational impact on large groups of people is the initiation of a secondary informational wave. An event is proposed that will pick up and begin to circulate the media. At the same time, other media can pick up the initial coverage in one media, which will increase the power of information and psychological impact. This creates the so-called "Primary" informational wave. The main purpose of this technique is to create a secondary information wave at the level of interpersonal communication by initiating relevant discussions, assessments, and rumors. All this allows you to enhance the effect of the information-psychological impact on target audiences.

- Seventh block of manipulations

Manipulative Techniques Used In The Course Of Discussions And Interactions

1. Dosing of the initial information base

Materials needed for discussion are not provided to participants on time or are given selectively. An "incomplete set of materials" is handed out to some participants in the discussions, "as if by accident." Over time, it turns out that someone, unfortunately, was not aware of all the available information — working documents, letters, appeals, notes, and everything else that is "lost" that can affect the process, and the discussion results are disadvantageous. Thus, incomplete informing of some participants is carried out, which makes discussion difficult for them, and for others creates additional opportunities for the use of psychological manipulations.

2. " Excessive information"

Reverse option. It consists in the fact that too many projects, proposals, solutions, etc. are being prepared, the comparison of which in the discussion process is impossible. Especially when a large amount of materials are proposed for discussion in a short time, their qualitative analysis is difficult.

3. Formation of opinions through a targeted selection of speakers

The word is given first to those whose opinion is known

and suits the organizer of manipulative influence. In this way, the formation of the desired setting is carried out among the participants in the discussion because changing the primary setting requires more effort than its formation. To carry out the formation of the settings necessary for the manipulators, the discussion can also end or be interrupted after the speech of a person whose position corresponds to the manipulators' views.

4. A double standard in the norms of assessing the behavior of participants in discussions

Some speakers are severely limited in compliance with the rules of relations during the discussion; others are allowed to move away from them and violate established rules. The same thing happens about the nature of the statements made: some do not notice harsh statements addressed to opponents, others make comments, etc. A variant is possible when the regulation is not specifically set so that you can choose a more convenient line of behavior along the way. In this case, either smoothing the positions of opponents and "pulling" them to the desired point of view is carried out. Conversely, the differences in their positions are strengthened up to incompatible and mutually exclusive points of view, as well as bringing the discussion to absurdity.

5. "Maneuvering" the list of the discussion

To make the "necessary" question easier to pass, first, "steam is let out" (initiate a surge of emotions) on insignificant questions. When everyone is tired or impressed by the previous battle, a question is raised that they want to discuss without intensified criticism.

6. Management of the discussion process

In public discussions, the word is alternately given to the

most aggressive representatives of opposition groups that allow mutual insults, which are either not suppressed or suppressed only for appearance. As a result of such a manipulative move, the atmosphere of discussion is heating up to critical. Thus, a discussion of a relevant topic can be stopped. Another way is to unexpectedly interrupt an unwanted speaker, or deliberately move on to another topic. This technique is often used during commercial negotiations, when, according to a pre-agreed signal from the manager, the secretary makes coffee, an "important" call is organized, etc.

7. Limitations in the discussion procedure

When using this technique, suggestions regarding the discussion procedure are ignored; unwanted facts, questions, arguments are circumvented; no word is given to participants who, through their statements, can lead to undesirable changes in the discussion. The decisions made are fixed rigidly, it is not allowed to return to them even when new data are received that are important for the development of final decisions.

8. Referencing

There is a brief reformulation of questions, proposals, and arguments, during which there is a shift in emphasis in the desired direction. At the same time, an arbitrary summary can be carried out. In the process of summing up the results, the emphasis in the conclusions, the presentation of the opponents' positions, their views, and the results of the discussion in the desired direction are changed. Also, with interpersonal communication, you can improve your status with the help of a certain furniture arrangement and resort to several techniques. For example, to have a visitor in a lower armchair, to have a lot of master's diplomas in his office on the walls, and in discussions and negotiations, he will demonstratively use the attributes of power and authority.

9. Psychological tricks

This group includes techniques based on the irritation of the opponent, the use of feelings of shame, carelessness, the humiliation of personal qualities, flattery, playing on self-esteem, and other individual psychological characteristics of a person.

10. The annoyance of the opponent

They are unbalancing with ridicule, unfair accusations, and other means until he "boils." It is important that the opponent becomes irritated and makes a statement that is erroneous or disadvantageous for his position in the discussion. This technique is actively used in the explicit form as a belittling of the opponent or a more veiled, in combination with irony, indirect allusions, implicit, but recognizable subtext. Acting similarly, the manipulator can emphasize, for example, such negative personality traits of the object of manipulative influence as ignorance, ignorance in a certain area, etc.

11. Self-praise

This trick is an indirect method of belittling an opponent. It's just not explicitly saying "who you are," but according to "who I am" and "who you are arguing with," the corresponding conclusion follows. Such expressions can be used: "... I am the head of a large enterprise, region, industry, institution, etc.", "... I had to solve large problems..." "...before applying for it... you need to be a leader at least ... "... before discussing and criticizing... you need to gain experience in solving problems at least on a scale ... ", etc.

12. Use of unfamiliar words, theories, and terms for the opponent

The trick succeeds if the opponent hesitates to ask again and pretends that he took these arguments, understood the meaning of terms that are unclear to him. Behind such words or phrases is the desire to discredit the personal qualities of the object of manipulation. Particularly effective from the use of unfamiliar to most slangs occurs in situations where the object of manipulation does not have the opportunity to object or clarify what was meant and can also be aggravated by the use of a fast pace of speech and a lot of thoughts that change one another during the discussion. Moreover, it is important to note that the use of scientific terms is considered manipulation only when such a statement is made consciously for the psychological impact on the object of manipulation.

13. " Lubrication" of the arguments

In this case, the manipulators play on flattery, vanity, arrogance, the increased conceit of the object of manipulation. For example, he is bribed with the words that he "... as a person of insight and erudition, intellectually developed and competent sees the internal logic of the development of this phenomenon ..." Thus, an ambitious person is faced with a dilemma — either to accept this point of view or reject a flattering public assessment and enter into a dispute, the outcome of which is not sufficiently predicted.

14. Failure or withdrawal from the discussion

A similar manipulative action is carried out with a demonstrative use of resentment. For example, "... it is impossible to discuss serious issues with you constructively..." or "... your behavior makes it impossible to continue our meeting ...", or "I am ready to continue this discussion, but only after you have calmed down... "etc. Disruption of the discussion with the use of provoking a conflict is carried out by using various techniques to get the opponent out of himself when the discussion turns into ordinary bickering completely unrelated to the original topic. Also, tricks such as interruption, raising the voice, demonstrative acts of behavior, unwillingness to listen, and disrespect for the opponent, can be used. After their application, statements are made according to the type: "... it's impossible to talk with you because you do not give a single intelligible answer to any question "; "... it's impossible to talk with you because you are not allowing expressing a point of view that does not coincide with yours..." etc.

15. Reception "stick arguments"

They are used in two main varieties that differ in purpose. Suppose the goal is to interrupt the discussion, psychologically suppressing the opponent, a reference to the so-called higher interests without deciphering these higher interests and without arguing the reasons why they are appealed to. In this case, they use statements like: "Do you understand what you are trying to encroach on?! ...", etc. If it is necessary to force the object of manipulation to at least outwardly agree with the proposed point of view, then such arguments are used that the object can accept for fear of something unpleasant, dangerous, or to which it cannot respond by its views for the same reasons. Such arguments may include such judgments as: "... this is a denial of the constitutionally fixed institution of the presidency, the system of higher legislative bodies, undermining the constitutional foundations of society ... ". It can simultaneously be combined with an indirect form of labeling: "... it is precisely such statements that contribute to provoking social conflicts ..." or "... Nazi leaders used such arguments in their vocabulary ...", or "... you knowingly use the facts that contribute to inciting nationalism, anti-Semitism ... ", etc.

16. "Reading in the hearts"

It is used in two main versions (the so-called positive and negative forms). The essence of using this technique is that the audience's attention shifts from the content of the opponent's arguments to the alleged reasons and hidden motives why he speaks and defends a certain point of view, and does not agree with the arguments of the opposite side. May be enhanced by the simultaneous use of "stick arguments" and "tagging." For example: "... you say that protecting corporate interests ...", or "... the reason for your aggressive criticism and irreconcilable position is obvious — this is the desire to discredit progressive forces, constructive opposition, disrupt the process of democratization ... but people will not allow such pseudo-defenders of the law to impede the satisfaction of its legitimate interests ... " etc. Sometimes "reading in the hearts" takes the form when a motive is found that does not allow speaking in favor of the opposite side. This technique can be combined not only with "stick arguments," but also with "smearing the argument." For example: "... your decency, excessive modesty, and false shame do not allow you to recognize this obvious fact and thereby support this progressive undertaking, on which the solution of the question, impatiently and hopefully expected by our voters, depends ...", etc...

17. Logical and psychological tricks

Their name is because, on the one hand, they can be built on violation of the laws of logic, and on the other, on the contrary, use formal logic to manipulate an object.

Sophism was known in antiquity, requiring the answer "yes" or "no" to the question "have you stopped beating your father?" Any answer is difficult, because if the answer is "yes," then it means that he beat earlier, and if the answer is "no," then the object beats his father. There are many variants of such sophism: "... Do you all write denunciations?...", "... Have you already stopped drinking?..." etc. Public accusations are especially effective, and the main thing is to get a short answer and not allow a person to explain. The most common logical and psychological tricks include the conscious vagueness of the thesis put forward, or the answer to the question, when the idea is formulated vaguely, indefinitely, which allows it to be interpreted in different ways. In politics, this technique allows you to get out of difficult situations.

18. Failure to comply with the law is sufficient

Observance of the formal logical law of sufficient reason in discussions is very subjective because the participants in the discussion conclude the sufficient basis of the defended thesis. According to this law, arguments that are true and relevant to the thesis may be insufficient if they are private and do not provide grounds for conclusions. In addition to formal logic in the practice of information exchange, there is the so-called "Psycho-logic" (theory of argumentation), the essence of which is that argumentation does not exist on its own, it is put forward by certain people in certain conditions and perceived by concrete people who possess (or do not possess) certain knowledge, social status, personality qualities, etc. Therefore, a special case, elevated to the rank of regularity, often passes.

19. Change in emphasis in statements

In these cases, what the opponent said about the

particular case is refuted as a general pattern. The reverse trick is that one or two facts are opposed to general reasoning, which in reality can be exceptions or atypical examples. Often, conclusions about the problem under discussion are made based on what "lies on the surface," for example, side effects of the development of a phenomenon.

20. Incomplete refutation

In this case, the combination of a logical violation with a psychological factor is used in those cases when they select the most vulnerable from the positions put forward by the opponent in their defense, break it down sharply and pretend that the other arguments do not even deserve attention. The trick passes if the opponent does not return to the topic.

21. The requirement of a clear answer

Using phrases like: "do not shirk ..", "say clearly, for all ...", "tell me directly ...", etc., the manipulation object is offered to give a definite answer "yes" or "no" to a question requiring a detailed answer or when the unambiguity of the answer can lead to a misunderstanding of the essence of the problem. In an audience with a low educational level, such a trick can be perceived as a manifestation of integrity, determination, and directness.

22. Artificial displacement of the dispute

In this case, having started discussing a situation, the manipulator tries not to give arguments, from which this statement follows, but suggests immediately proceeding to refute this. Thus, the possibility of criticizing one's position is limited, and the argument itself is shifted to the argumentation of the opposite side. If the opponent succumbed to this and begins to criticize the advanced position, giving various arguments, they try to argue around these arguments, looking for flaws in them, but not presenting their system of evidence for discussion.

23. "Multiple Questioning"

In the case of this manipulative reception, an object on the same topic is asked several different questions. They act depending on his answer: either they accuse him of not understanding the essence of the problem, or that he did not answer the question completely, or of trying to mislead.

- The eighth block of manipulations

Manipulative Effects Depending On The Type Of Behavior And Human Emotions

1. The first type. A person spends most of the time between a normal state of consciousness and a state of normal night sleep.

His upbringing, character, and habits control this type, and a sense of pleasure, a desire for security, and peace, i.e., all that is formed by verbal and emotionally-figurative memory. For most men of the first type, abstract mind, words, and logic prevail, and for most women of the first type, common sense, feelings, and fantasies prevail. Manipulative influence should be directed at the needs of such people.

2. The second type. The dominance of trance states.

These are super-suggestible and super-hypnotic people, whose behavior and reactions are controlled by the psychophysiology of the right hemisphere of the brain: imagination, illusions, dreams, dreamy desires, feelings, and sensations, belief in the unusual, faith in someone's authority, stereotypes, selfish or disinterested interests (conscious or unconscious), scenarios of events occurring with them, facts and circumstances. In the case of manipulative effects, it is recommended to influence such people's feelings and imagination.

3. The third type. The dominance of the left hemisphere of the brain.

Such people are controlled by verbal information and principles, beliefs, and attitudes developed during a conscious analysis of reality. The external reactions of the third type are determined by their education and upbringing, as well as a critical and logical analysis of any information received from the outside world. To effectively influence them, it is necessary to reduce their analysis of the information presented to them by their left, critical, hemisphere of the brain. To do this, it is recommended to present information against the backdrop of trust in you. The information must be submitted strictly and carefully, using strictly logical conclusions, reinforce the facts exclusively with authoritative sources, appeal not to feelings and pleasures (instincts), but reason, conscience, duty, morality, justice, etc.

4. The fourth type. Primitive people with a predominance of cerebral instinctive-animal states.

In their main part, these are rude and uneducated people with an undeveloped left brain, who often grew up with mental retardation in socially dysfunctional families (alcoholics, prostitutes, drug addicts, etc.). Animal instincts and needs control such people's reactions and behavior: sexual instinct, the desire to eat well, sleep, drink, and experience more pleasant pleasures. When manipulating these people, it is necessary to influence the psychophysiology of the right brain: the previously experienced feelings, hereditary traits of behavior, stereotypes of behavior, the feelings that prevail at the moment, moods, fantasies, and instincts. It must be borne in mind that this category of people thinks primitively: if you satisfy their instincts and feelings, they respond positively.

5. The fifth type. People with an "expanded state of consciousness."

These are those who have managed to develop a highly spiritual person. In Japan, such people are called "enlightened," in India - "Mahatmas," in China - "perfect wise Tao people," in Russia - "holy prophets and miracle workers." Arabs of such people are called "holy Sufis." According to V.M. Kandyba, manipulators cannot influence such people, since they are "inferior to them in professional knowledge of man and nature."

6. The sixth type. People with a predominance of pathological conditions in their psychophysiology.

Mainly - mentally ill people. Their behavior and reactions are unpredictable, as they are abnormal. These people may perform some action due to a painful motive or being held captive by some hallucinations. Many of the people of this type become victims of totalitarian sects. Manipulations against such people must be carried out quickly and harshly, cause fear, a feeling of unbearable pain, isolation, and, if necessary, complete immobility and a special injection, depriving them of consciousness and activity.

7. The seventh type. People whose reactions and behavior are dominated by strong emotions are one or more of the basic underlying emotions, such as fear, pleasure, anger, etc.

Fear is one of the most powerful hypnogenic (generating hypnosis) emotions that always occurs in every person with a threat to his physical, social, or other well-being. Feeling fear, a person immediately falls into a narrowed, altered state of consciousness. The left brain is inhibited with its ability to the rational, critical-analytical, verbal-logical perception of what is happening, and the right brain is activated with its emotions, imagination, and instincts.

CHAPTER 7

IS THERE A MANIPULATIVE PERSON IN YOUR RELATIONSHIP?

Manipulative people do not hesitate to play termites in a romantic relationship, exerting financial or sexual pressure, sometimes displaying exaggerated kindness. To undermine your foundations, several scenarios are possible. Learn to recognize them!

Being in a relationship with a manipulative spouse or a manipulator is not that rare ...

Kindness: a calculated maneuver

"When pushed to the limit, I threatened to leave, Philippe became gentle as a lamb, adorable and very unhappy. I had the right to flowers, travel proposals. I felt a little guilty, not knowing better why I was leaving," says Patricia, 40, 2 children.

Signs of manipulation: his attitude is a very calculated maneuver. "Instead of questioning himself and hearing the change request, he deploys a strategy, with the sole objective of bringing you back," decodes psychotherapist Christel Petitcollin. When we take a close interest in their thought system, we can quickly realize that it has a fair rudimentary ready to think, based on binary logic. All or nothing, now or never, leave or stay. "Often impervious to criticism or questioning, they can make an effort only in the short term, to serve their interests," adds Sarah Serievic. What to do?

Above all, resist their injunction and stay in touch with

your needs and requests for change. There is a good chance that the mask of kindness will pop off, reminding you very quickly of your desire to take your legs around your neck.

Money: constant pressure

"My husband and I have a good situation. Yet after shopping for several purchases, I hide them in the closet and show off a new one every three days. I feel spied on and fear that he calls me a spendthrift petty bourgeoisie, always in the tone of mockery, of course." Monique, 43 years old.

Signs of manipulation: "Manipulators often manage to make their victim live in an artificial financial shortage," remarked Christel Petitcollin during his consultations. Regardless of the amount of your income, you always have the diffuse feeling of being a budget gourd. You flirt more often than before with overdrafts. "In reality, the financial manipulation is real," reports Isabelle Nazare-Aga, behavioral therapist. He can forget his credit card at the restaurant, or make you believe that the distribution of charges is fair while you pay for groceries, school supplies, and half the rent ... And he just gas and gasoline.

What to do? This financial aspect often works against you. At the risk of sounding like a lie, do the accounts of who pays what, and adjust! If he refuses, you will be fixed on his bad faith and the decision to be made.

Sexuality: a misplaced requirement

"Receiving waves of coarse words whispered in my ear ... Caressing myself with a sex toy in front of him ... Sexually, I often felt uncomfortable. I didn't know how far I should go or not to satisfy him," admits Sylvie, 33 years old.

Signs of manipulation: Exploring new lands in terms of sexuality is always possible, as long as you feel particularly confident and respected. "A climate that does not create a manipulator who will not hesitate to spice up his lovemaking, especially to test your obedience," points out Christel Petitcollin. It is often a refusal in the face of sexual practice or a certain frequency that will make him obsessive. From there to feeling "stuck," there is only one step!

Conversely, Sarah Serievic underlines that "in manipulative women, abstinence, on the contrary, is often a means of pressure."

What to do? Going beyond your limits to "have peace" will not change anything. The manipulator will make a "fixette" on something else. Know yourself and respect yourself so that you can say no if you need to.

Communication: a great complexity

"I find it hard to communicate with my husband. The conversation is disjointed; he changes the subject, finishes the sentences for me. I have the impression that I can no longer think for myself, that I am struggling to keep track of my thoughts, "says Emmanuelle, 37.

Signs of manipulation: Manipulators seek to confuse rather than clarify. They jump from rooster to donkey, use ambiguous information, deliver half-truths. In reality, it confuses you, creates digressions, and ends these sentences with a "You see what I mean." But why? "Blurring the tracks, not taking responsibility for their words, are all means that the manipulators use to keep control within the couple" answers Christel Petitcollin.

What to do? Don't be fooled. Behind their communication's false complexity, remember that they are often immature, and intellectually lazy, their vocabulary is limited.

Manipulation and grip relationships

Getting out of a relationship of manipulation and control is not an easy thing. The first step to take is also the most difficult: to start and realize that there is a problem.

Mechanisms involved

The manipulation and the grip rest essentially on using three feelings: fear, doubt, and guilt, to establish a relationship of dependence.

Manipulators use mainly four techniques:

The seduction: The person flatters you, compliments you; you are physically and intellectually attracted, you touch, you door attention, and your values.

The victimization: If she has a problem with other people, she will always consider that it is the fault of others: people are wicked, people do her harm, she can not help because she is the victim.

Bullying: It can be physical, emotional, financial, etc. The manipulator can threaten explicitly or implicitly to harm you and withdraw your affection, support, or anything else.

The guilt: Another side of victimization is the person under the influence who is accused of being responsible for the current state, the discomfort, the problems the person is handling.

The classic path is:

Seduction phase

The manipulator undermines the foundation of a person's

balance (his or her values, he or she pulls on the sensitive chord, hits on the sensitive points, instills doubt in oneself and others).

The victim's isolation from his usual social environment, his family, his friends, his supporters. It can cause you to be suspicious or hurt your loved ones.

Establishment of dependency: the manipulative person has done you a service, helps you, gives you (attention, affection, services, compliments, gifts, etc.), then takes it back or turns off the tap, leaving you frustrated. It is this frustration, combined with the habit of her presence and her position of a savior, that she will use to confirm your dependence on her. She will change the rules, remind you that she has helped you a lot, that it is thanks to her that you have been able to succeed or accomplish such and such a thing, she will pretend that she wants your good, that she knows that which is good for you, to take control of your life.

How to get out

When in doubt: distance yourself. Move away from the person for a while, switch off the ignition, and take this time to listen to yourself, your feelings, your emotions. If you feel better and think that indeed the person with whom you were in contact was manipulating you or trying to get you under control, it will be necessary to completely and definitively break the link to protect yourself.

Do not try to help the manipulative person, and it is not your role. Your role is to protect yourself above all.

The older and longer the hold, the more difficult it is to move away and realize the manipulation. Over time, the victim of influence feels less and less capable and more and more isolated and impoverished since there is dependence and sabotage of the foundations of the victim and of other relationships that he could maintain.

After getting out of the relationship, it will take some time to rebuild: reconnect with your values, friends, family, find safety, mourn the relationship, express your emotions; turn to history, shed new light and a new look on it that will allow you to understand and put into words what happened, and turn the page. Kindness with oneself is a key ingredient in this process of reconstruction. A professional aid worker (psychiatrist, psychologist, psychopractor, or other) can support you in this psychological reconstruction process thanks to various tools (cognitive-behavioral therapies, active and empathetic listening, relaxation, personal development tools, and self-esteem, etc.).

In a relationship, do not accept "neither seduction nor aggression" (Jacques Salomé, ESPERE method) and remember to research your feelings and your emotions regularly. This will decrease the chances of falling under the influence of a narcissistic pervert or a pathological manipulator.

Remember that you deserve to be respected, loved as you are, and not to be used.

In love, do not let yourself be manipulated!

A relationship is normally based on trust, exchange, and respect. However, the spouse can sometimes instill guilt, devalue, sow discord ... In short, try to manipulate you! So how do you regain self-confidence when your lover turns out to be an emotional vampire?

"We live together, and we are not happy. Initially, everything is going well, and then day after day, the situation deteriorates ..." Nothing to do with the routine that can settle in a relationship. No, sometimes, these are real toxic relationships!

What to do when your spouse devalues you and makes you feel guilty, to manipulate you ultimately? "Prolonged contact generates feelings of aggression, fear, or sadness," says Isabelle Nazare-Aga, behavior therapist. Without separating, learn how to get over it and assert yourself in your relationship! The strategy is simple: identify the type of manipulative spouse, then protect yourself from this relational scourge.

The manipulator denigrates you without your knowledge.

He chooses you as his partner, and yet it is crazy how easy it is to say bad things about you, casually, to your friends. "Frederique, a cordon bleu, you must be kidding." The manipulative spouse bombards you with criticism, which undermines your self-confidence.

The Shrink's Opinion:

You find these reflections harmless. In reality, it is not the occasional scratch in your self-esteem that is dangerous, but the frequency of negative messages. To upgrade yourself, cultivate your professional environment skills, for example, far from its grip.

The manipulator isolates you from the rest of society.

He purrs at the thought of seeing you slaving away at work. But he is capricious if you show independence, like accepting an invitation (to dinner, to the theater, on weekends), without him. His thinking system requires that any free moment from one must be given to the other.

The Shrink's Opinion:

Your discomfort is diffuse, and you feel divided. As soon as you practice an activity without him, you feel guilty. If you give in to him, you are very frustrated. Position yourself without delay. Make the point that your desires are as valuable as his.

The manipulator is devouring jealousy.

He aspires to an exclusive relationship and does not suffer any possible "competitor." But the manipulator can practice a double game. In the evenings, his seductive number with the opposite sex frequently rubs his jealousy towards those who approach you.

The Shrink's Opinion:

You experience recurring scenes where he searches for evidence of your infidelity. Adopt the fog tactics: above all, do not start a showdown with him, you will only multiply his animosity. Just act surprised without actually arguing.

The manipulator preaches the false to know the truth.

Communication with him takes on the appearance of a difficult path. All pretexts are good to sow confusion. So he manages to ask a question including an erroneous element: Did you know that Eric had a mistress?

The Shrink's Opinion:

If your friend just falls, you may be in trouble. Try to hide your emotion and decode his words' underlying meaning (facial expressions, tone of voice, looks). It is exhausting but radical to distinguish between true and false.

CHAPTER 8

SUBDUING THE MIND

The computer that drives your mind, body, and soul, is your subconscious mind. This takes direction from your mind's conscious part and then carries out its function – to the letter. Who we are, what we do, and how we act are all down to the fact that we have no conscience? Imagine the power that is so immaterial that no modern computer can sense it. It is our cerebral cortex's spirit, the divine cord, which guides us in our life. What if I said you could train your subconscious mind and concentrate on making massive success?

You may. You can. Worldwide, people apply science or more mystical approaches to open the iron doors to the conscious mind and put their delicate hands on the subconscious. You change the threads that make you who you are— a reprogramming. A whole lifetime of conditioning is up against you. You can reprogram and rebuild your subconscious with the right techniques and application until it becomes a natural part of your life.

Have you ever seen somebody who likes to say, "I think you don't like to do that, subconsciously?" Regardless of how hard you try, you seem to be recoiling, constructing, and distaste progressive inertia. It can be changed; you can transform your entire attitude and make life much easier and meaningful.

By now, you could be wondering, how do I do this? Many approaches are available on the market, and many businesses specialize in deep brain stimulation. The key is to trick and subdue the mind to a profound trance, relax the mind, and shorten the normal defenses. When this is achieved, the subconscious becomes more malleable, and reprogramming can then begin. Breathing is very important here, and some businesses use that to build a sense of peace and glide the individual into a profoundly meditative state by using a screened floating tank.

This technology powers medical studies into Parkinson's disease healing or amnesia and dementia healing. It has also been extensively researched and used as an aid to improve the care of chronic patients and promote better prosperity. The mind state is a strong thing, and it can change universes within us. Just a few areas can be investigated with applied technologies, such as magnetic fields and sound frequencies for cortical stimulation.

Next time it is quite likely that you don't need aspirin if you have a headache. It's just the state of your mind that you could only alter. With a mind that thinks nothing can't be solved, almost any problem can be slowly eroded or strengthened.

Quieting the Mind and Being Present

The language of the heart is intuition. Intuition. Our intuition is mainly a self-speech. It also uses other methods of communication, but intuition serves as the ideas for the heart. Intuition almost constantly flows like thoughts, but it takes some time to be mindful of intuitions because they are much more subtle than thoughts. Thoughts normally get our attention over intuitions for that reason.

One of the advantages of meditation and other spiritual practices that suppress the selfish mind is that these practices offer more insight. Many need meditation or other spiritual practices to subdue the dominance of the egoistic mind. Once a certain superiority of the egoic intellect is reached, real progress towards our intuition can be made.

The egoistic mental is quiet because it keeps the mind occupied with a task by meditation or other activity that concentrates the mental mind. Any activity in which we fully participate can be a meditation. The mind is quiet and serves us only where needed if we focus all our attention on anything.

We tend not to dive into and experience the moment but to get by on life's surface. The egoic mind keeps us a long way off the real experience and replaces thoughts on it. It takes us away from now when life is full and living. By just realizing what's going on, we can be more aware at this time. Being more present usually takes away our thoughts and feelings and puts them on whatever else happens.

Exercise: Being Present

To be present is to reflect on all that is happening at present, not only your thoughts or feelings. If a thought comes into being, consider it, and then start to observe all else. When you do a job, and your mind wanders away, bring back your attention to the task, the current stimuli, and the experience. Through practice, it will become more normal to be involved in everything that is happening right now.

Another effective method is to do a more formal kind of meditation. Meditation regularly makes the intuition and, therefore, the guidance of the self more accessible and helps to establish a calm state of mind. Meditation is the most effective spiritual method available for moving into the experience of our true nature from the egoistic state of consciousness. It is neither more difficult nor complicated than being involved in a sport.

Exercise: Sitting in Meditation

Engage in meditating every day, even if for only a few minutes a day. Start with 10 minutes a day of meditation. Increase the time you meditate with rising pleasure. Make your meditation experience as comfortable, pleasant, and enjoyable as possible, so you look forward to meditation.

Come back to a calm place. Choose something that you want to concentrate on so you can enjoy your meditation. You might like to hear music or sounds in your room if you are auditory. If you are kinesthetic, you would likely like to focus on physical feelings and subtle energy sensations. You might like to look at a holy picture, a work of art, colors, flowers, or anything of nature if you are more visual.

Return it to what you concentrate on, whenever your mind wanders. Notice also what you feel while sitting in meditation. The experience is still happening, while the mind is busy with what it is focusing on. That's what you are, that experience! When you practice more meditation, your mind wanders less and less, and you spend more and more time in the moment.

As soon as you start to spend more time, meditation is extremely pleasant. It's now extremely enjoyable. It has all: joy, happiness, peace, enjoyment, success, devotion, insight, and wisdom. You're going to be asking if you ever had a stroll, but you're going to catch up again. The ego-mind, though the present is so cheerful and pure, is very seductive. Even those who primarily live in today are still roaming through the halls of the egoic mind.

We should learn to be present in our selfish thinking just as we are present to anything else that may arise. The idea may be like all other things that we also have. We don't

153

feel like we worry about our feelings when we are present to them, but rather as we know that they are thought, which is very different from our normal thinking. This is a workout that helps you to learn to be present to your thoughts:

Exercise: Being Present to Thoughts

If you practice your thinking, your relationship will change to learning. As ideas emerge, practice as much as possible.

Right now, notice what thinking is emerging. Look at it as if you were at a distance. What's the thought experience? Notice that thought appears to be in your head. What is thought-conscious? Do you have even the consciousness of your body? What is the size? Is it a frontier? What is this perception experience? That's the one you are. You are aware of the coming and going emotions.

The theories that emerge in your narcissistic mind are irrelevant to who you are. It's not up to you what comes into your selfish mind. You've only been given the conditioning. Without thinking, reflecting on your thinking, or keeping an opinion on thinking, simply observe how your thoughts come and go. From where will they come? Where do they go? Where are they going? Notice the lack of coherence between thoughts and how they jump from one thing to another. Often, it seems that they are designed exclusively for you. What else are you noticing? Are they tied up with different voices? Are you aware of certain subjects? What's their truth? Have they an influence on consciousness?

This way, we can be rational about thought. Being present to thinking. We should look at our feelings with objectivity so that it was not true when we were associated with them. During this test, much about our conditioning's essence can be discovered, and we can liberate ourselves from that awareness of our conditioning.

This new connection to the greedy mind is highly open. It can free us and allow us to understand the fullness of the moment. Based on the absence of the selfish mind's influence to define us, we are free to pay attention not only to our thoughts but also to our entire life. We find that part and parcel of what happens throughout life is that through intuition, the Self speaks to us.

CHAPTER 9
WHAT IS DARK NLP?

Neuro-Linguistic Programming (NLP) is a methodology focused on how our internal, mental and emotional processes work. Especially on the influence that language has on our mental programming and other functions of our nervous system.

NLP asks how we do what we do and the relationship between our behaviors and our experiences. It teaches us to "reprogram" (program) our minds using language (linguistics), which encodes the experience perceived by the neurological (neuro) system, to have successful results in any area of our lives.

NLP offers techniques for overcoming limitations, generating positive internal states, increasing self-confidence, unlocking emotional brakes, changing habits, influential communication, curing phobias, improving relationships, eliminating limiting beliefs ... It is a method that offers a healthy and positive way of communicating with the environment and with oneself.

NLP SESSIONS

NLP sessions are normally called NLP therapy because NLP is an effective communication model. This learning process trains people to increase awareness of the perception of their reality and to be able to change it. This process is very fast and effective because NLP has specific techniques to access the "files" that the client has engraved in their minds and provides the "updates" necessary to change the emotional response associated with the problem. These changes are lasting and profound because the client learns to use new strategies and behavior patterns to overcome fears, improve relationships, and resolve conflicts.

What is NLP for? Who is it for? What areas of action are required?

Neuro-Linguistic Programming is currently a valuable area of knowledge that provides techniques to improve communication with others and with oneself. By focusing on understanding internal processes, it provides control over what we feel and do and makes us more effective in any area of our life.

NLP to change habits

NLP has created specific techniques to change habits. A habit is a behavior for which hardly any effort or concentration is needed, and that is generated after repeating it for a time. One of the conditions that define a habit is that it is learned and not innate behavior.

NLP is well known for having a high percentage of success in treating harmful habits such as smoking, nail-biting, overeating ... The model of change of habits that Anna Flores applies includes an NLP technique that associates it with something unpleasant than to fix the process with an Ericksonian hypnosis exercise, installing in the unconscious the freedom to no longer depend on the habit.

NLP for emotional management

NLP achieves very good results in relatively short periods in emotional management. NLP asks us how we do what we do, how we "archive" experience in the brain, and how we respond to it, so we can change it. When a client wants to improve some aspect of his life whose emotional response does not satisfy him, there is no change in the situation or the environment. The change consists in the way the client perceives it; that is, it changes his emotional response.

These are some of the objectives most demanded by clients:

- Increased self-esteem
- Increased security and self-confidence
- Stress reduction
- Improving social skills
- Overcoming trauma
- Develop communication skills
- Increased concentration in studies or work
- Management of specific crises: divorce, dismissal, exams...
- Cure of phobias: insects, reptiles, fear of flying, fear of heights...

NLP for athletes

Neuro-Linguistic Programming gives excellent results in the world of sports; in fact, elite athletes use NLP techniques to generate an internal state so powerful that it helps them to program success. It is widely demonstrated that mood, mental concentration, and positive beliefs greatly influence the achievement of sports goals and that, often, these elements make the difference between a mediocre athlete and an excellent one.

It provides a new way of maintaining the attitude of success in the practice of the sport.

It provides internal security and trust tools to ensure success consistently and unconsciously.

It teaches mastery of space, body movements, sensations, and emotions to produce high performance.

Key points of NLP

- Increases awareness of own abilities
- Focuses on the solution, not the problem
- Provides new behavioral options
- It teaches flexibility of behavior
- Improves communication with others and with oneself

The ten Effective NLP Techniques

The most widely used NLP techniques are rapport, covert orders, anchorage, body physiology, eye access, external or internal reference, belief changes, and alternative illusion. In this chapter, we will explain them in detail.

Neuro-linguistic programming is a work methodology created in 1970 by Richard Bandler (computer scientist and psychologist) and John Grinder (linguist) in which they combine communication, personal development, and psychotherapy.

This approach seeks to achieve more self-knowledge, enhance contact with others, and inspire people to adapt and reach their goals. Research by the writers has shown that changes in psychiatric conditions like depression, phobia, psychosomatic problems, and learning disabilities can be made in the NLP ...

The authors of the NLP were Virginia Satir, Milton Erickson, Fritz Perls, Gregory Batson, Alfred Korzybski, or Noam Chomsky.

 One of them was Bandler and Grinder. In their research, these two scholars explore how neural mechanisms, language, and the spectrum of learned behaviors relate to each other. The latter can be changed to achieve the goals each person has in his or her life.

Therefore, Bandler and Grinder affirm that the NLP methodology can model people's skills until they achieve their aims. More recent scientist work has subsequently debunked the idea that all such issues can be solved.

However, the reality is that today it continues to be used in multiple areas such as emotion management, leadership, the development of creativity, the increase in communication, and the educational field.

Also, it has been used in psychology, personal development in general, commerce to promote sales, motivation in sports, and companies at both the individual and group levels.

Where does the name neurolinguistic programming come from?

Neurolinguistic programming owes its name to the relationship of 3 aspects of the human being that come together in this methodology:

Program

In Nitrolingual programming methodology. Similar to machines, our brain is a device. Mental programs coordinate our knowledge. Thus, these mental programs direct our actions to achieve our goals.

Neuro

All learning requires a neural network to carry out and store the learning in the short or long term. The human being develops his understanding of his experiences and everything around him through the nervous system.

The language

The latter term is based on NLP. For our interactions and learning, language is important to connect with others.

Ten professional NLP

NLP strategies help break out of the well-known comfort zone for all those who need a guide to conquer challenges and are resistant to change.

These are intended to provide you with the means required, but it is important to make the change and believe that it is feasible and beneficial to achieve it.

When you pursue your goals, your well-being will rise. The more energy you use in NLP's resources, the more likely the success will be. These tools are designed to be used to better your daily life.

First, I'll clarify the most commonly used NLP techniques.

Study

This strategy is used when we want to improve our contact with people, whether at work or in the community.

This seeks to establish a culture of collaboration and confidence in which there are no malentenduities, debates, or judgments. It is also possible to grasp the message that the other person wants to transmit and convey the message that we want to transmit to the listener.

We take advantage of the listing of things we know that connect us with our listener. The relationship is vitally essential in addition to the use of verbal words.

Covers orders

The questions are usually formulated according to this

technique and finish with an ascending musical intonation, while the orders are made with a descending intonation.

Thus, NLP provides the desired effect to tone the questions in descending order.

Mooring

Anchoring in a stressful situation is a technique to lessen an emotion of discomfort such as anxiety or anguish. It is based on the classical conditioning of learning psychology.

Physiology

They need to learn how the body works and how posture, breathing styles, and the heart rate affect our attitudes and emotions, among others.

As we adjust our body posture and learn to air correctly, we will alter our comportment and, hence, communicate well in other countries.

Entry to the eyes

The eye accesses are part of physiology, and they refer to the fact that the eye motion sequence corresponds to the person's purpose.

External or reference standard

References are a form of a mental model, unconscious and systemic.

Being conscious of both ours and other patterns helps us to build self-knowledge and empathy for others.

In particular, the reference standard allows us to know on which of our behaviors they based their requirements and value levels. This is where our decision-making process will reside.

Two comparison types can be distinguished:

External guide: People use this tool to reflect on their thoughts and feelings in the world. We would use topics such as how we feel about decision-taking and how we want to affect their opinion.

External reference: Individuals with this form of reference put great importance on others' views and are searching for agreement with the others around them. The sentences we use will expose our views since the person will consider them (e.g., My view is that...).

Audio / visual / kinesthetic

The person has different choices (visual, auditory, or kinesthetic) for decision-making.

We're going to use this to imply, for example, our target if we are going to convince a person whose preferred medium is auditory ("I'll tell you about the travel plan I prepared").

It is changing in values and personality strength

If we can identify our present beliefs, internally disputed ideas, and change in them on the basis that beliefs determine our situation, we can change our situation.

An alternative illusion

This strategy is designed to convince others to do what we want. There are several options for the person to choose from, but everyone is geared to what we want to achieve.

For example, we would ask you to reach the beach by car or train, if our goal is to reach the beach. Or won't you go to the beach instead?

Possibility or requirement modal operators

According to NLP, metaprograms are solid, unconscious thought techniques for people. These include modal operators in the form of implicit instructions for our internal dialogs of the possibility or need.

These implicit orders are expressed in the form of words; I need, need, need, etc. Each one produces a person's emotions.

So that it can be better understood, here is a practical example. It is very common to use the sentence: "I can't" to excuse failure, and the question we always come back with is, why can't you?

The person will give an infinite list of reasons if we return the question of why he cannot perform the actions. If the question is, on the other hand, "What stops you?" we direct the individual, instead of thinking about excuses, to consider possible solutions to their problem. In other words, the emphasis is on the solution.

Exercise realistic

First, the NLP technique is being developed to increase motivating strategies to achieve a goal or condition.

We begin to think of something that motivates us to do a great deal. Imagine a film that takes place and knows the strengths of this action, which takes all its specifics into account. Terminate activity and relax.

See and breathe deeply around you. Then think of something that you don't want to, pay close attention to what you hear.

See the picture and its qualities. Rest again, and take a deep breath. Compare activities or pictures, focusing on all of your details. Write down a list of motivational elements in this process.

Finally, you should take a picture that belongs to a pleasant and varying visual characteristic, size, distance, movement, etc.

Of all the changes that have been made, stick to the combination of qualities that make you happier and more inspiring. Write them down so that you can use them later for a motivational scenario.

Benefits from NLP use

The methods used in NLP provide several advantages that cover a broad range of needs and objectives that anyone can consider at some stage in their life.

Build knowledge of oneself

Emotional management: in any situation, a person should control and manage emotions and actions (such as being able to effectively face a job interview).

Through our communication techniques, NLP uses anchors to achieve goals or solve problems when dealing with stressful situations. One of the most common issues in the field of communication is the fear of publicity. This usually gives rise to fear and anguish. Through the anchoring strategy, an enjoyable, comfortable, and optimistic time that we recall is "anchored" and is correlated with the stressful situation at the exact moment using visualization techniques.

Learn strategies for innovation

Improve motivation strategies: improve motivation strategies and make them more effective in the achievement of personal or professional goals.

Understand our and others' learning styles: our questions

are often guided by lessons that have been learned over time. Associations of experiences and contexts have produced a pattern of thought because they have occurred again and again and are hard to modify.

Enhance our ability to achieve personal goals: reasons concealed in the unconscious and that necessarily promote delay in achieving our goals. This involves identifying and understanding the reason so that subsequent adjustments can take place and decisions to take action.

Develop effective strategies for decision-making

Understand, embrace, and learn how to manage cycles of personal and professional transition.

Remove phobias and fears.

CHAPTER 10

COMMUNICATE WITH NLP

Neuro-Linguistic Programming (NLP) is an approach developed in the 1970s in the United States by Richard Bandler, computer scientist and psychologist, and John Grinder, linguist and psychologist. They observed how well-known and valued communicators went about being efficient. Their thesis is based on the idea that if we can identify how a person goes about succeeding by decoding his "program," we can use it to succeed.

The "program" in question here reproduces the attitudes and behaviors, what the person thinks when he acts, his emotions, the values that guide him, and the objectives he pursues.

In terms of communication, we are effective when we can make ourselves understood, and when this communication leads to action. This is true when the interlocutors find interest and desire to maintain the relationship.

The effectiveness of communication, therefore, does not lie in its intention, but the results obtained. We communicate to share facts, feelings, values , and above all, to influence others.

Five principles for excellent communication

According to NLP, there are levers for developing excellent communication, including the following five principles:

- Pursue a defined and precise objective
- Create a quality relationship right away

- Pay attention to your interlocutor
- Adapt flexibly
- Stay consistent and relevant

1 / Pursue a defined and precise objective

Before starting communication, you should know in advance what you want. Is it to inform, to convince, to be appreciated? Before starting a meeting, an interview, and memo, it helps to ask yourself: "What do I want to achieve?" If, for example, you have a long e-mail to write, a report or an article to write for the job, it is recommended that you start with the conclusion first, before preparing the outline and content of the message.

If you want information from a seller about a state-of-the-art flat screen, advertise your goal. If you want to go on vacation in August, say so. You will thus avoid the risk of manipulating or entering into a situation of incomprehension. Encourage your interlocutors also to express their objectives clearly as quickly as possible.

2 / Create a quality relationship straight away

The popular adage: "It's the first impression that counts" holds in communication. If you create an unpleasant atmosphere for your interlocutors from the start of the meeting, they will not want to listen to you, much less to dialogue with you. Some communicators recommend applying the "eighty" rule. They know they have little time to catch the attention of their interlocutors.

What is this "eighty" rule? The first twenty seconds, the first twenty words, the first twenty gestures, the first twenty steps, and the twenty square centimeters of the face.

For example, if at a meeting you start your speech

hesitantly, looking at the ground, the scowl, using words like "we can try to," "maybe," " ... ", you risk creating an atmosphere of doubt, apathy, or demotivation.

On the contrary, if you address your audience with active terms, looking at your interlocutors and accompanying your words with opening gestures, you will immediately capture your audience's attention.

3 / Pay attention to your interlocutor

When you talk to people, focus your attention on them. You will notice their attitudes of agreement, disapproval, or doubt. For example, when a person says "yes" to you, they can very well mean "no" with the tone of their voice, the movements of their head, and their shoulders. A mother knows very quickly when her child tells her a lie.

Focusing your attention also means listening to the comments and fears of your interlocutors. There is nothing more eloquent than someone who says nothing.

4 / Adapt flexibly

In communication, what matters are results, not intentions. The best-orchestrated arguments may be incomprehensible to your audience. You may be right on the merits; if your words offend or scare others, they do not want to listen. In these cases, with your sense of observation, change your arguments. To persist, repeating the same arguments, would be equivalent to sinking yourself even further into error. Experience is sometimes a way of repeating the same mistakes more quickly. Parents who get angry with their children during evening homework at home understand this impasse. The hardest part is finding another communication strategy. "To learn Latin at Luculus, you have to know Latin, Luculus, and especially the method adapted to Luculus."

5 / Stay consistent and relevant

How many changes fail because of the gulf between saying it and doing?

Take the example of a leader who advocates responsiveness and flexibility and signs the letter in eight days. When you give a compliment, have a smiley face. When you issue an objection, accompany your statements with an appropriate gesture, without displaying an ironic smile. When you want to get an important message across, you can spoil your effect by saying, "I have a little talk to you."

The presentation of these five principles could imply that they occur in chronological order: first, have a specific objective, create the relationship, etc. In practice, these five criteria also apply simultaneously.

The state of mind first!

To learn and apply NLP tools, let us emphasize that the state of mind is just as important as the method itself, and it is based on five hypotheses:

- We know a lot more than we think we know. We have within us the necessary resources to carry out our existence.
- The more choices we have, the more efficient we are. Choosing is a mark of freedom.
- We cannot communicate; we only communicate.
- What we believe to be reality is, in fact, only our interpretation of this reality through our filters, and judgments.
- What validates the effectiveness of communication is not the intention but the result.

To communicate well with others, listen to them, accept

that they have other convictions than yours, find acceptable compromises to live and work together. Be open to others, even if it means making mistakes. These technical blunders are preferable to negative intentions in the service of manipulation and abuse of power.

NLP presuppositions

Getting your messages across and making yourself understood requires relevant communication tools. This is what NLP (Neuro-Linguistic Programming) offers models and techniques to learn to communicate more effectively, be successful and faster, and change easily. It is based on fundamental postulates, the presuppositions which we describe below.

1. The map is not the territory

This notion corresponds to the fact that we perceive the world (the territory) through our five senses. We make an internal representation of it (the map), which is not exactly the reality. Therefore, each of us has our world map, and there is no map better than another.

2. A positive purpose accompanies every behavior

The good intent determines all behavior. It means giving them a sense of quality if a manager's employees are too demanding for example. He does it for his employees' benefit, in his opinion.

Intending rather than a description of "problem" actions may be simpler and more productive. The question is: what could the good motive behind the other's actions be?

3. You can't communicate

In the morning, you are lost in thought, and you meet a colleague without saying hello. You did not have an intention towards him but receive a message from him. The words (the verbal) represent only 7% of the message, speaking (the para verbal), and the non-verbal represent the remaining 92%! In the presence of the other, even if we do not intend to communicate, we communicate anyway.

Since individuals cannot help but influence each other, a good question to ask is: to what extent am I helping maintain this situation?

4. We are not our behaviors

It is useful to distinguish a person's identity from their behavior. Indeed, while it is relatively easy to help a person change their behavior, it is impossible to change their nature. It's about changing problematic behavior while respecting the person.

5. Body and mind interact

What happens in the mind has repercussions in the body, and vice versa. If we observe the modifications of the non-verbal, we can deduce concomitant modifications at the level of thought.

6. It is possible to reproduce the performance of others

The NLP designers studied the behaviors of excellent therapists and deduced techniques to reproduce their performances and generalize them. In NLP, it is therefore considered that it is possible to reproduce and model individuals' effective behaviors.

7. The meaning of what we communicate is in the response we get

Have you ever met someone's eyes without any particular

intention, and yet this person gives you a black look or even invective? Even if you are unaware of what you are communicating, you get a response that matters.

Therefore, it is important to assess how the message is understood and, if so, how to change it to aim for more efficiency. It is about being receptive to the impact of your messages (feedback) and taking it into account to adjust your communication to the model of the world of your interlocutor.

8. The more choices, the better

At a given time, people adopt the best possible choice, taking into account their possibilities and capacities and according to what they perceive to be valid for them in their world model.

It is the variety of choices that makes it possible to face the complexity of a situation, and which allows that, when it does not work, we can change the way we do it, and therefore try something else. One of the NLP goals is to give people more options, more choices, and make them more flexible.

9. Each person has all the resources to get what they want

Each individual has within him the resources to obtain what he desires. You just have to teach him how to use them or discover them. This presupposition invites everyone to regain power over their lives. It considers that a person's limits are only the representation he makes of them.

10. There is no such thing as failure, and there is only feedback

While failure and error can make you feel guilty and

demotivated, viewing an unexpected response as feedback from a context empowers and invites action: a different outcome than the desired one is to consider additional information about how we are doing.

11. If you don't achieve your goal with a behavior, change that behavior

When you can't reach a goal, try something else. One of the basics of NLP is flexibility.

What assumptions do you want to use?

CHAPTER 11

HOW TO USE DARK SEDUCTION IN YOUR LIFE

The dark side of seduction: how to prevent progress with women from bringing you more unhappiness.

In this chapter, we focus on a very important topic for all those who are on the path of improving skills with women, especially aimed at those who are just taking their first steps and also those who already have enough experience with women but still feel very unhappy.

I want to talk about what I call "the dark side of seduction." By this, I mean when our progress at the social level and with women brings us more suffering and unhappiness instead of giving us that feeling of confidence and happiness that we seek to achieve.

What we all look for when improving skills with women

Almost all of us who seek to consciously improve our skills with women look for one specific thing. At first, our main reason is sex. We are motivated by the need to have as much sex as possible with women.

But deep down, we all have a deeper motivation that is difficult to detect during our early years of progress with women. Beyond seeking to have as much sex as possible with as many women as possible, deep down, our greatest motivation is to feel secure in ourselves and feel happy.

In other words, we seek confidence and happiness. At a superficial level, what motivates us to improve skills with women is sex, but at a deep level, what motivates us is to reach a point where we feel confident and happy. Beyond sex, what motivates almost all of us who seek progress with women are those two things: trust and happiness.

Our biggest dream with women

So, almost all of us embarked on this path, dreaming of obtaining those three things: sex, trust, and happiness. We assume that when we start to get the experiences and results that we seek with women, we will get those three things.

We assume that when we start having enough sex with many women and have one or more girlfriends, we will feel confident and happy. That is the great dream of almost all of us who embark on this path of progress with women.

Now, the problem is that perfecting your skills with women will give you the ability to have more sex, but it will not increase your confidence or happiness. Becoming more skillful on a social level will allow you to achieve all your goals with women. You are going to be able to get the amount of sex you want, you are going to get the type of women you want, and you will get the girlfriends you are looking for. But all those results are not going to bring you confidence or happiness.

I know this is difficult to accept, especially if you are starting. If you are taking your first steps and do not believe in what I just told you, then I do not blame you because many find it difficult to believe.

So if you do not believe it, what I recommend is that you ignore what I just told you and go out with everything to get the results you are looking for and check for yourself if it is true or not.

Improve your skills with women if it is going to give you the ability to get all the sex you want. Even your results are going to make you feel confident and happy in the short term. For example, during a night when you conquer a very hot woman, you will feel very confident and happy. The next day after having sex with her, you will feel very confident and very happy.

But after a few days, that feeling will disappear, and you will again feel a kind of emptiness as if something is missing. That feeling of confidence and happiness you get from having sex with her will start to diminish until you return to your natural state.

In the long term, the results with women will not give you the confidence and happiness you are looking for. As I said before, I know that this is very shocking to hear for those who are starting because it goes against that initial dream that we all have to find confidence and happiness in our achievements with women. It is normal that when someone tells us something that goes against our dreams, we close ourselves.

But I mention it because it is important to know, especially from the beginning so as not to fall into the "dark side" of which I will speak later in this chapter.

The two stages of growth: strengthening the ego and letting go

To explain what I mean by falling into "the dark side of seduction," I must first outline something very important. This idea is one of the greatest discoveries made in these years of progress. It is extremely valuable because it offers you a lot of perspectives to grow healthily and not get lost along the way.

The process of personal growth has two stages:

Strengthen the ego

Before talking about this stage, I want to clarify what the ego is. The ego is your mind. Thanks to having a mind, you can identify yourself as an entity of your own and separate from others. Thanks to having a mind, you can say, "this is me, these are my thoughts, emotions, and actions."

Now the ego is not bad. Within personal growth, the ego is often spoken of as something evil and disastrous. The truth is that it is not bad; it is extremely necessary to evolve as people. Without the ego, that is, without the mind, we could not grow personally. The problem is when we become attached to the ego, and we will talk about that later.

So this stage of growth is to strengthen your ego (your mind). When I refer to "strengthen," I mean progress and growth. There are many ways to strengthen the ego, but the main ones are:

- Acquire new knowledge
- Acquire new experiences
- Acquire new skills
- Face emotional challenges

When we acquire new knowledge, experience, skills, or face emotional challenges, we provide the necessary stimulus to our minds to grow. This type of stimuli strengthens us, and makes us grow mentally. It is as if our mind is a computer, and we are updating it to a new version when we provide these stimuli.

In seduction, we strengthen the ego when we educate ourselves on the subject, for example, we read an article, watch a video, buy a book, or buy a course. When we acquire new experiences with women, for example, we manage to have sex with a woman that we like the same night.

But above all, our ego is strengthened when we improve our skills and face emotional challenges. That is why it is very important to constantly go out as it is the only way to improve skills. Going out once in a while can bring you new experiences, but it won't improve your skills much. On the other hand, when you constantly go out, your skills improve a lot, and you gain a lot of emotional strength thanks to frequently facing all the great fears that arise when meeting new women.

So when you get an education, new experiences, and when you constantly go out to improve your skills with women, you are strengthening your ego. You are growing mentally, and you are becoming more efficient. This stage of growth is what we all know. Now let's look at the other stage, which almost everyone ignores.

Let go

This stage consists of disidentifying yourself from your ego. In a way, it is the opposite of the other stage. In the previous one, we got fully into the ego and strengthened it. Instead, at this stage, we detach ourselves from our minds.

Achieving this stage of growth is more difficult to explain because it is more subjective; it is a process that occurs entirely internally in the person. The previous stage is easy to recognize because there are clear actions that let you know if you are fulfilling it. Instead, at this stage, the actions are "internal."

The way we accomplish this stage of letting go is simply

one step. Which is to remind ourselves that we are not our mind, that is, we are not our ego. The objective of this stage is to detach ourselves from it.

Achieving this is very simple; we only need a few minutes (or even seconds) of internal reflection to remind ourselves that we are not our minds. We have to remember that it is only a tool that we use to our advantage.

There are many ways to achieve this, and each one has his internal process by which he lets go and reminds himself that a mind is just a tool.

However, I share two very practical actions that will help you let go:

Thank you: when someone gives you something you say thank you. After an outing to meet women, you are grateful for all that you accomplished, and you are also grateful for rejections and difficult situations. When you have a girlfriend, you thank her every day for having her. When you get a breakthrough in your skills with women, you appreciate it.

Share your knowledge, experiences, and skills: when a friend asks for advice about women, you give it to them. When you are at a party with friends, you are looking to approach women to bring them to the group and introduce them. When you are with a friend and he is doing poorly in an interaction with a woman, you seek help, say, or do something that increases his social value. When a friend with less ability asks you for help to conquer a girl, you help him.

I put examples relating to seduction. However, you can thank and share in any area of your life.

These two actions: thank and share; they automatically train you to let go because to do them, you have to be detached from your ego. It is impossible to thank and share when you are attached to your ego.

When you are fully identified with your mind, it is as if you are trapped within it. When you are trapped inside your mind, it is impossible to say "thank you" because you only consider what you do not have and what you need. On the other hand, you cannot share either because of that state, and you only seek to obtain things for yourself.

Instead, thanking and sharing automatically lead you to disidentify with your mind and leave the ego. They are actions that, to perform them, require being in a state in which you do not identify with your mind but experience it only as a tool.

The dark side of seduction: when we forget to let go

Now that I have explained the two phases of growth, I can explain much better what I mean by "falling on the dark side of seduction."

To grow healthy, you need to go through these two stages constantly. First comes a stage of ego strengthening, and then it must be accompanied by another in which we let go. When we start to go to an extreme and focus on just one stage of growth, we start having trouble making progress.

If we start to strengthen the ego without letting go, then we will have problems. On the other hand, if we start letting go all the time without strengthening our ego, we will also have problems. Each end will cause different problems when we seek to progress.

To clarify, neither of the two stages is bad. Each one is just as important and necessary. If you have read about personal growth, it may shock you a little when I say that it is important to strengthen the ego. As I said before, it is common for the ego to be interpreted as something evil since there is a lot of information that refers to it as something evil that must be destroyed and eliminated.

The ego (mind) is not bad, and it is necessary to evolve. Nor is it bad to seek to strengthen our ego. The bad thing is when we forget the other part of growth, which is letting go. To grow healthy and progress towards our goals, the two stages of growth are necessary.

At each stage, one enters a different state of mind that is necessary for growth. When we strengthen the ego, we focus on ourselves, and we focus on acquiring resources and becoming more efficient. When we let go, we focus on others, we focus more on sharing the resources we have accumulated, and we become more powerful.

Now falling on the dark side of seduction means forgetting the stage of letting go and getting stuck in the stage of permanently strengthening the ego.

In the seduction case, when we fall on the dark side, we desperately seek to progress to find the confidence and happiness that we dream of obtaining from the beginning. As we make a little progress with women, we realize that we are not obtaining the confidence and happiness that we seek, so we began to look harder to grow faster.

Little by little, we are progressing; each time we start to get better results, we become more efficient. We started to achieve things that we thought were impossible, such as kissing unknown women, generating a lot of attraction in them in a few minutes, and having sex with them the same day we met them.

But as we progress and achieve more, we realize that we have not yet achieved the confidence and happiness that we seek. This becomes an endless cycle of suffering because we always believe that confidence and happiness will be found when we reach a certain level of ability and obtain certain results.

We become obsessed with obtaining better results. We are always looking for better women and doing more impressive things on a social level because we believe that when we advance enough, we will finally get the confidence and happiness we are looking for.

Many have fallen victim to this way of acting. They start to get excellent results with women and achieve things that very few men achieve with girls, but instead of becoming more confident and happier, they become more fearful and unhappy.

It is something very hard to experience; when one falls into this pattern of suffering, it is difficult to overcome it. It is also very difficult to see how close friends destroy your life by falling into this cycle.

The way out of the dark

The way to overcome this endless cycle of suffering is to let go. The problem is that it is difficult to do it when we have been stuck for a long time, strengthening our ego. These two stages of growth are like a synchronous car. It is necessary to stay at a certain speed, but there comes a time when it is necessary to change gear to enter the next stage. If we forget to put the change, then the car begins to suffer.

The problem with being stuck for a long time in the ego-strengthening stage is that as time passes, it becomes more difficult to change in and move on to the stage of letting go. The more months and years we spend staking strengthening the ego indefinitely, the more difficult it is to let go again.

This occurs because as time passes, our suffering begins to grow. Our unhappiness and anxiety begin to increase when we get stuck, strengthening the ego indefinitely. So the more unhappy and fearful we become, the more difficult it makes us let go.

When we are unhappy and afraid, the last thing we want to do is thank and share with others or any other action that helped us let go. Paradoxically, what we least want to do when we are stuck in our minds will help us focus and continue growing healthily.

The solution to this endless cycle of pain is to let go, either by thanking, sharing, or taking time to reflect. We need to distance ourselves from our minds and remember that we are not our knowledge, experiences, skills, or results. All these things are simply tools, but they are not us.

We have to see our mind as if it were a sword. When we have a sword, we can perfect it, reform it, sharpen it, and polish it to make it better. We can do the same with our minds, and we can perfect it. The problem is that unlike the sword, our mind is something very close to us, and in the process of improving it, we forget that it is just a tool.

Being very close to us, then it is very easy to identify with it as we perfect it. The more we perfect it, the greater our tendency to identify with it. However, we can always remember that it is only a tool; it is like a sword that we use to obtain certain things.

Getting the experiences and results you are looking for

with women will strengthen your ego and get the amount of sex you are looking for. However, it will not give you the confidence and happiness you are looking for. This is something that you will only find as you increase your ability to let go.

Letting go is an internal skill that must be practiced constantly, especially after very intense stages of ego strengthening. Otherwise, you are going to start falling on the dark side.

If you are someone who already has experience in this game and have obtained great results with women but still feel unhappy and insecure, you need to learn to let go. You have to start thinking and sharing more. I know it's the last thing you're going to want to do if you've been trapped in that cycle of suffering for a while, but it's the only way out.

If you are just beginning, then always remember that you have to complete the stage of letting go so that you can grow and evolve healthily. Above all, remember it in intense stages of growth, for example, when you go out almost every day for months in a row to improve your skills with women. In those intense stages of growth is when it is easier to start forgetting that your mind is just a tool.

It is very hard to see how a great initial dream begins to turn into a nightmare as one progresses. I want your dream of progress to stay the same and keep motivating you day by day in a healthy way. To achieve this, you must always remember the stage of letting go.

CHAPTER 12

START YOUR MENTAL GAME

Imagine that you go to dinner with your partner; you go to a restaurant, observe the environment, they serve you the food, you smell and taste the food, you feel how your partner looks at you, and emotion is born in you... This whole situation triggers a series of stored data in our minds, which gives rise to different mental processes.

How are mental processes defined?

Mental processes are ways in which our mind stores, processes or translates the data provided by our senses to be used at present or in the future. The mind is defined as a set of mental processes.

What characteristics do mental processes have?

Three different characteristics of mental processes can be distinguished:

Intentionality. It refers to the direction towards an object. For example, in love, there is an intention towards something or someone who is loved. Intentionality is precisely what differentiates a physical phenomenon from a psychological one. Intentionality presupposes an attitude: I think, I hope that...

Consciousness. It involves realizing or knowing our mental processes. One can also speak of direct consciousness, referring to an object and reflex consciousness, which refers to a certain mental process.

The representational character. It is a fundamental characteristic of mental processes; if we think of a pool, we do not have a pool in mind, it is simply a representation of that object.

Types of mental processes

Among the mental processes, we can highlight the following:

Intelligence. It involves an ability to recognize what we feel, to find our motivation. Intelligence is not based only on knowledge and skills; it is based on knowing how to manage our own emotions and understand others (emotional intelligence).

The learning. It is a process by which behaviors, knowledge, beliefs, and values are acquired. It can be learned in many ways, through observation, study, or experience, among others.

The feeling. It supposes the result of an emotion.

The emotion. Emotions guide our behavior and influence our thoughts. An emotion can bring us closer to a person, an environment, or an object or, on the contrary, move us away. Emotions, therefore, have psychological, physiological, and behavioral effects.

Perception. It allows us to see and realize what is happening in a given situation. It helps us interpret and give meaning to a situation.

Awareness. It is not a type of mental process, but a set of mental processes that involve various aspects such as physiological or reason. Based on consciousness, a person can act in one way and another, in a different way. The ways of acting, therefore, can be determined by our genetics and by what we learn through our lives.

Attention. It assumes that our mind is focused on a specific stimulus.

As you can see, the mental processes are multiple and

sometimes quite complex, so it is a challenge to know them and to know how they work in each person.

Five tips to win at mind games

Never underestimate the playfulness of spirit. Here are a few tips that you can use to win the upper hand.

Do not underestimate the impact of small mental activity. While 'Towergate' may be the direction of Roger Federer to threaten Novak Djokovic with a little psychological warfare right before they were about to face off, not every game of mental thinking should have an evil genius. Mind hacking can help you in business, not through manipulation, but through understanding how your mind functions. This can help you to prevent a difficult situation and get to know your reactions.

Mind Hack 1

Your opponent is a mirror. It helps to reflect your body language when you talk to someone older to you. This helps build a sense of familiarity and comfort as our brains like to assume that they are like us when someone acts like us. But don't go over the top and immediately mimic their shifts in body language. This small hack is particularly good for raising or leaving. They see you like them by looking at their body language.

Mind Hack 2

Only take your time. Take your time. It works better than any serum of reality. Do not prompt additional questions when you ask someone a question about a touchy subject and they respond with an unclear response. Just wait a few moments, and in those awkward silence between you both, more information is usually bubbling than was desired.

Mind Hack 3

President, for you, this one. Limit your options. When you want to convince someone to do something, it is nice to limit their choices and make them know they are doing what they want. They do what they want. When choices are made, people typically stick to the options given, as it is difficult and hostile to offer others.

Mind Hack 4

Sit high. Workers be careful if your boss is trying this psychological trick. You will almost always find that the guy in your highest position sits on a better chair above yours when he joins your boss for a meeting, an interview, or a conference. The guest should be bullied. Counter it with the same height as the employer by adjusting the chair. Ha!

Mind Hack 5

Ask, and you shall receive. When asking your boss or colleague for a favor, start big, and then go small. Starting with a big favor, which you know they are likely to say no to, means that they will feel bad and agree to the smaller one. And if they say yes to you at first, well, that's a win-win situation.

Keep your mind active: tips to preserve memory

Challenge your senses in every possible way; the mental activity is necessary not only to avoid boredom but also to stimulate abilities and prevent cognitive decline.

Here are some tips to keep your mind active and, while you're at it, feel more attentive to what's going on around you, focused and sharp.

Use your brain. It seems like a no-brainer, but if you don't use it, you lose it. Exercising your brain helps maintain your mental acuity. People who often practice mind-challenging activities are the fittest. There are many to choose from, and they don't have to be complex: reading books, listening to the radio, playing games, visiting museums, learning another language...

Change your way of acting, challenge your senses. Do you remember when you were a child and tried to speak backward? Researchers from Duke University (USA) created exercises called "neurobics" to challenge the mind and force it to find new ways of thinking. Your five senses are the key to learning, so you can use them to exercise your mind. If you are right-handed, try to use your left hand. Go to work by a different path than the one you usually use. Close your eyes, and try to recognize foods for their taste. These are small challenges for your senses that help keep your brain in shape.

Physical exercise to stay alert. Exercise, especially the ones that raise the heart rate, such as walking or swimming, also provides mental benefits. Experts aren't sure why, but the truth is that physical activity increases blood flow in the brain and improves the links between brain cells. Staying active can help memory, imagination, and even the ability to plan tasks.

A healthy diet to improve your intellectual capacity. Do your brain a favor and choose healthy heart and waist foods. Obesity in middle age multiplies the odds of dementia later by two. High cholesterol and hypertension also increase that risk, believe it or not, because they negatively affect neurons. Try cooking your food in the oven or on the grill instead of frying them. Cook with "good" fats, such as olive oil, and avoid butter and fats from meat. Eat fruits and vegetables of all colors. Include fish in your diet.

Watch what you drink. Drinking alcohol affects judgment, speech, movement, and memory. But did you know that it also has long-term effects? If you drink too much for a long time, the size of your brain's frontal lobes may be reduced. And the damage can last forever.

Video games to train your brain. Take the "joystick," and let's play! Several studies claim that playing video games stimulates the brain's areas that control movement, memory, planning, and fine motor skills. Some experts do not share this opinion. The results are not conclusive, but why not try the fun?

Music helps your mind. Thank your mother for insisting on signing up for piano or guitar lessons. Playing an instrument as a child is worth it because it stimulates mental functions such as memory and the ability to plan. It also favors greater coordination between the hands. Plus, it's fun, and it's never too late to start.

Make Friends. Be a friendly person, relate to your environment. Talking to others sharpens your brain, whether at work, at home, or on the street. Studies show that social activity improves your mind. Think about whether you want to volunteer, sign up for a course or workshop, or call a friend!

Stay calm. Too much stress can damage your gray matter, which contains the cells that store and process information. You can relax in many ways: Take deep breaths, find something that makes you laugh, listen to music, try yoga or meditation, or find someone to talk to.

Sleep to take care of your brain. You have to get enough sleep before and after learning something new because it helps the brain learn. If you start tired, it is difficult to concentrate. Sleeping after learning something allows the brain to fix that knowledge so you can get it back later. A good night's rest is the best thing you can do for your memory and also for your mood. An adult needs 7 to 8 hours of sleep each night.

Tricks for memory. Everyone is distracted from time to time. As you get older, it becomes more difficult to remember things, and it is not as easy as before. It is a normal situation that happens to many older people. To avoid this forgetfulness affecting your daily life, you can: Write down what you don't want to be forgotten. Use the calendar and reminder function on your phone, even for simple things ("Call Mom"). Concentrate on a single task, avoiding several at once. Learning new things step by step, even if it is slower, will be easier for you.

The game of names. Do you have difficulty remembering names? Repeat the name of the person you are talking to several times throughout the conversation, at least in your head, if you don't want to do it out loud. You can also make up a picture or a simple rhyme that you can relate to their name.

CHAPTER 13

HOW TO DISTINGUISH BETWEEN PERSUASION AND MANIPULATION

Not all appear to be deceptive in non-rational conditions.

Calling a person dishonest is a critique of the character of the individual. The complaint that you were mistreated is simply a complaint. Manipulation is at best unreliable and at worst unethical. What is that, however? What makes manipulation wrong? Human beings always and in all sorts of ways influence each other. But what differentiates and makes manipulation immoral from other influences?

Attempts to exploit us are continuous. Here are some examples. Some situations involve encouraging someone to doubt their judgment and trust the manipulator's advice. Guilt trips make someone feel excessively guilty for not doing what the manipulator wants them to do. Spell offensives and peer pressure induce someone to worry so much about the manipulator's approval that they will do what the manipulator wants.

Advertising manipulates when it encourages the audience to form false beliefs. When we are told to believe that fried chicken is a healthy food, or defective association, as when Marlboro cigarettes are linked to the robust vigor of the Marlboro Man. Phishing and other scams manipulate their victims through a combination of deception (forged telephone numbers or URLs) and play with emotions like greed, fear, or sympathy.

Then there is a more direct manipulation; perhaps the most famous example is when Yago manipulates Othello

193

to create suspicions about Desdemona's fidelity, play with his insecurities to make him jealous, and load him with a rage that leads Othello to murder his beloved. All of these examples of manipulation share a sense of immortality.

What do they have in common?

Manipulation is not always harmful

Perhaps manipulation is wrong because it hurts the person being manipulated. Certainly, manipulation often hurts. If successful, cigarette manipulative ads contribute to illness and death; use of phishing, malware, and other types of identity robbery; social media can promote hostile or unhealthy relations, and political manipulation can encourage discord and undermine democracy. Manipulation, however, is not always dangerous.

Suppose Amy's abusive partner has been abandoned, but in a moment of weakness, she will be tempted to return to him. Imagine now that Amy's friends use the same techniques as Othello used for Lago. They manipulate Amy so that she (falsely) believes and is outraged that her ex-partner was abusive and unfaithful. If this manipulation prevents Amy from reconciling, it could be better than if her friends hadn't manipulated her. However, to many, it could still seem morally dangerous. Intuitively, her friends would have been morally safer to use non-manipulation to help Amy avoid recurrence. However, when these benefits rather hurt the exploited individual, something remains morally questionable about manipulation.

So the damage may not be the reason why manipulation is wrong.

Perhaps the manipulation is wrong because it involves inherently immoral techniques of treating other human beings. This thought might be especially attractive to those inspired by Immanuel Kant's idea that morality requires that we treat each other as rational beings rather than mere objects. Perhaps the only adequate way to influence other rational beings' behavior is through rational persuasion, and therefore any form of influence other than rational persuasion is morally improper. But despite its appeal, this answer also falls short, as it would condemn many morally benign forms of influence.

For example, much of Lago's manipulation involves appealing to Othello's emotions. But emotional appeals are not always manipulative. Moral persuasion often appeals to empathy or conveys how it would feel to have others do what you are doing to them. Similarly, making someone fear something really dangerous, feeling guilty about something immoral, or feeling a reasonable level of confidence in one's real abilities does not appear to be manipulation. Even invitations to doubt your judgment may not be manipulative in situations where, perhaps due to intoxication or strong emotions, there are good reasons to do so.

Not all forms of non-rational influence appear to be manipulative.

It seems, then, that whether an influence is manipulative depends on how it is used. Lago's actions are manipulative and wrong because they are meant to make Othello think and feel the wrong things. Lago knows that Othello doesn't have to be jealous, but he still makes Othello jealous. This is the emotional analog of deception that Lago also practices when he fixes things (for example, the fallen handkerchief) to trick Othello into forming beliefs that Lago knows to be false. The central point of manipulation occurs when the manipulator tricks another into distrusting what the manipulator recognizes as good judgment. In contrast, advising an angry friend to avoid making quick judgments before calming down is not manipulative, if you know that your friend's judgment is temporarily inappropriate.

But moral persuasion rather than manipulation is a strong call for empathy for real persons who suffer from unexpected misery. If an abusive partner attempts to make you feel bad about the presumption of unfaithfulness that they already have, they are deceptive, and they try to deceive guilt. However, when a friend makes you feel guilty of having left him in his time of need, it does not seem manipulative.

What manipulates the power and does not do it is the same: the manipulator tries to adopt what the manipulator regards as an inappropriate belief, emotion, or another state of mind. In this way, manipulation resembles lying. What makes a statement a lie and morally wrong is the same: for the speaker to try to get someone to adopt what he considers to be a false belief. In both cases, the intention is to get someone else to make some kind of mistake. The liar tries to make you adopt a false belief. The manipulator could do that, but he could also try to make you feel inappropriate emotion (or inappropriately strong or weak), attaching too much importance to the wrong things (for example, the approval of another person) or doubting something (for example, your judgment or the fidelity of your beloved) of whom there is no good reason to doubt. The difference between manipulation and non-manipulation depends on how a person wants to make anything of what they think, feel, doubt, or care about.

In addition to pure rational conviction, we influence one another in a human condition. It is endemic.

196

These factors often enhance the decision taking situation of the other person by making them believe, doubt, or feel or be vigilant about the right things; often, they undermine decision-making by making them believe, doubt, or feel that the wrong things are done. However, manipulation requires the deliberate use of these forces to prevent an individual from making the right decision: this is the basic immorality of manipulation.

This manipulative way of thinking tells us how to recognize it. Manipulation is a form of control, and it is tentative to think. As we have shown, without manipulation, the forms of stimuli that can be used for handling can be implemented. It is not what power is used to define coercion, but how the effect is used to make a decision better or worse for the other person. And we should not look at the type of power to understand exploitation. However, the purpose of the individual using it is the root and inherent immorality of coercion, as it is meant to undermine someone else's decision-making situation.

A matter of ethics

We all need to convince others to come up with some proposal of ours. From the seller who tries to get his client to choose the brand he promotes, the publicist who seeks to increase the consumption of a product, the politician who wants to win the votes of citizens, to the director who tries to convince his staff of the vision he has created for the company coming true.

All this indicates that persuasion is a subject of great use and utility. This led to social psychology and communication research, and a range of techniques have been developed for making convincing messages more effective. But it has been left aside on several occasions, be it ethical or not to use this device. This section aims to identify the differences between manipulation and ethical persuasion and invite the reader to avoid the first and make use of the second.

General Persuasion and Ethical Persuasion

The principle of persuasion should first be described. Collins (2009, p. 4) states that persuasion is "a change, intentional and internalized, in attitude, belief or conduct, that is, a communication that gives the beneficiary a certain degree of choice freedom." For example, Cablevisión, with its television advertisements, intends that Internet users cancel the service that Telmex provided and switch to Yoo, for which they offer a series of arguments, including speed and cost. Here it is intended to achieve a change in the belief that the fastest Internet service is that of Telmex so that the user transforms behavior and leaves one provider for another; his motto is "Change now."

Upon analyzing the concept of persuasion explained previously, we discover that it has no ethical consideration. Rather, one would speak of effective or ineffective persuasion, depending on whether they have achieved their purpose. Gadner (2004, p.212) expresses this practical conception of the art of persuading in the following words: "It is up to us to choose the use that we give (to the techniques of persuasion) and to do it selfishly and destructively, or in a way that is generous and makes improvements in life." In this way, the techniques proposed by the communication theorists would be neither good nor bad, since their ethical value would depend on the purpose for which they were used. From this perspective, the end would justify the means.

On the contrary, several authors (Messina 2007, Reardon 1991) insist that persuasion must be applied with ethical parameters. Among them, Baker and Martinson (2001) stand out, who propose that for persuasion to be ethical, five principles must be met:

- **The truthfulness of the message:** Telling the truth without distorting the information.
- **The authenticity of the one who seeks to persuade:** Be genuine and act in harmony with what one believes.
- **Respect for the recipients:** That they are treated as ends and not as means; avoid using them for personal benefit or the company.
- **Fair use of the persuasive message's appeal:** Avoids just talking about the positives of the proposal. Especially with vulnerable audiences, such as children and people with little education. They must be treated according to their limitations to understand the costs and potential harm they are asked to do. Otherwise, persuasion would be abusive and manipulative.
- **Social responsibility:** It is necessary to consider the effects of persuasive communication on the community and society as a whole. It would be unethical to try to achieve a company's sales goals or profitability at the expense of the common good.

In summary, it can be affirmed that, for persuasion to be ethical, it must respect the recipient's dignity, allowing him to make a voluntary, informed, rational and reflective choice.

If we analyze the great deceptions that some pseudo-entrepreneurs or directors of companies have carried out, we see that they have been efficient in their persuasion attempt, but unethical. For example, the fraud carried out by the private investment fund company Stanford

Investment that offered investors the promise of extraordinary profits, higher than the average of the financial instruments available in the Mexican market (very well marked the benefits of its proposal). Still, they failed to say that the Mexican Stock exchange institution was not registered, and if losses were incurred, no institution would protect them. His proposal was deceptive and manipulative. The result was that investors lost their money and couldn't find a way to get it back. As for the company director, he was left as a scoundrel, who has closed the doors to return to do business in Mexico and many countries of the world. When we see so many forms of deceit and manipulations in the business world, it would seem that the human being has a malicious pixie that leads him to want to abuse others, to achieve wealth or power quickly. But the wise part of the human being seeks to counteract that pixie through laws and regulatory institutions.

There are accounts of several brokers in Mexico who want to encourage potential clients to invest in their business instead of Stanford Investment. They accept their plan for sound reasons, backed by comparative performance figures on the market for their funds. When talking to the customer, they show enthusiasm about their products and make explicit the benefits they will obtain, avoiding deception and, above all, respecting the person's freedom. The consequence of this ethical persuasion will be that the client will have trust and loyalty with the institution and with the executive, which will allow them to continue doing business with them, instead of leaving with the competition. In the long run, ethical persuasion pays off.

How to Protect Yourself from Unethical Persuasion

While there is an ethical responsibility in the persuader,

the recipient also has to do his part: protect himself from abusive and deceptive attempts at persuasion. To achieve this, Pratkanis and Aronson (2001) suggest that we take the following measures:

Know the ways of persuasion and recognize that one can be a victim of propaganda. For example, we can develop the habit of analyzing ads that offer products that seem magical (such as those that promise to erase wrinkles in 60 seconds) and wonder if they will do everything that the advert promises.

Monitor our emotions. If you feel that your emotions have been played with, get out of that situation and analyze what is happening to you. For example, if you find that you have been scared or guilty about buying a service, consider whether you need it.

Explore the motivations and credibility of the source of the communication. Ask yourself if the communicator is an expert and trustworthy. For example, it is obvious that a seller is interested in closing the sale to earn the commission, so we may doubt that he wants to help us choose the product that best meets our needs, even if the competition sells it.

Think rationally about the proposal they make to you. Take on the devil's advocate's role and reflect on the arguments against what you are being asked to do, the seller will tell you about all its benefits, and it is up to you to identify all its defects.

Review the full range of alternatives before making a decision. Do market research before buying a good or service. For example, if you have decided to buy a laptop, visit several stores and check several brands to compare the price and the functions they offer.

Do not base your evaluation on what the persuader says, but on what he does. For example, if Televisa stresses in its propaganda that the mass media have a social commitment, and we observe that the company supports campaigns like the Telethon, we can believe their words.

If the proposal is too beautiful to be true, it may be misleading. If Stanford Investment investors had followed this recommendation, they might not have lost their money.

Human beings like others to do what they ask of them, be they an entrepreneur, a publicist, a manager, or a politician. To achieve this, you can apply the principles and fundamentals of effective persuasion, regardless of deception or manipulation. The unethical persuader may accomplish his or her purpose. Still, as soon as the recipients become aware of the abuse, the trust will be broken, and it will be almost impossible to restore it. In the business world, trust is essential. If a manager or company director speaks the truth, is authentic, respects his clients' dignity, and his employees, they will trust him, and they will be able to establish lasting relationships. Ethical persuasion has its costs, but it is well worth paying?

CHAPTER 14

CONCLUSION

We are used to thinking that we own our body and mind; after all, who else would it belong to, if not us? However, our mind is somewhat confusing and complex since it keeps many secrets in it that until today have not been fully discovered. And what's even more interesting is that it can manipulate us when we least expect it. For example, if we are hesitant about starting a new job in something completely unfamiliar to us, the good news is that this means we are more likely to succeed in doing so. So in this final chapter of this book, we have compiled ten quite curious mind games that our mind plays on us without us knowing.

Halo effect

It is a popular and well-known influence by marketers and advertisers; behind this is the belief that a person can easily determine a product or service based on an individual. Therefore we have many supermodels and actresses who are the "face" of great make-up lines or clothing companies. We like to assume that renowned people have the slogan "I cannot do something wrong," and unintentionally pass it to the product they want to sell. In general, we are less stringent with famous or recognized characters than we will ever punish ordinary people when it comes to some form of crime or accident.

Spectator effect

This psychological effect is a bit sad: While in a crowd of people, a person is less likely to help someone who needs it because we unconsciously believe that someone else will. A few years ago, several experiments were carried out on this effect and revealed that when one person in the crowd decides to help in an emergency, others immediately followed his behavior. But the most difficult and most important thing was to find the "hero" to start the movement.

Spotlight effect or epicenter effect

Have you ever thought too much about the impression you make on others? Did you think you were too clumsy or did you wear the best outfit for the party? This is known as the Spotlight effect, we literally think all the time that we are the center of attention and that any missteps we take are immediately going to be noticed by other people. This psychological effect tricks our minds into believing that people fixate on ourselves as much as we do, and that everything we do will be judged and examined by other people when, in reality, this mental exaggeration is far from true.

Disinhibition effect on networks

The media have contributed greatly to the development of this effect behind online "trolls" and cyberbullying. On the Internet, where we can use an alias, we tend to be more severe, critical, and harsh than we normally are in real life. It is much easier than doing it face to face, and not everyone can resist the temptation to show their anger instead of being calm and polite.

The "cheerleader" effect

Aren't cheerleaders beautiful? We are not all so exceptionally beautiful, and it is the "animating effect" or "attractive effect" that is a huge help in the field of public relations. So much so that it was given that name. The essence of the effect is this: a person appears to be more beautiful when surrounded by a group of attractive friends; It is also known as the "group attraction effect." This happens because your brain calculates the "average attractiveness level" in the group you are in.

The Dunning-Kruger effect or syndrome

This is a very peculiar thing. Have you ever seen someone who is inexperienced in a specific field and who has rarely, without any knowledge, been very successful in doing this? Conversely, a professional in your field, struggling for years to succeed without being able to make further progress? It's Dunning-Kruger, which explains how beginners have a breakthrough in any area because, unlike professionals who know all things already, they're less familiar with limitations and rules.

Déjà vu

Most of us know this French term that means "something already seen." Déjà vu is the feeling that you have already experienced a situation happening to you in real-time. Before psychology gave it this name, the déjà vu effect made people believe they had a first psychic experience as if they were witnessing a warning or a prophecy. Psychology still does not have a clear answer to the question that we all ask ourselves: What triggers these feelings? To this day, the déjà vu effect remains an unsolved phenomenon.

Google effect

For so long, Google has made a major contribution to the trend of information being lost easily, especially when we are confident that everything is quickly accessible on the Internet. This is why this effect is known as the Influence of Google.

Pareidolia

Taking advantage of the use of Latin words, pareidolia is an effect that makes us see things that are familiar to us in unknown or unusual places.

The phenomenon of the broken ladder

This phenomenon deceives our physical reaction. That's when we expect something to happen, but this isn't going to happen. It is most evident in scenarios such as when we wait for the last step when we go down the stairs, and it is not there, or when we step on a broken escalator, and it does not move. Our body begins to feel nauseous or like we are tripping over our own feet, or that we are losing our balance; this is exactly what the "phenomenon of broken escalators" is.

Have you ever experienced any of these phenomena? Try to remember when you first fell into a trap that your mind played on you.

Manipulation, NLP

and

Body Language Stoicism

The Complete Step-by-Step Guide to Win the
War of the Mind and Discover the Dark
Secrets of Persuasion and Kamikaze Mind
Control

Blake Reyes

INTRODUCTION

We'll be exploring a very important topic in this eBook, because of which many people are interested in psychology. This is a type of exploitation that we experience in life all the time. I'm unlikely to be mistaken if I say somebody is constantly trying to manipulate us, and we try to manipulate others as well. And more often than not, we do this unintentionally, intuitively and thus ineptly, because of which our manipulations do not always lead us to the desired result, nor do other people manage to successfully manipulate us. Even so, people accept attempts to constantly manipulate one another. Therefore, understanding that issue is very important. We will explore in this book what coercion is, how it operates, how effective it is and what can and should be done.

Manipulation is a secret psychological tool by which you can compel any person to do the acts you need against his will and interests. But that is the default exploitation description. Let's offer a wider and more practical definition of that talent. Manipulation is a psychological weapon which, like other types of weapons, gives a person the same (and even greater) advantage over other people. You can strike and catch with one arm and you can also protect and defend with it. It helps with survival and success.

A good manipulator, that is, a person who is skillfully in possession of hidden psychological techniques, is far stronger than a person armed to the teeth. Why? Because he can spread the actions he wants to a variety of people and thus solve any problems and activities. And how many problems and tasks can a person armed with a firearm embedded in our understanding solve? Just a couple, right? One weapon's strength has its limitations. But there are no limits to manipulation. Without exception you can manipulate all people, both the most ordinary and the most powerful. Your talents are the only weakness.

The more perfect your skills in manipulation, the more people you can manipulate. There's no limit to the manipulations themselves—you can manipulate any guy. Without exception you can control all men, both the most average and the most powerful and strong. Your talents are the only weakness.

For some, the most terrible thing is people's inability to accept the fact that they are being exploited. If you tell a person that he was a victim of abuse by someone, then he will most likely deny it and continue to do what he has done. Like showing himself and you that his decision is his choice, and no one is controlling them.

As a manipulated person, my conscience, too, doesn't want to admit that I'm being exploited, but I know for sure. My thoughts, decisions, and actions can't be completely clear of others' influence; it's simply impossible to achieve that. And I understand that so to speak, many of my decisions aren't entirely correct, because I make them under the influence of other people coming to me from facts. I don't have to deny that—I have to regulate that.

Those who doubt they are abused deprive themselves of the chance to defend themselves against it. This is the power of manipulation—it affects people not only secretly, but they also don't want to reveal it themselves. If conventional weapons are used, we turn the aggressor into an enemy quickly, and start fighting with him. Yet people don't see the manipulations, they don't want to see, so they follow them obediently. So, think about what power you can achieve if you know how people can be manipulated.

MANIPULATION, NLP AND BODY LANGUAGE STOICISM

CHAPTER 1

MIND CONTROL TECHNIQUES

Mind control means using the human psychology of one to guide the other person to the conclusion he or she desires. Know these techniques in advance to avoid being fooled by cult groups and illicit traders!

1. Returnability

When a person gives me something such as a gift, praises me, "You're a wonderful person," or helps someone in trouble, I feel the need to respond to it. That is the returning nature.

Usually, a person cannot be favored unilaterally, he must be sure to give something back.

For example, it is the psychology that salespeople use with customers, such as providing bouquets and concert tickets, sending handwritten letters and birthday cards, helping out with the garbage, and holding their shoulders. After that, people who have received benefits are likely to accept solicitations, saying, "The least I can do is to buy a product."

2. Consistency of commitment

With the psychology that you want to do something once and consistently perform actions, or want to be seen by others as consistent, it is very difficult to change what you have decided or promised later.

When you make a decision to do something, of your own choice and without being coerced, you will tell yourself that you can't turn back when you are asked to fulfill it, and more.

3. Authority

Everyone is weak to authority. They tend to follow the instructions of authoritative people without thinking deeply.

Therefore, if you emphasize a relationship with authority or a celebrity who seems to be considered to be authoritative, it is easy to trust the person or organization.

To take advantage of this psychology, dubious associations and bother-to-representatives shoot or show photos with celebrities that represent that they have a good relationship with the person of authority or influence.

4. Low ball

First of all, the solicitation technique started by gently throwing a "low ball" that is easy for the opponent to receive.

If anyone asked you all of a sudden, "Would you like to enroll in religion?" or said "Pay a donation," "Buy this picture," you would refuse immediately.

However, if they said to you, "I'm studying palms," or "Are you interested in art?" you'd feel more comfortable with them. Those who have been solicited ask themselves "Is it okay to go out with them?" And become more likely to be drawn in.

5. Favor

It is easy for anyone to accept requests from people they like. They also think that they must accept such requests.

Especially for men and women who have romantic feelings,

it becomes "naturally answered when asked by someone you like." In that case, the psychology of wanting to be liked by listening to the wishes of the other person also works.

Also, even if you do not think of it at first, you gradually give favor to those who compliment your appearance, sense, work style, or those who feel that your hobbies and outlook on life are suitable. And so, you fall into the same psychological state.

6. If you refuse, concession

With this technique, at first, the person poses an excessive request on the premise that the other party rejects it. At the time it is rejected, concessions are calculated as expected, and the other party is likely to accept the switch to smaller requests easily.

7. Social proof

The psychology of making decisions based on what others think is right, and what they choose, whether or not things are right.

Even if you are not an expert in the field, when you hear that someone around you or a celebrity chooses it, it feels correct and wonderful, and this acts as a powerful judgment.

Therefore, disseminating the story that "a particular entertainer XX selects and uses it" will result in a very high advertising effect.

8. Rarity

The harder it is to obtain, the more valuable the opportunity given to you to obtain it.

"Limited 100 pieces only," and "Now only" gifts are good

examples of this technique.

Recruiting cults and the like go one step further with phrases like, "You are one of tens of thousands of people selected," "You are lucky." They skillfully tackle the psychology of the other person.

9. Perception of Contra strike

Human perception and cognition have a large contrasting effect when subjected to contrasting stimuli.

For example, if you show a cheap item immediately after you show an expensive item, people will see it cheaper than it really is.

Another example of applying this mechanism; A person drives an invitee into a desperate psychological state by showing a video that radically edits unfortunate events in the world such as war, disaster, and crime. Immediately afterward, he solicits, saying, "Only the truth taught by the gurus will save you."

10. Fear

It is a common practice of cults to stir up the other person's fear.

Also, those who offer a defection repeatedly show an example of people that became unhappy because they lacked that defection. In that case, not only the person himself, but also his family and descendants, or even the ancestors of that world, become more unhappy, and the effect is further enhanced.

Mind Control with NLP for Love and Relationships

In a relationship, a word said unconsciously or with conviction can be worth more than a thousand images. For example, the belief that "men always leave me" leads to an experience that turns that idea into truth, so that in the end men leave you, cheat on you, or want to go to bed and nothing else.

Those words that come from the drawer of advice and proposals of love and desire are mental schemes that help to disturb or improve relationships, from the most intimate, without consciously noticing it. 'Intuitive Intelligence' is a way of interpreting the purpose of NLP, which is defined in what the acronym describes: Neurolinguistic programming, the dynamics between the mind (neuro) and language (linguistic) and how the relationship between the two affects the body and behavior (programming). FUCSIA magazine proposed the application of Neurolinguistic Programming in couple relationships to the greatest expert on the subject.

1. What is NLP?

Neurolinguistic Programming (NLP) is the study of the structure of subjective experience and what we can calculate from it. It is a model that goes beyond the obvious and helps us make better decisions according to our objectives. But it is a subjective model. We will discuss more of this in this book.

2. And what is that subjectivity?

Our beliefs, what we know and believe to be true. NLP helps us to know how our mind works, how we communicate and behave. Everything we see, feel, and hear is veiled by our subjectivity.

3. Can NLP techniques be applied in pairs?

Yes, NLP makes evident to us the resources we have within ourselves to relate to in any field, obviously including the couple relationship. When we relate to others, we encounter two different realities, two different belief structures, knowledge, information, physiology, and development. In relationships, it helps create harmony and install positive state mechanisms in our minds, what in NLP we call 'anchors.' It leads us to focus on what we want.

4. Do these 'anchors' produce states of pleasure?

The anchor is a neuro-association between an intense internal state (emotion) and an external stimulus (touch, see, hear). Also, the place, the aromas, the environment, the objects are anchors. So, if you consciously create anchors between the two, you can stimulate the intense desire to be together.

5. In other words, subliminal techniques with the partner?

In NLP, we do not use subliminal messages, and we direct the unconscious mind to start generating the results it wants. But, only you and no one but you decide to change.

6. So, do the parameters of 'good sex' and the orgasm quest change?

Perhaps all humans act on those parameters. The parameters are created by who? Has there ever been a time when you have intensely enjoyed being with your partner, and it has been more fabulous than an orgasm? Surely yes! But what makes us believe that "it must be" clouds these beautiful experiences. Again, we return to beliefs, and for this, it would be good to answer yourself: what beliefs do I have that are mine? Have they been useful to me? What do I believe now of many subjects I have questioned myself?

7. How to use anchors in the sexual game?

When you feel extremely good, so much that your heart is

pounding and you are enjoying it to the fullest... in the most exciting moment of the experience, say something in your mind! Project an image into your mind. Do something now, and your brain will create a connection, a neural network with this state that will be increasingly pleasant. So, the two in unison will begin to create mind maps that generate full understanding and vital focus.

8. Does love count in NLP mind maps? Is there a technique to fall in love?

Love is not had, and it is not a thing; it is a state that you create and decide to live. In the brain, in the neural connection, every thought is translated into a chemical that generates emotions. If your brain is loaded with the 'love chemical,' let's put it that way, everything that person says, everything they do is perfect.

9. Why is it that sometimes, what is said and what is desired does not flow in the relationship?

The apparent contradiction happens because we do not realize what the other is saying to us with his body. So we do not listen to the body, the tone of voice, the looks and the gestures, and although the information is there, we become blind.

10. Would NLP apply to sex therapy interventions?

A lot of sexual problems between couples are the expectations created by the environment of what should or should not be; of what is satisfactory or not; of taboos, the bad, the accepted, the not accepted. Couples come into the relationship littered with so much trash that it doesn't allow them to explore and wonder what each one wants. What is most important in the relationship? What do you like? What do you not like?

For good lovers

Thus, in sexual matters, that breathless phrase "life is not measured by the times you breathe but by the moments when you are out of breath," is very applicable. The search for enjoyment, affection or orgasm can go through periods of dissatisfaction, blockage or trauma, that if you only look for explanations on the outside, in the body, you do not achieve any sense or a pleasant response to express love, which is the fundamental thing in the relationship.

Of course, there is negative mental programming, especially the one imposed subliminally by machismo, which presupposes that "women only enjoy sexuality psychologically." The truth is that orgasm is part of a process that women learn, while the male climax is more automatic and early. And hence it turns out that there are women who fake orgasms to not detune in a duo or because reaching the climax is not so important.

But how can we ensure that the expectations of having a sweet, deep relationship, with greater contemplation, contact, and caress are fulfilled in the couple we want? Perhaps, changing, not of the partner, but convictions, reprogramming what mentally produces negative responses in the way relationships are established.

In this way, there are traces of a map to apply neurolinguistic programming in the life of a couple. Consuelo Martínez gives sexuality a greater dimension, which is not restricted only to genitality, but also highlights the importance that mental structures have on affectivity, desires, and relationships.

The good lovers, in short, are those who know that the map is not the territory. But they do know how to get to the "You are here" point.

The most Powerful Mind-Power Tool

1- Self Test emotional: We should often ask ourselves how we are, and if we perceive that there is a lingering emotion, or attention, we should ask what is the message that brings. The answer does not usually take long if we are honest with ourselves.

Let's also learn to name emotions. Let's ask ourselves in what way it did not sit well if we feel that someone else's comment did not sit well with us. Has it caused anger? Frustration? Sadness? Envy? If we manage to give a name to the emotions, it will be easier to recognize and speak to them over time.

2- Let us live the Present with voluntary intensity: We do not invest too much energy in the memories of the past and the expectations of the future. The past does not exist now. It is the memory of present moments that have passed. The future does not exist now. It is the projection of future moments that may come at some point. Sant Agustí already wrote it sixteen hundred years ago. In essence, consciousness is diluted if we overthink about the past and future, and it does not allow us to maintain contact with the Present, with reality.

3- Let's do different things: If we always get up at 7, let's get up one day at 6.30 and another day at 7.05. If we still drink apple and orange juice, let us add a mango and a papaya juice to our palates. Let's learn to do everyday things with the hand that we use the least, let's play with our bodies and with the things that surround us to stimulate adaptation to something new, although small. A brain that adapts quickly is a brain that does not stagnate in the problem, but naturally seeks other (emotional) opportunities and outlets.

4- Let us grant ourselves the power to choose what kind of thoughts to have: In the same way as when we go to the market to buy things. We have more or less definite ideas of what we are going to buy when we are aware of a constant negative thought, let's ask ourselves: Is this thought useful for my personal development? Does it help me to be a better person? Can it help me achieve a loving and content mood? Is it essential for the development of my skills at work or in relationships with others?

If the answer is no, then we thank the thought and "we accompany him to the exit." Emotions and feelings should never be cast or denied or mistreated. We always accept its existence, and we intervene when choosing what stays and what does not.

5- Let's learn to smile more. At first, it may seem forced and uncomfortable, but over time a genuine and harmonious smile will emerge. Let's start in the morning in the mirror: we smile at each other and pay ourselves a compliment like "Today you are doing super well, flat! You deserve it !!" Let's be ironic; let's say nonsense from time to time; let's be able to take ourselves not so seriously. Life is short and is to love.

6- Let's be grateful. Let us thank everyone and everything. The world smiles at those who smile. The world gives to whom it provides. If you think you could spend so much, well, you're wrong. Thanksgiving is an act of love and trust. It never is enough. If it seems too much, it is because you are afraid of love.

CHAPTER 2

WHAT'S EMOTIONAL MANIPULATION?

You may already be used to hearing about emotional manipulation, the manipulator's behavior, and the victims he leaves in his path. Undoubtedly, it is one of the behaviors that generate the most harmful effects on the victim, mainly due to its silent and lethal character.

The emotional manipulator has a perfectly defined action plan in his head. He knows his victim's weaknesses and how to remove his defenses to impose himself. He acts as if he were the victim, and the other is to blame: he convinces the other person to give him a reason and do what he wants.

They manage to generate certain emotions in the other, depending on what interests them. The plan, as we said earlier, is already outlined. They do not hesitate and use all possible means to manipulate the other's will, using it as a tool for their purposes.

Cognitive dissonance: the origin of emotional manipulation

Manipulators use what in psychology is called "cognitive dissonance." The cognitive dissonance refers to the internal conflict that we feel when we have two contradictory or incompatible ideas in our minds, or when a thought does not fit into our belief system or behavior.

This internal conflict, this tension that corrodes the thought, ends up generating a very curious result. We deceive ourselves to avoid this sensation of cognitive

223

uprooting where we enter without realizing it. This sense of internal inconsistency stuns us to such an extent that we will do our best to eliminate it.

We need to feel an internal coherence between what we feel and what we think, between our beliefs and our attitudes... between what we think and how we act. When we find ourselves at this crossroads, we will leave it at any cost, even if caught in the hands of self-deception.

Self-deception is the subterfuge par excellence of all cognitive dissonance

We will do everything necessary not to endure this feeling of internal inconsistency for long. We will avoid becoming aware of all information that increases this dissonance and "closes our eyes" to anything that may destabilize us even more.

The emotional manipulator knows how to act in the face of cognitive dissonance by deceiving himself to achieve his goal. For example, some people are unable to end some relationships; then, they will do everything to reverse the situation and for the other to end this relationship.

Jorge wants to leave Maria because he met another girl for whom he felt a special "connection." Maria, on the other hand, doesn't know any of this, doesn't want to end the courtship because she is very much in love with him. Faced with this situation, Jorge will do everything possible for Maria to end this relationship once and for all. Later, she will feel the sole responsibility for the end. Jorge will say: "Oh, no! You were the one who left me, and I never said that!"

The handler transfers the blame to the other and gets rid of it

He is faced with the discomfort caused by the confrontation between who he is and what he would like to be, someone loyal. What is being done at that moment is that Jorge chooses to manipulate Maria emotionally so that she can resolve the situation... be the culprit for the breakup. Maria probably does not understand what is happening, because few can conceive having a partner who does this. On the other hand, Jorge's behavior may not be conscious.

In this case, Jorge does not see himself ending a relationship, much less than the reason is that another girl appeared in his life. In his mind, he doesn't want the role of the villain in the relationship, and to protect himself, and he plays the victim. In order not to accept this reality, not to assume his responsibility, he manipulates Maria until the rope breaks definitively, regardless of how much she may suffer.

If Maria is the person who left him, he will need not feel guilty about wanting to leave her for someone else. Because it "goes bad" and can tarnish your reputation. Instead, in this way, he resolves the internal conflict and "benefits" from this battle.

For all these reasons, emotional manipulation is often the result of cognitive chaos from which the person seeks to get rid of it anyway. They will look for an executor, a culprit who will make them victims or put them in a situation that justifies their thoughts or behavior.

The other will always be to blame. They will always be the unhappy victims in their relationships overtaken by emotional manipulation.

Types of Emotional Manipulation

The very word manipulation already calls for something unpleasant and undesirable. One of the types of manipulation is emotional manipulation, and often a person consciously allows it to happen because he does not know how to deal with it. This section will explain some of the actions of emotional manipulators and how to deal with them.

Cheating the victim: Is something we face every day. They never want to take responsibility for their actions, but constantly play the victim and blame others for something they have done wrong. As a result, someone apologizes to them in the end, because they are skilled in playing the role of someone helpless.

Presenting their problem as bigger: Is also a common occurrence. If a person starts complaining about their problem, they will immediately start comparing. Even if your two problems are not connected, they will find a way to connect them and thus tell us to "tie-up," because no one has a bigger problem than them.

"Gaslighting": Has the consequence that the person who is a victim of gaslighting begins to wonder if he is sane because the emotional manipulator begins to convince him that he has heard or seen something wrong. In that way, they establish control because people often react to it by starting to question themselves, and it mostly ends by convincing themselves to imagine.

Making jokes: Is sometimes very difficult to recognize as manipulation because people generally do not associate humor with anything bad. However, there is a difference between a harmless joke and harassment. Emotional manipulators will constantly belittle us and deliberately provoke us where they know it hurts, claiming that they are just kidding, to establish superiority over someone. If someone decides to oppose them, he will immediately blame them for being too sensitive or accusing them of making a scene, maybe even in front of friends and acquaintances. This allows them to behave as they wish because no one likes to be labeled as a "party breaker".

The question is, how to protect yourself from emotional manipulators? The most important thing of all is to learn to recognize when someone is trying to manipulate us. Once we do that, the next step is not to let them have control over us. Ask yourself, why allow yourself to feel unnecessarily bad? It's easier said than done because they often play on our empathy, and it's hard for some people to stop it. However, the sooner we start trying, the easier it will be later. Although sometimes it seems to us that there is no way out of the black hole, we are the ones who set the boundaries, and if we allow the manipulators to cross them once, they will do it again.

Hold on to yourself, and don't let others sway you.

Behavioral and Character Traits of Manipulators

Throughout your life, you will encounter manipulative people, who pursue their selfish purposes, for which they have no qualms about causing harm to you.

Generally, manipulative people have no qualms or compassion when they find a new victim for their plans since they are individuals dedicated to exploiting other people's weaknesses to achieve their benefit, regardless of what they have to do for it.

The manipulative method used in this approach focuses on emotional blackmail, involving people with false words and deeds. In this way, their victims trust and yield to the supposed good intention of this manipulative mind, which pretends to feel sympathy and appreciation for others.

Hence the danger posed by manipulative people to anyone's life, as for them, there is no moral limit or obstacle between their goal and themselves. This allows them to easily crush, use, and dispose of people affected by the way they act.

Despite knowing the threat that manipulative people pose in their life, it is quite difficult to differentiate them into a group of acquaintances or coworkers since you can even fall victim to someone without realizing it until you are affected by their bad influence.

That is why we present five typical characteristics of a manipulator, to help you identify and recognize this type of predator that lurks in your social circles.

Five common traits in manipulative people

Innate speakers

Manipulative people demand their best speech skills to convince their victims of their false good intentions to deal with the gift of speech effectively.

They can transform any situation they find themselves in to convince others of their innocence. Coming to create a false image in the minds of those who fall for their mind games.

They maintain excessive control over the situation, always obtaining the greatest benefit in exchange for others' hard work. His word tends to confuse and manipulate his victims efficiently, to the point of remaining unaware of a bad way of acting.

Manipulative people are greedy

Manipulators do not pursue a simple goal that they can achieve on their own; on the contrary, they are always looking for a greater objective that constantly compresses their victims.

The hunger for power and control is also a reflection of the great ego that manipulative people tend to possess—those who over-rely on their manipulation to the point of feeling invincible, lest they set future limits.

They tend to assume the role of the victim

Being a victim implies great vulnerability and innocence, so it is the preferential role of manipulative people. Since people around them never think that the victim is the victim.

In this way, they manipulate other people emotionally, playing with their feelings. Therefore, confrontation with a manipulator can make you believe that he is the victim, and you are the aggressor.

Create a false image of the need

Piety is the emotion that manipulative people tend to hold on to. To do this, they use an image of weakness and fragility, to which their victims fall easily, wanting to help someone in need.

After deceiving people with their false need, a manipulator makes his victims feel responsible for their health, food, money, and any other benefits they can obtain from that individual.

Manipulative people always lie

Inevitably, lying is part of any manipulator's repertoire. They deal with this ability naturally, without showing doubts or any characteristic that allows their victims to detect the truth behind their false facade.

Manipulative people are masters of lies, to the point of lying in any aspect of their lives, regardless of whether it is minimal or important. Because, through deception, they can approach the goal they are pursuing.

For lack of a moral compass, there is no limit to the lies of a manipulator. For him, lies are part of the tools he needs to achieve his goal, regardless of who he causes harm.

CHAPTER 3

PSYCHOLOGICAL MANIPULATION TECHNIQUES

The sophisticated technique that many fraudsters use to gain benefits is to manipulate people. Human psychology is so powerful that it can be controlled. In the commercial talks process, the sides seek to place pressure on each other to support their position. And to defend yourself from outside threats, you need to learn to know various forms of coercion.

It's usually hidden away. It's harder to suppress the will openly. It needs a person who is easily exposed to it. There are very few of them and the hidden coercion of individuals is being used in this respect.

The multiple arts of management

Psychology is multiple sciences. And the art of manipulation is direct proof of that. There are a huge number of methods you can use to learn to control a person. But no manipulator would use all means. They usually choose some of the most appropriate methods. Why is human manipulation so popular?

With the help of management skills, you can not only influence the actions of the interlocutor but also achieve your goals.

You have to feel the mood of the people

It would help if you did not think that everyone is subject to management. Some people are difficult to hypnotize.

Therefore, they are also not subject to manipulation. The attackers are trying to avoid such people. How do you know who to avoid and who can be controlled? Manipulations by people, psychology - to be a professional in these areas, you need to feel the interlocutor's mood. Otherwise, all abilities will be reduced to zero.

1. Distribution of Attention

We, therefore, remind you of the still current Techniques of manipulation.

A key element of social control is a strategy of distraction or obstruction that will distract the public from important issues and changes that the political and economic elite decide through continuous interference by placing insignificant information. Distraction strategy is important for preventing public interest in basic knowledge from science, economics, psychology, neurobiology, and cybernetics.

2. Create Problems and Offer A Solution

The method is also called "problem-reaction-solution." This method creates a problem, a "situation" that provokes reactions in public, after which solutions are offered that would, under normal circumstances, be opposed by the public.

For example: Let urban violence develop and intensify or arrange bloody attacks so that the public can demand new security laws and rules on its own, albeit to the detriment of personal freedom. Or: create an economic crisis and accept the recession as a necessary evil and ultimately reduce social rights and reduce public services.

3. Strategy of Graduality Of Change

Make the public accept the unacceptable, i.e., apply

gradual acceptance of change, drop by drop, step by step.

4. Use of Children's Language

A better future facilitates their acceptance.

5. Disposal Strategy

Another way to prepare the public for unpopular changes is to announce them much earlier, in advance. They should also be presented as "painful and necessary" to gain public consent for future changes. People do not feel all the weight of change at once, because they get used to the very idea of change. Also, the common hope for most advertisements aimed at the general public use speech, arguments, characters, and especially children's intonations, as if addressing small children or mentally underdeveloped people. The more they want to mislead the viewers, the more they apply infantile tones. When addressing adults as if you were addressing children, we achieve two beneficial effects: the public suppresses their critical awareness, and the message has a stronger effect on people.

6. Use of Emotions

Emotional abuse is a classic technique used to cause a short circuit in the process of reasonable judgment. Critical consciousness is replaced by emotional impulses (anger, fear, etc.).

7. Keep the Public in Ignorance And Average

Render the population incapable of recognizing the technology and techniques used to regulate and enslave it. The quality of education in the lower social strata should be as low or below average as possible so that the chasm between the upper and lower strata remains insurmountable.

8. Encouraging the Public to Be Satisfied with Its Average

The promotion of the public's attitude is that it is modern and desirable to be stupid, vulgar, and uneducated.

9. Creating A Feeling of Guilt

To lead a person to assume that he is the only one to blame for his failures, because of the weakness of his intellect, negligence, or lack of effort. Thus, instead of rebelling against the economic environment, the person does not act because he blames himself for mistakes, contributing to distressing societies whose sole function is to discourage intervention.

10. Getting to Know an Individual Better Than He Knows Himself

The rapid development of science in the last 50 years has created a larger gap between the knowledge possessed by the average man and the knowledge possessed and used by the ruling elites.

The system can understand the common man better than he knows himself. This means that, in most cases, the system has more control and has more power over the individual than the individual has over himself.

CHAPTER 4

THE ROLE OF DEFENCE

Signs that You're Being Manipulated

There is a category of manipulators who try to influence people, fully aware of what they are doing. To manipulate is to persuade a person to fulfill one's will to gain profit. A person unconsciously manipulates from an early age. Already, preschoolers can use primitive manipulation techniques to get what they want from their parents.

Most adults also use manipulation techniques, but more often, they do it unknowingly. But there is a category of manipulators who try to influence people, fully aware of what they are doing. Such people are called energy vampires and maintaining close contact with them is sometimes very dangerous.

How to recognize who is in front of you—an experienced manipulator, aware of his actions, or just a person acting out of habit, unconsciously? Consider the following signs that you are being manipulated consciously.

1. The model of behavior

If we talk about experienced manipulators who are used to achieving their goals by controlling people through their subconscious fears and weaknesses, they differ in a certain behavior model. Conscious manipulations gradually lead to personality deformation. Several behavioral features are considered typical. The first thing you need to pay attention to is excessive, ostentatious emotionality.

Second, such people are attentive and observant, and you

235

can notice how they sometimes peer at people. A professional manipulator will never listen to a person inattentively. He listens sympathetically, actively participates in conversations, can assent. And of course, the third—the manipulators take small pauses between the emotional reactions and the events that provoked them. This happens only because their body needs a little more time to synthesize emotions, which are often an instrument of control and influence.

2. Unpredictability

As a rule, it is impossible to predict such a person's words and actions in advance. This distinguishes manipulators—they have flexibility, and they always adjust their actions depending on the situation, and on how open the interlocutor is. Unpredictability is inherent in every person, but usually, the actions and words of such people in most cases can be predicted. Manipulators often use it as a technique that discourages the interlocutor, disorients, and plunges into confusion. It is at such moments that people are most open to manipulation, and one who uses this method of influence consciously often uses unpredictability.

3. The lack of direct answers

As a rule, an unconsciously manipulating person does not care that their victim can figure it out. However, professionals know what they are doing and why, and are as cautious as possible in their speeches. Therefore, they often answer evasively or may even evade answers if it is not convenient for them to answer questions.

4. Inconsistency of gestures and emotions

This is a typical sign of insincerity that accompanies all the speech of manipulators using unclean tricks in dealing with people. You can replace the difference between what kind of emotional tone a person speaks and what his gestures are. As a rule, manipulators actively gesticulate, and it is difficult not to notice it. Unconscious manipulation is distinguished by the fact that a person does everything automatically, and the pros perfectly understand their insincerity and try to hide behind an emotional background.

5. Conversations in private

Each of us sometimes needs to discuss something with someone in private. This is the norm and does not contain any toxic elements. But a consciously manipulating person almost always calls his potential victim into a solitary conversation, since in this case, he will have to face the least resistance. A person who realizes that he plans to persuade someone through psychological pressure to fulfill his will not do this in public, where there is a high risk of exposure.

6. Valuation judgment

Pro manipulators use value judgment more often than ordinary people. They intend to expose the world, people, phenomena, and actions in black or white, without shades. They have only "very good"—this is usually what is beneficial to them. And "very bad" is what they do not need at all.

7. Eye-to-eye look

As a rule, psychologists recommend recognizing liars and manipulators by a wandering gaze. People often look away when they are not completely sincere, but this is most often done by those who do this unconsciously. An energy vampire who knows his job, on the contrary, tries to look directly into the eyes of his interlocutor, and rarely looks away. Because of this gaze, people get confused quicker and can make concessions easier.

8. Speed

The manipulator, acting consciously, does not give the interlocutor time for thought and does it very skillfully. He requires an immediate response, and always adjusts the circumstances in such a way as to increase the likelihood of agreement. They do everything very quickly, do not insert pauses in conversations, and are always in a hurry. Modern psychologists have begun to study the fraud's problem to uncover as many criminal schemes as possible aimed at taking away other people's money. Relatively recently, psychologists around the world have become interested in the so-called "toxic charges." We are talking about fraudulent fundraising, allegedly for sick children. Law enforcement authorities have uncovered several such cases. And psychologists noted that in all messages of scammers, there was an emphasis on urgency.

9. The tendency to downplay

This is another psychological technique that is not always used consciously. The tendency to downplay is inherent in absolutely all categories of manipulating personalities, but those who do this consciously use this technique more often and more persistently. Such a person likes to periodically accept the victim's image because having caused pity in the interlocutor makes it easier for him to manage him.

10. Aura of hopelessness

If the manipulator acts consciously, it does not just play down, which thickens colors to hopelessness. The complete hopelessness that he can draw in the imagination of the interlocutor is not a reliable reflection of reality. The manipulator presents only negative facts, skillfully hiding the positive aspects and keeping silent about them.

To learn to recognize manipulators and understand whether they manipulate consciously or unconsciously, experience and practice are needed. Unfortunately, it is far from always possible to figure out an energy vampire right away, but with experience, this skill will come.

Factors that Make You Vulnerable to Manipulation

Manipulation comes into play in many of our relationships, but to what extent does it affect you? You are not exempt from others' influence; if you usually do things that you do not want at the suggestion of others, you may be a somewhat manipulatable person.

You need to understand that being a manipulatable person is something that many people around you can take advantage of. Being aware of this issue can make you reflect on how the opinion of others determines your behavior, to try to modify this aspect.

If you want to know to what extent other people take advantage of you and end up manipulating you, you should check for yourself if you are a manipulatable person. Through this simple test, we show you.

Test to know if you are a manipulatable person
- It makes me nervous when I realize that they are trying to blackmail me. T or F
- I consider that the opinion of others is something that matters a lot to me, sometimes even too much. T or F
- I usually have a hard time expressing my opinion and offering my point of view. T or F

- I generally do things to please others. T or F
- I need the approval of everyone, or most people. T or F
- When I make a mistake, I feel guilty and give many justifications. T or F
- If someone gets mad at me for not doing what he asks me, I do what is necessary so that he doesn't get angry. T or F
- I always try to follow social fads or trends. T or F
- I feel that my decisions are based primarily on the needs and wants of others. T or F
- I have a great need for other people to be okay with me. T or F
- If I realize that someone does not like my clothes, I will not wear them again. T or F
- I usually feel guilty about any anger from others. T or F

Answers:

Score one point for each true answer. If you have earned six or more points, you are a person who can become easy to manipulate by others.

You must be aware of this matter so that some people do not take advantage of you. Reflect on how you relate to your environment since you are in time to change this situation.

If you have scored less than 6 points, congratulations! You do not allow yourself to be influenced too much by others, value your opinions, and have your criteria to face life.

You don't need too much of the approval of others, and you know how to distinguish between what is your responsibility and what is not.

How to Defend Yourself from a Manipulative Person

Manipulation is a rather unpleasant word. Especially when it is used about your person. But, one way or another, each of us is faced with manipulation daily.

This can include both attempts by someone from the environment to influence our actions and decisions, as well as the usual impact on us of advertising from billboards or gadget displays.

Logically, you will immediately want to defend yourself against attempts by anyone to incline you to certain actions and deeds. Then it is necessary to understand what methods of protection against manipulation generally exist clearly. We'll talk about this.

How to resist manipulation in real life?

It is not difficult to protect oneself from manipulation. After all, everything has a recipe and solution. But before we touch on the topic of the mechanism of protection against manipulation, it is worth learning three basic and quite important points. Their understanding will help in using those techniques that will be described in the future.

So, three conditions must be observed:

Your speech and language should be clear and concise.

Your intonation should be appropriate to the situation and be intelligible.

Each of your answers to the replica of the manipulator (a person trying to impose his will and his decisions on you) must be thorough and confident.

Have you learned? Fine, then move on. After all, these three aspects are based on everything that will be listed below. And below are the main ways to protect against

241

manipulation, which were once painstakingly collected by the famous American social psychologist, Philip Zimbardo.

Methods of protection against manipulation

Do you feel that a colleague, relative or any other person is trying to impose their opinion on you, forcing you to do what they need?

Such actions can be either in the form of an active emotional conviction of the interlocutor or in an attempt to "put pressure on pity," or even blame something. To become the master of our own decisions, we will look at 12 ways that will certainly help to resist manipulations of this nature.

Recognize and mirror manipulation

"Exit the template."

This is a method that consists of the following - learn to behave in a dialogue, going out of your typical form, and manner of communication. Try on yourself the role of a person with the opposite character. For example, react as the manipulator does not expect at all. The main thing—do not even think while making excuses or bickering.

Accept your mistakes and shortcomings.

State clearly that you made a mistake. Having agreed on what you are accused of, you will disarm your interlocutor and discard the burden of unnecessary obligations based on remorse.

Do not be fooled by the manipulator imposing his picture of the world.

Suggest an alternative to how you see the situation under discussion. Be prepared to take a step back in time and declare your rejection of the vision that is being imposed on you by another person.

Do not be afraid of a short-term refusal of goods.

Which may follow the termination of contracts with the manipulator (the same money or other material resources). If a person openly imposes on you actions that are beneficial to him, break your relationship, and consider the knowledge gained from this as a useful experience.

Be prepared to refuse to communicate with the manipulator.

This item is paired with the previous one but is still somewhat different. This is about intangible things. Do not be afraid to say the word "enough" to the person manipulating you. Accept that you are self-sufficient and able to live without being favored by anyone. It can be both a refusal from companionship and the sympathy of the opposite sex.

Do not let them rush you.

Often the manipulator rushes you in making decisions. And he can do it skillfully and quite emotionally. Do not fall for such tricks, in any situation, take time to think.

Insist on clear and concise explanations of a given situation.

Also, do not respond to provocations aimed at making you stupid. If any explanation was ambiguous—require specifics!

Don't play too much in the host-guest relationship model.

Being in conditions that ascribe guest behavior to you, do not get too carried away with this role. Indeed, often such rules significantly limit your freedom of action, hiding behind the generally accepted model of behavior.

Do not expect from a person baseless sympathy and even love.

This is one of the most important principles on which defense mechanisms against manipulation are based. No, that doesn't mean that you need to expect a trick and set it up everywhere. It only means that it's worth looking at relationships (especially with strangers) a little more pragmatically.

Try yourself as an impartial and cold person.

Oddly enough, at the same time, you can safely remain a kind, sympathetic, and a good person. However, critical thinking and evaluating other people's actions without an emotional component will significantly increase your chances of a calm and confident achievement of your own goals.

Eradicate guilt dictated to you by someone from the outside.

Consider mistakes as experience and try not to make them, but never "digest" everything that has already passed in your head. It is the regular experience of situations from the past, based on a sense of guilt that can unsettle and make you subject to a human manipulator.

Act not based on established habits and laws, but the basis of your judgments.

Accept the idea that you can change—you are a living person. Even if you're used to expecting one thing, but you decide to do otherwise, you have every right to do so.

Doing as profitable does not mean to be bad.

Do not forget that almost everyone in the world is trying to capitalize on it. Often, people differ only in the fact that some accept this idea, while others consider it something completely unacceptable and themselves suffer because of this. If you want to succeed, consider yourself the first type. This does not mean that you will become selfish. On the contrary, you can look at many things with a cold head and free yourself from the shackles of far-fetched obligations and rules that manipulators skillfully use for their purposes.

Practical Tips for Dealing with Predators

When dealing with an emotional predator, we should have a good social and psychological support.

The victim of an emotional predator does not always have adequate resources to cope with this behavior. Thus, it is common that it is completely conditioned to the personality of the first, who feels the victim of a psychological prison and trapped in turn by fear.

In these cases, in addition to making use of adequate psycho-emotional skills, it is always vital that we have social and healthcare support. As striking as it may seem to us, all of us can fall into such damaging links at some point in time. Regardless of our gender, social position, or previous experience.

The emotional predator inhabits almost any setting. Furthermore, there is a narcissistic profile sometimes behind these behaviors, a personality type that highly specialized in psychological manipulation, blackmail, and domination. Knowing how to act is key in all cases.

Identify the emotional predator

There is a first aspect that we must take into account. We must be sensitive and know how to react in time to all processes of emotional predation. We cannot forget that this reality occurs too frequently and defines a highly common type of psychological abuse.

To do this, we must put aside the blame and gradually abandon the position of tolerance, recognizing that the person we are with may have a possible personality disorder or simply be someone with dangerous behavior.

Therefore, it is important to understand their tactics and how they work, counting as far as possible with psychological help and support from our environment.

Let's see some characteristics.

How is the emotional predator?

- He yearns for control at all times.
- He despises and humiliates the other person. In case he offers reinforcements or positive acts; it will be done for personal interest or to get something.
- He manipulates reality, makes us believe that we are wrong or that we are naive.
- He victimizes himself to be in control.
- Ironic, critical, sarcastic language.
- Grandiose airs.
- He punishes us often with indifference and with the idea of severing the relationship.
- Projects the blame on us.

As a curiosity, according to a study carried out at the University of Innsbruck, Germany, by doctors Ursa Nagler and Katharina J. Reiter, the emotional predator is highly skilled in Emotional Intelligence. However, be careful because that ability is used to control others.

Stop justifying yourself

It is important to keep this message in mind when you are faced with an emotional predator. The victim will indeed want to justify himself since the aggressor's speech is riddled with lies, but the explanations and justifications will only lead to getting more stuck at that moment:

- The emotional predator will use all the mistakes and inaccuracies that his victim has made against them, even if they had good intentions.
- Therefore, silence is better, since anything we do or say can turn against us.
- If we are facing a moment of separation, the harassment process can be carried out by phone or through messages.

For such cases, it is recommended, if possible, to change the number or email, filter them, or have a third person to help us. It is whoever intervenes since if it is the victim who responds again, they can re-immerse themselves in the process of emotional predation, destabilizing their separation and independence.

Act

As the mental process of separation progresses, and the victim finds himself strong and resilient, he can change his strategy and act firmly, without fear.

The crisis will allow the victim's life to be reborn again. We must end this link clearly and definitively.

To resist

It is important to know that to resist psychologically, you have to have some kind of support that is capable of restoring the victim's self-confidence that has been lost.

Valid supports are content to be by the victim's side, available when the victim needs them, without making judgments or being fooled by reproaches and manipulations.

Further, it is advisable to go to professionals (psychologists, psychiatrists, etc.) to help us reestablish our well-being and personal autonomy, as well as to recover our confidence and face our fears.

Justice intervention

It may happen that a crisis or a conflict of this type can only be resolved with justice. However, in these processes, the provision of evidence is necessary. This is where there are usually more complications because humiliations, contempt, insults, and offenses are difficult to demonstrate unless there is a third party when they occur, which may be the key.

It is also suggested to keep all written documents that can be recognized as evidence. It is an arduous process, and full of uncertainty, since many judges are suspicious.

Perhaps the only way to protect the victim is to establish rigid judicial orders and avoid any contact between the parties. Being finally, a matter of justice, the adoption of adequate protection measures to avoid the resurgence of the relationship of emotional predation.

CHAPTER 5

THE ART OF BODY LANGUAGE

Why is body language an art? Why is it so crucial to understanding getting better at decoding the opposite sex? One simple answer may answer these questions: most communication is considered non-verbal, up to 90%. Those who use non-verbal communication of 90% are very good at it and have practiced it more than once. Think about it this way: can you use non-verbal communication to tell a person how you feel, and what you think? Probably not.

Thus, you fall into the 70-80% of people who lack sufficient non-verbal competencies. Those who fall in the 20-30% of people who are capable of non-verbal communication, find themselves lucky because it is a powerful skill. What are the keys to success, then? All circumstances are unique, but patterns are permanent, so the following things to be looked for are not set in stone but are a great guide to construct from.

The first and largest type of nonverbal contact is with your eyes. One cannot overemphasize how important the initial eye-contact is because this is the first form of non-verbal contact that one normally encounters when communicating with an opposite-sex person. This doesn't mean that if somebody stares at you, they're interested in you and you should look back. NO! NO! It is all focused on contextual situations. This is an appropriate assumption in a bar because it befits the atmosphere. But, if you're enjoying a family dinner at the restaurant, you're likely to have something on your chin or mouth. So, there are

249

certain ways to tell if someone, in this case, is also trying to communicate with you non-verbally.

The transition from eye language to body language is much faster in the first situation at the bar; therefore, it is easier to decipher as a purposeful nonverbal communication. In the restaurant's second scenario, eye language is the prominent form of non-verbal communication, since the person cannot use their body to communicate their feelings/thought. Therefore, if there are repeated occasions where eye contact continues for longer than 1.7 seconds, this can be viewed as purposeful flirting. Why those 1.7s? Based on many studies conducted by people who are interested in interactions with others, most of the situations that include eye flirting last for about 1.5-1.7s per eye contact. Also, if you want to test whether they look back at you or not because you started to look at them, using your peripheral vision is simple. Try and catch them looking at you. If this occurs on more than one occasion, then your initial thoughts are confirmed. Rule of thumb, if the eye language studies concentrate on the language of the brain, DO NOT start incorporating subtle facial gestures because you may look stupid and give the wrong impression if done wrong.

The Five C's of Body Language

Do you want to know exactly what people think when they talk to you? Their lips say yes, but they say no with their eyes and their bodies. We unconsciously pick up on those signals. Have you ever had a bad feeling about someone who's been justified?

The human ability to understand body language meaning was essential to life. The earliest cavemen wanted to know whether others were friends or a threat, so they easily determined this by reading their non-verbal signals. One

Princeton study found a first impression took 100 milliseconds to form.

Body language goes beyond detecting threats. Protecting ourselves is about human nature. Sometimes that means masking our real feelings and intentions. Decoding such motives lets you know whether you are interested in a future date, a working relationship is going poorly, or someone is trying to take advantage of you. This won't hurt, either, as a party trick.

We can understand body language. If you've ever "seen" someone wasn't interested in you, you've picked up the language of their body. You can appear to read minds by learning more about the more than 30,000 unconscious clues we send off.

Body language goes in both directions. You will learn to interpret another person's actions, while others can read your thoughts and intentions. Be mindful of this so that you can align your body language with your intentions, including emphasizing authenticity and not signs of deceit.

Charles Darwin believed that six facial expressions were genetically inherited: joy, sorrow, anxiety, disgust, surprise, and rage. Later work verified that such terms are used and accepted in the world.

Perhaps you'd like to brush up on how to understand body language. It's not enough to memorize body movements and expressions to know what someone feels; a movement is often not a true signal, but a spontaneous gesture. To further refine your body language skills, you will need to apply the following 5 C's to what you are doing.

1. Context

Our eyes are moving in different directions, depending on what part of our brain we control. We search for constructed images (up and right for visual, right for auditory and down and right for kinesthetic) and left for recollected images (and again, up / left for visual, left for auditory, down / left for kinesthetic).

To check that, ask a friend a question like, "What is your favorite song's second line?" (They would look to the left) or "What if I were a woman/man?" (They would look up and down). They usually look left when they remember something, while their eyes flit to the right for imagination.

Does that mean that someone lies when they look right? It depends on a lot of things; meaning is one of those. Looking left into a courtroom may be a sign of deceit. But what if the jury is on the left and the accused gazes at their reaction nervously? Are they always looking left, or was it only in response to a particular question? You can already see how a manufacturing environment can make someone look more guilty than their natural self would produce.

Say you're talking to someone, avoiding eye contact, looking at your phone, and folding your arms. They assume you are bored but knowing "Signal A = B" is not enough. We are not living in a vacuum, and our world constantly affects us. Think about what's going on in the nonverbal signal before you leap to a conclusion.

Firstly, what's the chat about? Has the other person suddenly shifted his or her body language when a particular topic arose? It could be the subject that renders them uncomfortable. Try to change the subject then see what's going on.

Second, consider your surroundings. Crossed arms are a sign of defensiveness, which creates a barrier, but it may be cold and they're just trying to keep warm. Look for all the details. Perhaps their ex just walked in or they have bad memories of that place.

Finally, think about the person you meet. They may be checking their phone because they're expecting some important news, they've received a message that's putting them on edge, or they've had a stressful day and have not yet disconnected.

Contextual awareness will save you from embarrassment. Imagine conversing with an attractive man or woman. You think they flirt from the way they turn their body towards you. Often a woman's interested in you when she crosses her legs toward you. Other signs of interest are leaning in and shifting their body to face you.

To get meaning from the body language, look at the context. During a date, aspects of the person's body towards you are strong signs of attraction, but there are other circumstances where people can expose their attitude to you; therapists, interviewees, and sales staff know how to do that.

Never underestimate contextual meaning. The way someone conducts themselves at work, with their mates, and on a date is very different. The atmosphere and the attitude of an individual has a profound impact on how they behave. Don't apply the same rules for every situation.

2. Clusters

People send off hundreds of signs in body language. It's easy to hone in on one thing after learning a body language text, e.g., the way they rub their nose (which can indicate lying) or their upper arm (which can indicate attraction). By doing so, you miss the other signs people are sending off.

There is nothing in solitary confinement. While talking about sports or baseball, the word "bat" takes on a different meaning. If a friend rubs her eyes, you can agree that she's bored. Look at the picture as a whole, and you might also note that she is yawning and rubbing her temples; she's just really tired.

If she is rubbing her eyes, avoiding contact with your eyes, crossing her arms defensively and pouting, you can put the pieces together and know that she's upset. You will strengthen your friendship by reading your friend's feelings. You might inquire whether she is okay, or whether she needs a cup of coffee.

Search for three to five behavioral elements that go together before making an assumption. Eye contact, laughing, gently rubbing your shoulder, playing with her hair, and even revealing her wrists (showing vulnerability) is a typical sign of female flirting. It's not enough to see just one of those signs to deduce that she is flirting with you.

Note how much a behavioral cluster deviates from the normal behavior of that person. Your colleague may stumble over their words, move their eyes around quickly, hunch their shoulders, and speak quietly. They may be lying or afraid, but if they still act like this, the chances are that they're just a nervous person.

Ask yourself for every possible reason when you catch one piece of body language. Maybe that girl smiled at you because she's a smiley person, and she crossed her legs to point away from you because she feels more relaxed physically that way. Wait for several arrows before making your deductions to point toward the same thing.

3. Congruence

Imagine a man stopping you down the street and telling you the wonders of the commodity he sells. His words are meant to win you over, but a glance at his body language shows you he cannot be trusted. Do his words fit his actions?

These are congruent because words and acts tell the same story. When lying, people usually avoid eye contact, blink more than normal, and become anxious. When people say the truth, they gesture with palms up. The motion is a sign that they have nothing to conceal. Although body language reveals the facts, a story may sound convincing:

When somebody's words, tone of voice, and body language are in sync, you get a true signal. When your girlfriend says, "Honestly, I'm great!" you pick up an incongruent symbol as she crosses her arms and turns her body away from you.

Know how your body is betraying your true intentions of trying to match it to your thoughts. If you're trying to persuade a prospective boss to be comfortable in your job, make sure your body language suits your doing. I've found video creation is a good form of self-analysis to increase your body language awareness.

An open stance, leaning back a little and taking up plenty of room implies confidence while hunching your shoulders, forming a physical barrier (with arms, legs, or items), taking in as little space as possible implies the opposite.

4. Consideration

Consideration implies "using someone else's feet." Effective communication has to take into account the audience, i.e., the views of the audience, context, attitude, level of education, etc. Make an effort to think of the audience, their desires, feelings, and problems. Ensure the audience's self-respect is maintained, and their emotions are not harmed. Change your words in a message to suit the needs of the audience while completing your message. Considerable communication features shall be as follows:

Emphasize your approach to the "you."

Empathize with the audience and show public interest. That will encourage the public to react positively.

Give the viewers optimism. Emphasize "what's possible" instead of "what's impossible." Lay emphasis on such positive words as jovial, committed, thank you, warm, healthy, help, etc.

5. Culture

You come across a man who touches you while talking to you. Touching isn't completely inappropriate; he just brushes your arm lightly, catches you as he smiles, and sits close to you.

Physical contact is typically an attractive sign. A single touch's sense differs across cultures. People from New York or London need a great deal of personal space, while cultures from the Middle East or South America naturally touch as a sign of friendship. They may find your inability to make physical contact cold and unfriendly. When somebody's words, tone of voice, and body language are in sync, you get a real signal.

Understanding how the gestures vary from culture to culture is becoming increasingly important. Though nodding your head up and down usually means "yes," it means "no" for Eskimos and Belgians (whereas shaking your head from side to side means "yes").

Know the patterns of the body language of the cultures you come across. In Western culture, eye contact is a representation of interest, respect, and trust. Don't believe a lack of eye contact often indicates timidity or rudeness. Extended eye contact is seen as intrusive and awkward in a variety of Asian, African, or Latin American cultures.

Understand how cultures will disagree about a word's meaning. In America, the A-OK symbol (a circle with your thumb and index finger) is used to signify that all is OK. In the Middle East, Latin America, or Germany, this is a rude gesture. The reverse "heart" sign (holding two fingers away with the back of your hand) is as bad as giving anyone in the UK a "finger."

Reading body language is harder than memorizing a series of signals. Anything from a person's childhood and personality to their present mood and the setting they're in can influence what their body tells you. By looking at the larger image and using the 5 C's of body language, you will soon be able to tell others what is really in mind.

The Subconscious Mind and The Limbic Brain System

In this section, we will talk about the limbic system, the neocortex of their history of occurrence, and major functions.

Limbic system

The limbic system of the brain is a combination of complex neuroregulatory structures of the brain. This system is not limited to just a few functions—it performs a number of the most important tasks for a person. The purpose of the limbus is to regulate higher mental functions and special processes of higher nervous activities, from simple charm and alertness to cultural emotions, memories, and sleep.

History

The limbic system of the brain was formed long before the neocortex began to form. It is the oldest hormonal-instinctive structure of the brain responsible for the survival of the subject. For long evolution, it is possible to form 3 main goals of the survival system:

- Domination - A manifestation of superiority in various parameters
- Food - The nutrition of the subject
- Reproduction - The transfer of the genome to the next generation

Because man has animal roots, the limbic system is present in the human brain. Initially, a reasonable man had only an influence that affects the physiological state of the body. Over time, communication evolved according to the type of vocalization. Individuals who were able to convey their condition with the help of emotions survived. Over time, the emotional perception of reality took shape more and more. Such evolutionary stratification has allowed people to unite into groups, groups into tribes, tribes into migration, and others into entire nations. American researcher Paul Mac-Lin first discovered the limbic system in 1952.

System structure

Anatomically, the limbus includes areas of the paleocortex (ancient cortex), the archicortex (old cortex), part of the neocortex (new cortex), and some subcortex structures (caudate nucleus, amygdala, pale sphere). The listed names of different types of crust denote their formation at a particular time of evolution.

Many neuroscience experts have addressed the question of which structures belong to the limbic system. The latter includes many structures:

- Cingular gyrus.
- Hippocampus.
- Ribbon for ribbon.
- Parahippocampal gyrus.
- Zubati gyrus.

258

- Amygdala.
- Transparent partition cores.
- Mastoid bodies.
- The central gray matter of the water supply to the brain.
- Scented bulb, triangle, and fragrant tract.
- Anterior and middle nuclei of optic tubercle.
- Cord core.
- Midbrain nuclei.
- A collecting system of pathways that ensures communication between visceral brain structures.

The system is closely related to the reticular formation system (the structure responsible for brain activation and the state of wakefulness). The anatomy of the limbic complex rests on the gradual stratification of one part onto another. So above lies the cingulate gyrus, and further down:

- Corpus callosum.
- Vault.
- Mammary body.
- Tonsil.
- Hippocampus.

The peculiarity of the visceral brain is its rich connection with other structures, which consist of complex pathways and two-way connections. This system of branches forms a complex of closed circles, which creates the conditions for prolonged excitation circulation in the limbo.

Functional limbic system

The visceral brain actively receives and processes information from the outside world. What is the limbic system responsible for? The limbus is one of those structures that work in real-time, allowing the body to adapt effectively to environmental conditions.

The human limbic system in the brain performs the following function:

- Formation of emotions, feelings, and experiences. Through the prism of emotions, a person subjectively assesses objects and the phenomenon of the environment.
- Memory. This function is performed by the hippocampus, which is located in the structure of the limbic system. Mnestic processes are provided by echo processes—a circular motion of excitation in closed neural circuits of the seahorse.
- Selection and correction of appropriate behavior models.
- Learning, retraining, fear, and aggression.
- Development of spatial skills.
- Defensive and food search behavior.
- Express speech.
- Acquisition and maintenance of various phobias.
- Work on the odor system.
- Caution reaction, preparation for action.
- Regulation of sexual and social behavior. There is a concept of emotional intelligence—the ability to recognize the emotions of people around you.

When expressing emotions, a reaction occurs that manifests itself in changes in blood pressure, skin temperature, respiratory rate, pupil reactions, sweating, hormonal mechanisms, and much more.

Perhaps among women, the question arises as to how to include the limbic system in men. However, the answer is simple: there is no way. For all men, limbus works completely (except for patients). This is justified by evolutionary processes, when a woman in almost all periods of history has been engaged in raising a child, which involves a deep emotional impact, and thus a deep development of the emotional brain. Unfortunately, men no longer achieve a woman's limbo level.

The development of the limbic system in infants largely depends on the type of upbringing and the overall relationship to it. A stern look and a cold smile do not contribute to the development of the limbic complex, unlike hugs and sincere smiles.

Interaction with the neocortex

Numerous pathways tightly connect the neocortex and limbic system. Thanks to this unification, these two structures from one whole of the mental sphere of man: they unite the mental component with the emotional. The new bark acts as a regulator of animal instincts. Human thought, as a rule, undergoes a series of cultural and moral inspections before taking any spontaneous action caused by emotions. In addition to controlling emotions, the neocortex also has an ancillary effect. The feeling of hunger occurs in the depths of the limbic system, and already in the highest cortical centers that regulate behavior, they look for food.

Such a brain structure at the time did not bypass the father of psychoanalysis, Sigmund Freud. The psychologist claimed that every neurosis is formed under the yoke of suppressing sexual and aggressive instincts. Of course, there was no data on limbo at the time of his work, but a great scientist speculated about similar devices in the brain. Thus, the more cultural and moral layers (superego - neocortex) in an individual, the more his primary animal instincts are suppressed (id - limbic system).

Violations and their consequences

Based on the fact that the limbic system is responsible for different functions, this set may be susceptible to different damages. Like other brain structures, the limbus can be exposed to injury and other harmful factors, including tumors with bleeding.

Syndromes of the destruction of the limbic system are rich in quantities, and the main ones are the following:

- **Dementia.** The development of diseases such as Alzheimer's and Pick's syndrome is associated with atrophy of the complex limbic system, especially in the localization of the hippocampus.
- **Epilepsy.** Organic hippocampal disorders lead to the development of epilepsy.
- **Pathological anxiety and phobias.** Disorder of amygdala activity leads to mediator imbalance, which, in turn, is accompanied by emotional disturbance, including anxiety. A phobia is an irrational fear of a harmless subject. Also, neurotransmitter imbalance causes depression and mania.

The most powerful techniques you can use to fake your body language and manipulate Anyone's

We all want people to trust us. Trust means that someone relies on you to do what you say you will do or to act like the person you say you are.

That's why it's especially crucial to earning the trust of those you work with. When people trust you, they are much more likely to believe in you, bond with you, and buy from you. Your actions ultimately determine whether you will earn someone's trust; however, your verbal communication and body language also play a big role.

Given that studies show that the vast majority of the messages we send are transmitted through our body language, it is imperative that you think not only about what you say but also about how you dress and behave.

Body language can be much louder than verbal communication. For example, if someone is holding a dormant position or arms crossed, we can assume that they are tired or uninterested in speech. If someone avoids eye contact, we may think it's because they have something to hide. None of the above may be true, but we must pay attention to how we behave; otherwise, people will perceive us negatively.

Here are eight simple tricks to perfecting the body language that can help people trust you.

Laugh... sincerely

This seems obvious, but the smiles that most of us use daily are a bit fake. The key to a real smile is to smile with your eyes, to show your teeth when you smile, and to remove the smile from your face slowly. A real smile will make you more sincere, and therefore more reliable.

Lean forward

This mainly refers to leaning towards someone when sitting because you are showing attention and involvement in the conversation. When people feel that you are interested in them, it will make them more likely to trust you.

Look people in the eye

If you do not look people in the eye during the conversation, they may assume that you are not telling the truth, or that you are not completely sure of yourself or what you are saying. One should pretend that those eyes are glued to the partner you are talking to. Research shows that subjects significantly reported greater feelings of respect and affection for colleagues who used this technique.

Nodding

Nodding means agreeing with the person talking to you, which will make them more open. When you evoke this positive emotion, you are more likely to be trusted.

Point your toes when standing

Pointing your toes at someone means you are completely facing them. Nothing is more encouraging than someone who gives you full attention and consciously ignores other people and distractions to dedicate himself to talking to you. When your feet are pointing in the other direction, it sends the message that you are ready to go—and who would believe someone who always looks like he can't wait to "give in to the wind."

Keep your hands out of your pockets and visible

You don't want anyone to think you have something to hide, do you? Expert Katherine Noel states, "Make sure your hands are always visible, that you never hide them. Crossing your arms has a similar negative effect, making you look closed and unacceptable." Invite people and let them trust you using more open body language. Avoid positions that appear defensive.

Don't spin or squirm in place (but don't be too stiff)

A few signs that someone is lying are: they constantly move their feet, cover their mouths, and "wave" their hands. But we should also pay attention to those interlocutors whose bodies do not move at all. This can be a sign of a primitive neurological 'struggle' rather than an 'escape' from the response, as the body positions itself and prepares for possible conflicts. When you speak and participate in normal conversation, it is natural to move your body in subtle, relaxed, and mostly unconscious movements. So, if you observe the rigid, catatonic attitude of the interlocutor, without movement, it is often a huge warning sign that something is not right.

If you want people to trust you, relax.

Imitation of body language

This strategy is called mirroring (as mentioned before). When talking to someone, try to copy their body language, gestures, and facial expressions. Researchers from the University of New York documented the "chameleon effect" in 1999, which occurs when people unconsciously imitate others' behavior and that mimicry eases taste.

In the study, 78 men and women worked on a task with a partner. The partners dealt with different levels of mimicry, while the researchers secretly recorded the interactions. At the end of the interaction, the researchers and participants showed how much they liked those partners who mimicked their body language because they found them more harmonious and reliable.

CHAPTER 6

MASTERING THE SECRETS OF NON-VERBAL COMMUNICATION

Body language is hard to fake, but there are ways to learn to use positive body language while communicating with others and eliminate negative body language that can send the wrong message.

Most employers recognize communication as one of the basic skills that every employee must have and develop to adapt to the workplace's needs and expectations. We can communicate in various ways—orally, in writing, with movements, facial expressions, clothing, and the goal of every communication is the exchange of information, ideas, messages. In addition to giving and receiving information, ideas, or messages, an important part of successful communication is the interpretation of the same, i.e., whether the information, ideas, or messages are understood in the way and a sense intended by the sender. Like the same music, picture, or movie can produce different experiences for different people so that different people can understand the same message in different ways.

Manner of Transmission of The Message

In addition to the message's content, the way it is conveyed, and the context in which it takes place are also important. Nonverbal elements in speech such as voice tone, gaze, facial expression, gestures, body language, emotions (anger, happiness, fear, etc.) often cause the message to be misunderstood and seen more than we

MANIPULATION, NLP AND BODY LANGUAGE STOICISM

hear. Often due to uncoordinated verbal and non-verbal communication—when the interlocutor says one thing and his body language says something else—in some situations, we quickly realize that the interlocutor is saying one thing and thinking another and trying to "sell us a story" he does not believe.

As the folk saying goes: "One swallow does not make spring," so the true meaning of a gesture can have many different meanings if we look at it outside the context in which it takes place. One simple "scratching of the head," if we do not know the context in which it occurs, can be interpreted as a sign of lying, insecurity, forgetfulness, or that the interlocutor has "ears" or "dirty hair." Therefore, each gesture needs to be compared to other elements of nonverbal and verbal speech and placed in the context in which it occurs.

If at a bus stop, on a cold winter morning, you saw a person with his arms and legs tightly pressed and crossed and leaning against his body, with his head and chin pointing down—all these signs in this context would mean that the person is simply cold. But if you saw the same gestures on a person, you are in the same room with, in a meeting, and want to sell them a product or service, and you would correctly conclude that such gestures mean that the person feels negative or rejects your offer.

Strength of Hand and Palm

Throughout history, open hands and palms have been associated with openness, truth, fidelity, and honesty. Outstretched hands with palms facing the interlocutor send the message: "Trust me, I'm not lying." The palm facing up suggests that we are not a threat, that we are willing to listen, and that we want to talk. On the other hand, the palm facing downwards suggests authority and giving orders, and provokes opposition and rebellion in the interlocutor. The outstretched index finger creates a sense of threat and aggression and suggests the command: "Do it or otherwise...". The goal of the outstretched index finger is to obey the interlocutor and, as a rule, causes a negative reaction because we experience it as a physical attack. Interestingly, if we connect the index finger with the thumb, we send a message of thoughtfulness, focus, and goal orientation.

The first impression of a person at a meeting is usually obtained by shaking hands. It is important to know that the handshake sends subconscious messages, which, although we are not aware, can significantly affect the outcome of the meeting and our impression of the interlocutor. If we shake hands with the palm facing down, we send a message that we are taking control and that we are in charge. If we shake hands with the palm facing up, we send a message to obey the interlocutor and give him the feeling that he is in control of the situation.

What we should strive for when shaking hands is that both interlocutors have their thumbs facing upward, which sends a message of equality. In addition to the palm's position, it is important always to apply the same grip force we get (so if our grip is stronger, we should give in, if it's weaker, we need to squeeze harder). The nonverbal messages sent by our body are a key part of our communication and are often even more important than what we say.

Communication skills, both verbal and non-verbal, are extremely important in human relationships because unsuccessful communication creates numerous misunderstandings, problems, and conflicts. In contrast, successful communication improves interpersonal relationships and contributes to a true understanding of the interlocutor.

Some interesting facts about hands:

Many people cannot lie convincingly if their palms are open to the interlocutor because gestures and feelings are directly related.

When we speak with our palms open to the interlocutor, we create pressure on the interlocutor, to be honest with us.

If we keep our arms crossed on our chests while listening to the interlocutor, we will begin to feel a defensive attitude.

Research has shown that 84% of listeners respond positively to content if the speaker holds their palms facing up, 52% if the speaker holds their palms facing down, and only 28% if the speaker uses an outstretched index finger.

How to Interpret Verbal Communication

Even being far from each other, people communicate. There are several ways to express your thoughts and get acquainted with a stranger. In psychology, this is called verbal and non-verbal communication. The first of them is the most accessible and understandable to others.

Verbal Communication in Psychology

The deaf and dumb also speak, but through gestures. You can speak out by changing the position of the body, facial expressions, eyes. These are all ways of non-verbal contact.

Verbal communication is the transmission and receipt of information through speech (it does not matter whether it is oral or written). All people do not understand sign language, but the sign system using words is available to most.

As a child, a person learns to communicate using speech as the most accessible and understandable way to express his desires and convey important information to his interlocutor. The phrases expressed aloud are more obvious than attempts to explain something with gestures. The power of the word helps the interlocutors to hear and understand each other.

Without verbal communication, a person feels closed in the "shell of loneliness." The lack of communication skills will not make it possible to learn the world, improve, and reach certain heights.

Speech has several features that allow people to interact with each other. These characteristics emphasize the importance of communication.

The components of verbal communication

Name Features

Total: Even communicating at a distance (by phone), you can get some information about the person you are talking to by voice, intonation, and said phrases: gender, approximate age, temperament, state of health, etc.

Personal: Any conversation evokes emotions, attuning to positive contact, or provokes indignation. With some, you want to communicate with others, and it is better to end the conversation immediately.

Emotional: Communication is a way of self-expression, an opportunity for harmonious development. Information can be obtained from books, textbooks, television. Mutual communication helps to get emotions, find a response to your feelings and thoughts.

Common preferences among people around or different views on life - this does not prevent them from contacting each other. Speech helps build relationships (family, neighborhood, production) and is a tool to achieve your own goals.

How verbal communication is used

Verbal speech is called a symbolic communication system in which the meaning of a transmitted or received message is not lost. It is based on two principles:

- Set of words of a particular language (this is vocabulary).
- Rules for creating units of speech (syntax).
- Non-verbal communication - what is it in psychology.

In psychology, speech and thinking are inseparable, because the first is a form of existence of the second. When people communicate with each other, this happens according to this scheme:

- The speaker mentally selects certain words.
- Using the rules of vocabulary and syntax forms phrases from them.
- Only then pronounces them out loud.
- The interlocutor decodes the information for mental perception and creates images in his head.

Note! Even with the clear transmission of information, distortions and semantic losses are possible, amounting to about 60%.

If the proposal were made according to the rules of grammar, communication difficulties would not arise. But only if people speak a language that is understandable to each other.

How to reach an interlocutor

The same applies to writing. To get information from print media (or at least read SMS), a person must know this language. To state your thoughts on paper (type text on the keyboard), you need to not only be able to speak, but also write.

Spoken or written words help to analyze objects, events, and phenomena, to find the main and secondary signs in them. Bare, concrete facts are inherent in business speech. For emotional contact, additional verbal means are needed:

- Voice modulation, intonation, pauses, rhythm in oral speech.
- The range of handwriting, and the angle of inclination, the pressure, and direction of the lines in the letter.

These expressive characteristics make it possible to understand how the correspondent himself relates to the message and the person he communicates with.

Types of Verbal Communication

Why is communication necessary for a person—what does it give, and why is it important for people?

Verbal means of communication is speech, which inaction is divided into two types: "say-listen," "write-read." In other words, speech is divided into oral and written. Each of them, in turn, is divided into components.

Speech Types

<u>Name Definition</u>

- **Oral:**

Dialogue: A consistent change in the roles of communicating individuals, in the speech of which there is a certain meaning, is characteristic. By exchanging phrases, the interlocutors make it clear to each other that they understand the essence of what the recipient said.

Monologue: A lengthy statement by one person that is not interrupted by others (for example, a lecture, a report, a campaign speech, a presentation of a product, etc.)

- **Written:**

Direct: Correspondence in real-time is carried out through SMS messages, the exchange of notes in the lesson, etc.

Delayed: Communication via paper or email.

There is another kind of speech—dactyl, which is used by blind and deaf-mute people. The signs used in it are a manual alphabet that replaces the usual letters.

Oral and written speech is classified as external, the existence of which is unrealistic without internal speech. It is formed in the head of a person before an individual voices it out or writes it.

Language and its functions

Types of communication in psychology - what applies to them, its functions.

Language does not just express the thoughts and feelings of people. It is impossible to imagine any aspect of life wherever speech is applied.

Language features

Name Definition

Communicative: It provides interaction between people, allowing you to communicate with your kind fully.

Accumulative: The ability to accumulate and store knowledge, passing it on to descendants (notebooks, abstracts, fiction, and scientific literature).

Cognitive: Language helps to gain knowledge from books, films, scientific treatises, lectures, etc.

Constructive: It makes it possible to put thought into an accessible, understandable to others conscious form in the form of written or verbal expression.

Ethnic: It unites people not only in groups of the same nationality. Through language, communication is possible between the peoples of the whole world.

Emotional: With the help of words you can convey to your interlocutor your feelings and emotions.

To successfully use the functions of language in one's own life, a person must learn to communicate and build relationships. The ability to speak is influenced by knowledge of one's own and foreign languages, the rules of speech production, as well as the mental aspect. Fear of contact with other individuals interferes with some people in communication. Inaction only exacerbates the situation.

Rules for verbal communication

To achieve the desired result in the development of relations, it is necessary to take into account some points and apply them in practice:

- It is necessary to show goodwill and respect for the interlocutor.
- Do not impose your point of view on the issues discussed and tactfully circumvent the "sharp corners".
- Observe logic in statements and consistency in conversation.

- Build a conversation on brief lines and the optimal amount of information.
- Present truthful information relevant to the subject of the conversation.
- Take into account the nationality, social status, and attitude of the interlocutor in the communication.

In the dialogue, it is important to observe the sequence of statements. A person who interrupts the speaker for no reason emphasizes the low level of his speech culture by such behavior.

How to make verbal communication effective

Thanks to communication, people coexist in this world, achieving certain heights in life. For communications to give positive results, and those around you want to communicate with a specific person, you must adhere to several principles:

- By his attention and interest, arouse a strong desire in the opponent to communicate.
- Sincerely and honestly evaluate people and events.
- Do not complain, condemn, or criticize.
- Show interest in the interlocutor, talk about things important to him.
- Learning not only to clearly state your thoughts but also to listen carefully to the opponent's speech.

Important! A thought that is clumsily expressed may be misinterpreted. But inattentive listening distorts the meaning of the information received. The ability to speak and listen are two components of communicative communication.

Interest in the interlocutor

It is important not only what they say, but also how the words are pronounced. For the interlocutor, the emotions and para verbal signals (articulation, speed, tonality, and accompanying sounds) present in the speech can mean more than the phrases said.

Some people can think clearly but are not able to formulate phrases in oral speech. Others speak well, but they are difficult to put into writing. Or vice versa — beautifully set out on paper, but in verbal communication tongue-tied.

To achieve harmony in all verbal speech versions, you need to improve your abilities and overcome psychological barriers.

What do languages have in common?

A person in life uses two types of communication. Non-verbal language is not the prerogative of the deaf-mute. It can be called an external manifestation of brain activity. Not having begun to utter phrases out loud, an individual with facial expressions, body posture, and gaze can unwittingly hint about the course of his thoughts.

But the interlocutor may incorrectly interpret such signals, or the individual intentionally distorts the information transmitted by body language. To understand the partner and get complete information, the analysis also requires voice contact.

Verbal speech and body language in harmony

So that communication does not tire the partner, both languages must be balanced. Monotony, emotionless speech, excessive gestures interfere with the perception of information and can alienate the interlocutor.

A misunderstanding leads not only to disappointment in relationships but also to serious conflicts. This is manifested at any level: in the family, business, and business communication, thereby complicating life. Having learned to speak body language and verbal, bringing both types of communication into harmony, a person will achieve great success in any field.

Verbal and non-verbal communication - what is it

Verbally - this word comes from the Latin "verbalis," which means verbally. Communication, in this case, occurs through words.

Verbal communication is of three types:

- Speech - communication through words (dialogues, monologues).
- Written communication - by hand, printing on a computer, SMS, etc.
- Inner - your inner dialogue (the formation of thoughts).

Nonverbal - other types of communication, except verbal. What could it be:

- Gestures, facial expressions, and postures - all this tells us a lot if you can read them.
- Visual - scanning a person in the first seconds when you see him: determining sex, age, assessing the appearance, and facial expression.
- Acoustic non-verbal perception is an assessment of the voice (its rhythm, timbre, volume, brightness, pauses, cough, parasite words).
- Tactile non-verbal communication - touch (it is very significant).
- Smells - some attract, and some repel.

- Mobility - enlivens perception, but if mobility is too high, fatigue occurs.
- The boundaries of personal space - their transition takes a person out of the comfort zone or, conversely, brings them closer together.

Verbally is our difference from another living world

Words that are compiled into speech are a unit of our communication with others. We use them both in oral pronunciation and writing. Or typing (typing on the keyboard), if we talk about realities that are closer to us. Such communication is divided depending on who plays what role: speak - listen, write - read.

To maintain verbal communication at a high level, it is necessary to develop its components. This is, first of all, vocabulary (what is it?). Reading books, listening to vocabulary, talking with intellectually developed people - all this greatly helps to replenish and expand vocabulary.

In written communication, it is important to know the rules of punctuation to present the information correctly. Often, by incorrectly placing dots and commas, you can distort the meaning or focus on something wrong. We all remember the cartoon where you had to put the punctuation mark in the right way and save your life: "You can't have mercy on execution."

Speech and written communication solve several problems at once:

- Communicative - provides interaction between people in its large-scale manifestations.
- Cognitive - a person receives knowledge and new information.
- Accumulative - display of accumulated knowledge

(writing abstracts, books).

- Emotional - you can express your attitude to the world, feelings using words.
- Ethnic - an association of the populations of different countries (in the language used).

Forms of verbal communication and barriers are not one way

Communicating verbally, we can use different forms and styles to convey certain information in a specific context and color. This can be well traced by the styles used in literature:

- Journalistic - the main goal of such a speech is to convey to people the idea, the essence of what happened.
- Scientific - different logic and clear statements using terminology, complex concepts.
- Official business is a dry language of laws, where everything is accurate and without any epithets.
- Artistic - a combination of any words and word forms, jargon, and dialect (dialectism) is possible here; speech is filled with unimaginable images and colors.
- Conversational - characterizes both individual dialogues in works and our communication with others or when we meet a friend.

Speech interaction can be divided by the number of people who take part in this:

- Monologue (one person).
- Performance - in meetings in front of someone or reciting a verse in front of the class.
- Report - important information, as a rule, is supported by figures.

- Statement - similar to a report but provides more extensive information and description.
- Lecture - providing useful information to the audience.

Dialogue (two or more people):

- Ordinary conversation - exchange of greetings and thoughts.
- Discussion - a discussion of the topic where the interlocutors act as representatives of different points of view.
- Dispute - here, too, there are two positions between which you need to resolve the resulting conflict.
- A dispute is a discussion within the framework of science.
- Interview - a conversation during which the employer considers whether it is worth hiring a person.

Even though we communicate in the same language, various barriers to verbal communication may arise:

For example, phonetic. The interlocutor may have a speech impediment, unpleasant diction, pick up unusual intonation, sprinkle with words parasites, etc...

The semantic noise grows between people from different countries, with a different mentality or even when raising children in different families.

The logical barrier is that the interlocutors have different types of thinking, levels of development, and intelligence.

The stylistic barrier is that the interlocutor incorrectly builds a chain of verbal communication to convey information. First, we need to draw attention to what we want to say to interest. Then lay out the basic information; answer questions that the opponent may have. After that, give time to think so that he draws conclusions or makes a decision.

Non-verbal communication - we inherited it

Non-verbal communication is body language (as in the rest of the animal world). Facial expressions, gestures, poses, touches. As well as visual and acoustic perception, smells, distance, and movement of communicating objects—all exactly like animals.

All this can carry a lot of information, so do not neglect this format to impress people (with a pleasant perfume and appearance, set by voice and manner of movement).

It is important not only to interpret these signals correctly but also to send them correctly to the interlocutor. Non-verbal communication is not only an addition to the conversation using words but can completely replace it in some situations.

Accents - this is something that can be successfully placed using non-verbal means if you cannot do it in full intonation. After all, it is often necessary to indicate to the interlocutor that you think what you focus your attention on is important. So that background information does not take much time for analysis and decision making.

Sadness, anger, joy, sadness, satisfaction - this is what can best be emphasized by verbal means (you can even completely show these feelings with your gestures and facial expressions). Therefore, if you are attentive to the interlocutor, you can read his condition without words.

The distance between the interlocutors can also be analyzed. The closer they are, the more they trust each other.

Differences between types of communication

Communication with words is characteristic exclusively for people because it requires a strong development of the brain. Other animals are not capable of this. But non-verbal signals send absolutely everything.

If a cat wags its tail — it is unhappy, if a dog does the same – it experiences joyful emotions. It turns out that even at the level of animals, you need to be able to correctly interpret the signs they give, given who exactly is standing in front of you. What can you see if you are facing different people?

It is worth noting that sign language is more sincere since we have almost no control over it. Therefore, it is so easy to deceive a person by phone or correspondence. But if a fraudster tries to do this while standing in front of you, then there is a chance that you will read through his facial expressions that he should not be trusted.

We are people, which means that both types of communication (verbal and non-verbal) are open to us, so you should use them to the maximum for your purposes. This is a great tool to achieve what you want and get everything you need from life.

Verbal communication: definition, types, and principles

COMMUNICATION (English communication, intercourse, interpersonal relationship) - the interaction of 2 or more people, consisting of the exchange between them of information of a cognitive and affective-evaluative nature.

Verbal communication - uses human speech as a sign system, natural sound language, a system of phonetic signs that includes two principles: lexical and syntactic. Speech is the most versatile means of communication because the transmission of information through speech is less unlikely to lose the meaning of the message.

The system of phonetic signs of the language is based on vocabulary and syntax. Vocabulary is a collection of words that make up a language. The syntax is a language-specific means and rule for creating speech units.

Speech is the universal means of communication because when transmitting information, the meaning of the message is lost to the least extent compared to other means of transmitting the information. Thus, speech is a language in action, a form of generalized reflection of reality, a form of thinking.

Indeed, in thinking, speech is manifested in the form of an internal pronunciation of words to oneself. Thinking and speech are not separable from each other.

The recipient (listener) perceives speech and decodes the speech units to understand the thoughts expressed in it correctly. But this happens when the communicants use a national language that is understandable to both developed in the process of verbal communication over many generations of people.

Speech performs two main functions - significative and communicative.

Thanks to the signifying function for a person (unlike an animal), it becomes possible to arbitrarily call up images of objects and perceive the semantic content of speech. Thanks to the communicative function, speech becomes a means of communication, a means of transmitting the information.

Words make it possible to analyze objects, things, and

highlight significant and secondary signs of them. Mastering words, a person automatically masters complex systems of connections and relations between objects and phenomena of the objective world.

A dictionary compiled on this basis, encompassing terms and concepts of a special field of activity, is called a thesaurus.

The communicative function of speech is manifested in the means of expression and means of influence.

Speech is not limited to the totality of transmitted messages. It expresses both the person's attitude to what he is talking about and his attitude to the person he communicates.

Expressive components are also available in written speech (in the text of the letter). This is manifested in the range of handwriting and the force of pressure, the angle of its inclination, the direction of the lines, and the shape of capital letters, etc. The word as a means of influence and its emotional and expressive components are inextricable and act simultaneously, to a certain extent affecting the recipient's behavior.

Types of Verbal Communication

Distinguish between external and internal speech. External speech is divided into oral and written. Oral speech, in turn, is dialogic and monologic.

In preparing for the oral speech, and especially for writing, the individual "speaks" the speech to himself. This is inner speech. In written language, the conditions for communication are mediated by text.

Written speech can be direct (for example, the exchange of notes at a meeting, at a lecture) or delayed (exchange of letters).

A peculiar form of verbal communication is dactyl speech. This is a manual alphabet that serves to replace spoken language when deaf and blind people and people familiar with fingerprinting communicate among themselves. Fingerprints replace letters (similar to letters in print).

The accuracy of the listener's understanding of the meaning of the speaker's statement depends on feedback. Such feedback is established when the communicator and the recipient are interchanged. Through his statement, the recipient makes it clear how he understood the meaning of the information received. Thus, dialogue speech is a kind of sequential change in the communicative roles of communicating, during which the meaning of the speech message is revealed. Monologue, the same speech, lasts long enough, and is not interrupted by replicas of others. It requires preliminary preparation. This is usually a detailed, preparatory speech (for example, a report, lecture, etc.).

Constant and effective exchange of information is the key to achieving any organization or firm's goals. The importance of verbal communication, for example, in management, cannot be overestimated.

However, it is necessary to pursue the goal of ensuring the correct understanding of the transmitted information or semantic messages. The ability to accurately express one's thoughts and the ability to listen are the components of the communicative side of communication. An inept expression of thoughts leads to a misinterpretation of what has been said.

Ineffective listening distorts the meaning of the transmitted information.

The main functions of the language in the communication

process include: communicative (information exchange function); constructive (formulation of thoughts); appellate (impact on the addressee); emotional (direct emotional reaction to the situation); fatal (exchange of ritual (etiquette) formulas); metalanguage (interpretation function. It is used if necessary, to check whether the interlocutors use the same code).

Thanks to the observation of non-verbal means of communication, we can draw a huge amount of information about our partner.

Verbal communication is "the process of establishing and maintaining purposeful, direct or indirect contact between people using language" (V. Kunitsyna, 2001, p. 46).

According to the authors of the book "Interpersonal Communication" (ibid.), talking people can have speech flexibility to varying degrees. So, some of them pay minimal attention to the choice of speech means, talking at different times with different people, in different circumstances, mainly in the same style.

Others, trying to maintain their stylistic appearance, can perform different speech roles, using a diverse style speech repertoire in various situations. However, in addition to the participants' characteristics in verbal communication, the social context influences the choice of the style of speech behavior.

The role-playing situation dictates the need to turn to poetic, then to the official, or scientific or everyday speech.

In cases of conflict with parents, it is better to adhere to the official manner of communication.

The principle of cooperation "the requirement for the interlocutors to act in a manner that would correspond to the accepted goal and direction of the conversation" - suggests that verbal communication should:

- Contain the Optimal Amount of Information. (It Should Correspond to The Current Goals of Communication, Redundant Information Can Be Distracting, Misleading).
- Contain Truthful Statements.
- Correspond to Goals, Subject of Conversation.
- Be Clear (Avoid Obscure Expressions, verbosity).

The principle of politeness, which implies expression in speech:

- Tact.
- Generosity.
- Endorsement.
- Modesty.
- Consent.
- Benevolence.

Pedagogical practice shows that an incorrectly built verbal message can lead to both partners not understanding each other and to open conflict.

That is why the literature devoted to the problems of constructive behavior in conflict is aimed at optimizing verbal communication (Grishina N.V., 2002).

Verbal communication

Verbal communication is a communicative, mutually directed action that occurs between one individual, several subjects, or more, which involves the transmission of information of a different orientation and its reception. In verbal communicative interaction, speech is used as a communication mechanism, which is represented by language systems and is divided into written and oral. The most important verbal communication requirement is the clarity of pronunciation, clarity of content, and accessibility of thought presentation.

Verbal communication can trigger a positive or negative emotional response. That is why each individual simply needs to know and correctly apply the rules, norms, and techniques of verbal interaction. For communication efficiency and success in life, anyone should master the art of rhetoric.

Verbal and nonverbal communication

As you know, the human individual is a social being. That is, the subject can never become a person without society. The interaction of subjects with society occurs through communication tools (communication), verbal and non-verbal.

Verbal and non-verbal means of communication provide a communicative interaction of individuals around the world.

Although a person has primary thought, for its expression and understanding by other individuals, such an instrument of verbal communication as speech is needed, which convicts thoughts.

The universal means of communication between people is the language, which is the main system encoding information, and an important tool for communication.

With the help of words, a person clarifies the meaning of events and the meaning of phenomena and expresses his thoughts, feelings, positions, and worldview. Personality, language, and consciousness are inseparable. However, in this case, the vast majority of people relate to language as they do to air, i.e., use it without noticing. Language quite often overtakes thoughts or does not obey them.

During the communication of people at each stage, barriers arise that impede the effectiveness of communication.

Individual differences in human needs and their system of values often do not make it possible to find a common language even when discussing universal topics.

Violations of the process of communication human interaction cause errors, mistakes, or failures in encrypting information, underestimation of worldview, professional, ideological, religious, political, age, and gender differences.

Also, the following factors are incredibly important for human communications: context, subtext, and style. For example, an unexpected familiar appeal or cheeky behavior can nullify the entire informational richness of the conversation.

That is, the idea of the interlocutor's true feelings and intentions, the subjects derive not from his speech, but with direct observation of the details and manner of his behavior.

In other words, interpersonal communication interaction is mainly carried out thanks to a whole range of non-verbal instruments—facial expressions and gestures, symbolic communicative signs, spatial and temporal boundaries, intonational and rhythmic characteristics of speech.

Verbal and non-verbal means of communication in the course of communication between people are perceived simultaneously; they should be considered as a single complex. Also, gestures without the use of speech are not always consistent, and speech without facial expressions is empty.

Types of Verbal Communication

Verbal communication refers to externally directed

speech, divided into written and oral, and internally directed speech. Oral speech can be dialogic or monologic. Inner speech is manifested in preparation for a conversation or, especially, for written speech.

Writing is direct and delayed. Direct speech occurs during the exchange of notes, for example, at a meeting or lecture, and delayed speech occurs during the exchange of letters, which can take quite a long time to get an answer. The conditions of communication in writing are strictly mediated by text.

It follows that dialogue speech is a sequential change in the roles of communicative interaction of the conversation, in the process of which the meaning of speech utterance is revealed. On the contrary, a monologue speech can last quite a while, not interrupting other conversants. It requires prior preparation from the speaker.

Monological speech includes lectures, reports, etc.

Important components of the communicative aspect of communication are the ability to express their thoughts and listening skills accurately. Since the fuzzy formulation of thoughts leads to an incorrect interpretation of the spoken. And inept listening transforms the meaning of the broadcast information.

The well-known type of interaction is also related to verbal communication—conversation, interview, disputes and discussions, debates, meetings, etc.

Participants in the conversation can ask each other questions to familiarize themselves with the interlocutor's position or clarify incomprehensible points that arose during the discussion. A conversation is especially effective when it becomes necessary to clarify a question or to highlight a problem. An interview is a specially organized conversation on social, professional, or scientific topics.

A dispute is a public discussion or debate on a socially important or scientific topic. A discussion is called a public dispute, the result of which is the clarification and correlation of various points of view, positions, search and identification of the correct opinion, finding the right solution to the controversial issue. The dispute is called the process of exchanging opposing views.

That is, it denotes any clash of positions, disagreements in beliefs and views, a kind of struggle in which each of the participants defends its innocence.

Interpersonal communication is carried out between several individuals, the result of which is the emergence of psychological contact and a certain relationship between communicating.

Verbal business communication is a complex multilateral process of developing contacts between people in the professional sphere.

Features of verbal communication

The main feature of verbal communication is that such communication is peculiar only to man. Verbal communication as an indispensable condition involves mastering the language.

Due to its communicative potential, it is much richer than all types of non-verbal communication, although it is not able to completely replace it.

The formation of verbal communications initially necessarily relies on non-verbal means of communication.

Any message built using a non-verbal sign system can be decrypted or translated into verbal human language.

So, for example, the red light of a traffic light can be translated as "no traffic" or "stop."

The verbal aspect of communication has a complex multi-level structure and can appear in different stylistic variations: dialect, spoken and literary language, etc. All speech components or other characteristics facilitate the successful or unsuccessful implementation of a communicative act.

Such a process is endless in its diversity

Words in verbal communicative interaction are not ordinary signs that serve to name objects or phenomena. In verbal communication, entire verbal complexes, systems of ideas, religions, myths characteristic of a particular society or culture are created and formed.

The way the subject speaks can form another participant's idea in the interaction about who such a subject is.

This often occurs when the communicator plays an established social role, such as the head of the company, the school director, the team captain, etc.

The choice of verbal tools contributes to the creation and comprehension of certain social situations. So, for example, a compliment will not always indicate that a person looks good; it can simply be a kind of "communicative move."

The effectiveness and efficiency of verbal interaction are largely due to the level of communicator's mastery of oratory and its qualitative characteristics. Today, proficiency in speech is considered the most important component of the professional realization of a person.

With the help of speech, not only the movement of messages takes place, but also the interaction of the participants in the communication process, which is a special way to influence each other, direct and orient each other. In other words, they strive to achieve a certain transformation of behavior.

How to Influence and Subdue Anyone's Mind

Having the full mastery of communication skills to defend ideas and present your point of view to others is a fundamental characteristic for anyone who wants to know how to influence people—especially in the business world. After all, people tend to trust those who demonstrate security in their beliefs deeply. Because of this, when a manager is unable to communicate effectively—nor sustain his speeches for a long time—we can perceive the negative impacts on results and organizational influence. In such situations, employees are likely not willing to experience what the leader propagates, which generates enormous institutional disorder. With that in mind, we have prepared this section to teach you some tips on how to influence people through simple, practical tips. Read on to find out how this is possible!

1. Know how to give and receive feedback—on any issue—whether positive or negative. It is essential to keep employees motivated and aligned with the organization and the team's performance. However, for this tip to be useful when influencing people, it is necessary to know the correct way to give feedback. To give assertive feedback, it is important to reflect on the relevance and integrity of what is going to be said, as well as to maintain a concise and direct communication. It is essential to recognize what is well done and give tips to improve behavior or performance. After that, carefully follow the case to see if the requested changes have occurred or if it will be necessary to intervene again in the process.

2. Treat everyone by name. One of the most practical ways to open efficient communication channels and get closer to the interlocutors is to refer to everyone involved. After all, it is the key piece of personal identity. Using it to refer to someone, you will certainly be able to create much greater intimacy and keep others interested in what you have to say. On the other hand, it is necessary to pay attention to excessive nicknames or that demonstrate proximity that does not exist between you and the listener. Do not forget that professionalism should be the focus of communication.

3. Mirror behaviors. This type of conduct—known as "mimicry"—is capable of making the person whose movements are mirrored more likely to act positively towards the person who imitates him. This is because the human being has an inherent tendency to sympathize with those who look or act similarly to him. It is a type of behavior that few people naturally adopt without realizing it. However, through good observation and a lot of training, it is possible to develop this skill and use it to influence people. Over time, it will become spontaneous.

4. Demonstrate proactivity. If you want to learn how to influence people, it is important to understand that, in general, we all have a real inclination to admire and follow those who are good examples. This is where proactivity comes in, based on self-responsibility and anticipating needs or problems. You probably have already realized that the most proactive employees are the most admired and, consequently, the most respected, right? With that in mind, don't forget to always be proactive in the workplace. As a result, you will inspire and influence more people.

5. Invest in emotional balance. Maintaining the balance of emotions in the workplace is a challenge for many employees in the market. The lack of this capacity, however, can cause several problems and also hinder corporate interpersonal relationships. To achieve the desired balance, it is necessary to develop emotional intelligence. With that, it will be possible to identify and control your emotions assertively. The good news is that there are several behavioral trainings to improve and make that ability flourish. What are you waiting for to start developing this skill?

6. Give praise. It seems obvious. But the truth is that many people do not take advantage of the potential that good praise has to offer for the art of influence. A lot of people don't know when and how to praise—let alone how to make it not feel forced. And this is exactly where our 6th tip comes in. Thus, when praising someone, be careful that the praise is really sincere, after all, the intention is to validate what the person feels about you and not create a doubt about the truth of what was said. By doing this—without exaggeration or flattery—you are sure to make the speaker more likely to accept what you say. Incredible, isn't it?

7. Plan strategic approaches. Applied to the previous tips, it is time to plan how you will present your ideas so that the listeners will accept them. Planning is very important in this process and must go hand in hand with those who want to learn how to influence people. Therefore, it is essential to develop a script for your approach and rehearse the best way to present it.

Also, be sure to prepare yourself for any questions that may arise and schedule convincing responses to avoid being taken by surprise. Knowing the importance of following the tips presented, it is interesting to note that good behavioral training can be a key piece in influencing people. Do not forget to look for a company that has experience and recognition in the market. Otherwise, you may lose time and money.

CHAPTER 7

HOW TO USE SUBLIMINAL MESSAGES TO MANIPULATE

Subliminal messages are emitted at a level below the limit of human perception so that the human eye cannot perceive them in time, which means that they cannot become aware of the brain due to their brevity.

Influence of subliminal messages on the brain

They usually appear in the duration of three-hundredths of 30 milliseconds in the form of words or pictures. This type of message stimulates different parts of the human brain, especially the area of vision important for perceiving shapes, colors and movements, as well as the temporal lobe, which is responsible for memory and object recognition, and the limbic system in which emotions are created. Even though they stimulate many areas in the brain, these three-hundredths are still not enough to leave an effect on the frontal lobe in charge of raising awareness of all these previously mentioned colors and shapes.

Most of today's films are made so that thirty pictures are placed in every second of the shot, which means that each picture lasts three hundredths. This leads us to the conclusion that constantly watching such moving content, we are stimulated in various ways. We are not aware. Producers and filmmakers use this method. It is also known that subliminal messages can be read from cartoons, such as those of the Warner brothers, in one with the famous character Duck Dodd, in a split second a shield of a metal figure appears in which engraved letters say "buy bonds", encouraging Americans to support the financing of the war. Such messages try to instill a certain intention in the subconscious part of the human mind. In the last few decades, this method is very popular. However, today it has become common to pause movies or videos whenever we want so that these same subliminal messages can still be made aware in some way. Interestingly, products sell better if they have some hidden meaning related to sexuality, but of course, such inappropriate images or words are not noticed at first glance.

Chronology of conducted experiments

In 1957, there was great interest in America in the idea of subliminal messages. Namely, at that time, James Vicary appeared to be a market researcher who began to deal with the concept of advertising through this method seriously. He experimented by inserting subliminal messages into the films, such as, "Are you hungry? Buy popcorn." Or "Are you thirsty? Drink Coca-Cola." also lasting three hundredths. After experimenting, Vicary said sales of popcorn and especially Coca-Cola had increased significantly. After that, he became a kind of marketing guru, and he was invited to television and radio shows where he spoke about the successful results of the freshly tried method. At the end of his career, he earned a total of $4 million at the time on his very idea, which would be $36 million.

In addition to the great interest in the new concept, a mass hysteria arose from the question of how much power and influence subliminal messages can have. A Cold War period soon followed, and Westerners thought that Russia might be interfering with American television waves and injecting messages like "Kill the President." This is why the US government's Federal Communications Commission (FCC) received a handful of complaints and letters from concerned citizens in the 1970s, to which it replied that it would investigate and report any such cases, for which there is no evidence or record—cases in which a person is sought or sued who could abuse the idea of subliminal messages.

The panic that spread seemed unnecessary because James Vicary himself denied the success of his experiment, stating that he had invented it. He said that the instructions he inserted about buying popcorn did not affect the increased sale of popcorn. Also, the scientists who later tried to conduct Vicary's experiment again did not get the results he first claimed to have obtained. This concept may have no power of influence, but since it is intriguing, it has continued to be discussed and researched, and ultimately proved that in certain circumstances it could have a certain influence on man.

In 2002, the true power of messages and images displayed in a short time began to be explored. This research was conducted by psychologists Erin Strahan, Steven Spencer, and Mark Zanna. They wanted to prove whether messages inserted into the subconscious can make people thirsty. James Vicary himself said that showing messages derived from the word thirst can make people feel subjective thirst and increase the likelihood of buying drinks. To experiment, they gathered a group of people to whom they displayed words such as thirsty, dry, and dehydrated. In doing so, the respondents had to concentrate on the center of the screen.

The research showed that the messages displayed on the screen had almost no effect on the group that came to the interrogation and they did not feel thirsty. The turnaround happened with the part of the group that came to the interrogation already a little thirsty and who were told not to drink anything for the next three hours. The results of research in this part of the group showed that subliminal messages had a very large impact on emphasizing and intensifying the feeling of thirst. As a reward, all respondents received a glass of juice at the end of the study, which was also part of the experiment because this is how the strength of thirst was tested, so some already thirsty people drank much more than the other part.

A few years later, in 2006, psychologists Johan C. Karremans, Wolfgang Stroebe, and Jasper Claus came up with the assumption that subliminal messages can amplify a particular feeling such as thirst but can affect people in terms of standing behind a particular producer. As an example, Lipton iced tea was used for the experiment. The researchers used part of the 2002 study by dividing the respondents into two groups; in one, the respondents were thirsty, and in the other, they were not. Also, as in the previous study, respondents were required to focus on the central part of the screen on which the Lipton logos were displayed separately within three-hundredths of a second.

And pictures of their iced tea. At the end of the experiment, the researchers offered the subjects two types of iced tea, one of which was Lipton, and the other iced tea was from an unknown manufacturer. It has been proven that already thirsty respondents preferred Lipton iced tea. It can be said that this 2006 survey served as a complement to the 2002 one, proving that subliminal messages can not only amplify a particular feeling but have the power to steer people in a particular direction to meet their unmet needs.

In 2013, psychologists Bryan Gibson and Katherine Zielaskowski researched a Las Vegas casino where they inserted thumbnails showing a US dollar symbol or a jackpot message on second-hand clips on slot machines. What followed is very interesting, and that is that some of the people who were shown these messages invested 55% more money on gambling and betting than other people in the casino. And as many as 45% of people after the bombardment of messages and the pictures were convinced that they would win something. Their mind interpreted that message as a sure win, an incentive to invest even more, and simply, as support for the opinion with which they had already come to the casino, and that is that there is a possibility of winning something and multiplying their money.

The question is, is there any protection against these cunning, flashing influences? Of course, certain agencies try to prevent subliminal messages from spreading through television and radio to viewers and listeners, but as soon as we step into a mall, casino, or any place intended for consumers, agencies do not influence because the owners of such places determine what to do. How to present to your consumers. One should be prepared for the fact that by going to any store, we will be exposed to subliminal messages. Lately, it is fashionable to show products on small screens, even in the nearest stores where we go to get basic groceries. The more technology develops, the more information is available to retailers about what consumers want.

On this occasion, it is convenient to say that one should never make decisions hungry, as it is not wise to go shopping hungry. If our needs, especially the primary, physiological ones, are not met, we are in great exposure to subliminal messages from various manufacturers. Just because all we have in mind is hunger or thirst, we won't even think about being exposed to commercials. The stroller gets piled up, and then, when we get full and watered, we realize that we probably don't need so many purchased things.

CHAPTER 8

HOW THE EYES CAN TELL US A LOT OF THINGS

Are you satisfied with your ability to communicate with people? Few will answer this question with a confident yes. More often than not, we only talk about how it will turn out and how it develops spontaneously on its own. And that means—we risk achieving a result that we did not want and did not expect at all. It happens, however, that we prepare in advance for a complex, responsible conversation. But even then, as experience shows, it is not easy to point it in the right direction towards the desired goal. Of course, some lucky people have such talent from birth. Well, if you are not one of them, try using the NLP technique.

To learn the skills of "effective" communication, a person must learn how to follow the course of their mental processes, to recognize emotional states, to assess the sincerity of statements, and the degree of agreement or disagreement with them.

First of all, you need to understand how the interlocutor's mind "processes" your words and prepares an answer. The first assistant here will be the method of observing the direction of a person's gaze. Summarizing and analyzing the vast amount of experimental material, the creators of NLP were convinced of the surprising informativeness and reliability of this simple feature.

In previous chapters it has already been said that according to the theory of NLP the human consciousness is connected with the external world and with its subconscious through three systems of sensations, images and notions: visual (sight), auditory (sound) and kinesthetic (muscular sensations, taste, odor). You can find out which of these systems is most active at the moment, what experiences the person now has.

The eyes are the mirror of the soul... It is unlikely to understand how real this old aphorism is. For example, clearly manifested in sight, even just in the direction of one's eyes, is the hidden structure of our inner world.

What do we do by orienting ourselves in the surrounding space or looking for the right object? Expressing ourselves not too intelligently, but very precisely, we shine with our eyes. But in the end, inner contemplation, the search for the right image, word, idea is said very similarly: "wander with the eye of your mind." And so—it turned out that this is not a metaphor at all! In such cases, we are looking at a very real, albeit very unusual, space arrangement.

On the one hand, it has a meaningful, "semantic" structure—it is divided into zones corresponding to three systems of representation (visual, auditory, and kinesthetic). On the other hand, these areas in our consciousness, for some reason, are tied to strictly defined directions of external, physical space. And the connection is so strong that any mental representation appeals to any area.

According to the scheme given in the book by NLP creators John Grinder and Richard Bandler, "From Frogs to Princes," six main lines of vision have the following semantic content.

Centuries (look to the left) - visual memories. This is an area of visual images of those objects that one has already seen once. For example, questions such as, "What color are your wife's eyes?" "What does your house look like?"

Bk (lookup) - visual constructions. Visual images of those things or phenomena that one has never seen or never seen in the way one should imagine. Typical questions: "What will an orange cow with blue spots look like?" "What will you look like in a firefighter's suit?"

AB (left side view) - audio memories. Auditory images of those sounds that one has already heard. Standard questions: "What did I just say?" "Remember the melody of your favorite song."

Ak (right side view) - audio design. Images of those sounds that people have never heard before. Standard questions: "Imagine the noise of applause against the background of singing birds," "How would your name sound if you said the opposite?".

A (look down left) - closed audio performances. Conversation with yourself, internal conversation. Standard questions: "Say something you usually say to yourself," "Repeat a passage from each text next to you."

K (right view) - kinesthetic images of any type. Emotional as well as tactile, muscular, etc. feeling. Standard questions: "How do you feel when you touch a pinecone?" "How do you feel when you run?"

Another case is possible when the view of the interlocutor is directed straight ahead. This most often means that some external visual images pass before his eyes, and he not only participates in the conversation but, to some extent, is influenced by them. The criterion is a change in the eyes' focus to "examine" imaginary objects and a slightly missing facial expression.

Also, note that observing the internal process of finding an answer to a question from the person you are talking to, you will notice not one but several consecutive views. The reason is the three-stage process of reflection, which is common to all people.

In the first stage—extracting the necessary information—one must gain access to his memory. This is done with the help of the "key"—visual image, sound, or bodily sensation. The presentation system (visual, auditory, or kinesthetic) used to "open" memory is called a presenter and reveals significant differences between people. NLP even introduces the terms "visualize", "kinesthetic," "audio"—according to the leading system specific to a person. If, say, the word "cat" is uttered, then Visualize will visualize it, Audialist may hear a meow first, and Kinesthetics will most likely recall the feeling of caressing soft hair.

In the second stage, the information extracted from the memory must be brought to consciousness. Here it will also be presented in the form of visual, sound, or kinesthetic images. The specific person used for this purpose by representations is called representative (representing). Each of us again has our favorite representation system (one of the three possible), with the help of which we are more accustomed to keep in mind the necessary information and work with them.

The last, third stage is to check the integrity of the information received. And this is aided by the inherent inner sensations of each individual of the same three types as if signaling the right or wrong solution to the problem. You've probably often heard phrases: "I feel something is wrong here!" Or "I see I'm wrong," etc., which unknowingly shows your criterion for a hidden test. The corresponding system of representations in NLP is called a reference (verification).

So, remember the three stages of thought when looking for the answer to the question:

1. The master system provides access to information stored in memory using images of one of three types (visual, sound, kinesthetic).
2. Representative system presents information to the consciousness, ensures its introduction and work with it in one form or another.
3. The reference system verifies the truth of the information and gives a signal for evaluation —also in the form of images of a certain type.

Here is a specific example of the analysis of the work of the line of sight consciousness. You asked someone you know to remember the color of his father's eyes and to observe, say, such a sequence of reactions. First, the gaze goes left up (zone Bb), then right down (zone K), and finally left down (zone A).

It can be assumed that the partner first saw his father in the imagination, then experienced the kinesthetic sensations he experienced in his presence, and finally orally commented on the result. Only after going through such a sequence (called strategy in NLP) will you hear the answer. To make sure the assumption is correct, ask the other person if this was the case. Most people are not used to following their internal strategies, but they are fully capable of implementing them.

You can find out in which system of representations a person's consciousness is currently working on learning how to analyze the oculomotor reactions of the interlocutor quickly.

The additional signs will allow you to understand how a person emotionally relates to his inner images, how important they are to him. There are many such secondary signs, although they are no longer so unambiguous. For example, in an irritated state in some people, the iris of the eyes darkens, while in others, the same thing happens at the moment of great joy. Facial pallor also has several "decipherments." It is even more difficult to interpret the changes in posture, micromotion of the arms, the tension of the facial muscles, etc. Nevertheless, Dr. Bandler strongly recommends that you strive to notice and make sense of as many signs as possible.

In the first stage of such training, it is better to ask questions to good friends, from which you can without hesitation indicate the results of observation. Noticing any new sign or reaction whose meaning is not yet clear to you, try to understand what they are feeling at the moment, in what condition they are.

As you acquire certain skills, start working with strangers, comparing questions to the situation, or just watching someone else's conversation. So, you can even train in transport on the way to work. Your goal at this stage is to learn how to move entirely to the analysis of the interlocutor. In NLP, this state is called actual time. In it, you completely forget about yourself and live only in the flow of information coming from the outside world. All inner feelings and sensations should be discarded as interference, or, rather, descending into the subconscious. Then the consciousness is released, and you can fully focus on the other person.

Here are some more sample questions that encourage the interlocutor to look for the non-verbal answers you need, that is, to create different imaginations.

Searching for images in memory (one sees the situation from the inside):

- Centuries "How many buttons are on your favorite jacket?"
- AB - Remember the sound of the surf.
- Ap - Imagine the feeling of a jet of water in the shower.

Look for images that are not in memory and need to be "constructed" (one sees the situation from the outside):

- Bk - Imagine your boss as an angel.
- Ak "How does a door creak in a Viking dugout?"
- k.k. - How would you feel when you parachute?

Training with such questions is best done by three people. One person seeks an answer but does not utter it immediately in words. Another, noting the direction of the respondent's gaze, makes assumptions about those images that have been replaced in his mind, and tries to talk about them as fully as possible (using additional characters). For example, if a person is asked to remember how he drove a car, then with a visual representation of the movement of his eyes, they can resemble the gaze of a fast-moving car. With a kinesthetic, you will notice the legs' involuntary movement, as if pressing the accelerator.

If the issue does not cause severe oculomotor reactions, it is necessary to complicate it. Then the respondent will be completely busy looking for the answer, and his reactions will become more natural.

The third participant complements the analysis of the second with his comments (another life experience will help achieve greater completeness of the result and will also create a useful atmosphere of the competition).

Then the partners change roles until each of them visits all three. The described exercise perfectly develops the first skills for observation of the interlocutor, without which it is impossible to become a master of interpersonal communication.

Eyes - a universal lie detector

The eyes are one of the most modern lie detectors. Through the movement of the eyeballs, you can determine what a person is thinking at the moment, whether he is telling the truth or lying. People move their gaze in certain directions, depending on the type of thinking. Eye observation is one of the simplest methods of obtaining information about a person's thoughts and emotions.

Studies show that the pupil expands completely by 45% if we like what we see and conversely narrows if we do not like it. It always happens that a human narrows his eyes when he or she feels unpleasant emotions. Such eye reactions last about 1/8 of a second, but you'll catch them if you look closely. One possibility for non-verbal cues involving the eyes is eye blockage. If a human, in reaction to visual or auditory input, covers his or her eyes with his or her hand, brushes his or her eyelid, or simply closes his or her eyes for a split second, it reveals negative emotions from the information received. Such a reaction can even provoke your thoughts. It is worth noting that during stress, the movement of the eyes is recognized. When a person experiences positive emotion, the eyes will be wide open, eyebrows raised. Also, the widening of the eyes is observed in a moment of surprise.

Decrypt eye movement

- The movement of the eyes to the left

(Image memory). If we imagine things from our

310

experience: "What color is your car?" then, along with the verbal response, you'll get a left-hand feel, characteristic of visual memories.

"When was the last time you ever saw this guy?"

- Defocusing the eyes

The eyes are out of focus, and their position is fixed, the pupil is slightly dilated. Visual images can be from memory or projected.

- The movement of the eyes up to the right

The constructed image. Visual representation of images, events, or objects that we haven't seen before, or representation of events and objects that we haven't seen before. "What's that cow going to look like?"

We have heard the auditory recollection of those sounds before. "How does your favorite song sound?"

Hearing construction. The auditory representation of sounds that we have never before heard. "How does your dream song sound?" "How would your phone sound, if you had your hand covering it?"

- Movement of the eyes down to the left

Internal conversation. The direction of the eyes matches the role of speech control when a person chooses the words he wants to pronounce. The interpreter can often see this view during the interpretation by the student regarding the defense of the diploma by the interviewer.

- Eyes down to the right

The sensation of emotions, tactile sensations, sensation of movement, smell. "How do you feel when you're upset?"

"When you play games, how do you feel?" "Do you remember how to bake a burn?" The important point is that it is impossible to construct sensations—we cannot imagine those feelings that we have not experienced.

There is a typical pattern of eyeball movement called the "Lie Detector": the direction of gaze from the visual structure (right up, right horizontal) to speech control (left down); in the inner experience it corresponds to such a sequence - First visualize, create how it might be, and then just state what it refers to, nothing more.

And now a few examples from life.

During an interrogation, the investigator asked the woman: What relations did you have with the citizen "K"?

Answer: "We were friends." — and lowers her eyes to the right down. It enters kinesthetics (sensory memories). Judging by the response of the brain, including the recollection of the senses, we can infer that the woman was telling a lie.

Similar situation: The spouse comes back from a get-away, the wife asks: "How could you bite the dust?" The spouse answers: "It was exhausting," and he brought down his eyes to one side. It goes into sensations (tactile recollections). It is too soon to finish up the falsehoods, yet we can say that he has something to recall.

Question: What happened at your gathering

Answer: "Not all that much, we talked and bid farewell." The eyes go left - up, while the pupils slender. The recollections evoked negative feelings. It tends to be expected that a squabble emerged at the gathering.

The gaze controls the course of the conversation, regulates the activity and distance of the interlocutors. The eyes help keep in touch when you speak. People look at each other from 1/3 to 2/3 of the talk time. The speaker usually looks less at the partner than at the listener. This allows him to concentrate more on the content of his speeches without being distracted. But at the end of his speech, the speaker usually looks directly into the listener's face, as if signaling the end of his speech. The one who takes the floor usually looks away first and then starts talking. If the interlocutors are seen too often, then perhaps they are more interested in the interlocutor than in what he says. If a person meets the gaze of a conversation partner for less than 1/3 of the communication time, then they accept it.

From the point of view, people are often in a hurry to make judgments about a person: for example, if a person's gaze is direct and open, then the person himself is such and if he "hides his eyes"—most likely insincere, unfriendly. Such a conclusion may be hasty. Some people do not want to be seen, that is, to be in the spotlight, which is why they "hide their eyes" in conversation. Others like to attract the attention of others, which may be the reason for their direct gaze, not for the openness of the character. Studies show that if interlocutors sit on opposite sides of a wide table, they look at each other more often than when they sit at a narrow table. In this way, the increase in the distance between the partners is compensated by increasing the frequency of viewings. The emotions experienced during the conversation also affect the appearance: positive emotions are accompanied by an increase in the number of views when discussing a pleasant topic. It is easy to look into the interlocutor's eyes. Negative feelings are characterized by a refusal to look at the interlocutor—we avoid doing this if it is something less pleasant.

The eyes can make different movements during a conversation. It is useful to be able to read these signals more effectively with people. Here are examples of such movements. Moving the eyes down (lowering the eyes) shows that a person is very worried about what others are saying. Eyes facing up and to the left mean that the listener is completely absorbed in the content of the speech. Eyes pointing up and to the right show that the listener is characterized by great care and experience to compare what is said with their own experience and knowledge.

A person's self-esteem and status affect how often people look at each other in the process of communication. You can observe two glances at the same time— "bottom-up" and "top-down." The first look "bottom-up"—the head is bent, and the eyes seem to be forced to look up. It can be seen when a person wants to help, to emphasize his attention, humility. Also, such a view is found in secretive people: aggressive and cautious (they still have stressed movements throughout the body). This view is often seen in anxious, restless people, modest and shy, conscientious, and executive.

If a person during a conversation looks down, as if he is trying for some reason to remove another from the field of view, perhaps he is unpleasant or uninteresting to him. Noticing this look from your interlocutor, you should keep in mind: something causes a negative reaction, and you need to change something, unless, of course, the partners are interested in successful interaction. But sometimes people in conversation close their eyes for a short time because they agree and approve of the words of a communication partner. Thus, the same sign, considered outside the context of communication, can be incorrectly assessed.

If the interlocutor looks at him for a long time, a stare ("glazed") look, this probably means that he misses half of what was said. Maybe something is pressing him, it is not easy for him, most likely at the moment when he does not have the situation under control.

When the interlocutor listens sincerely, he can unconsciously turn his eyes, this lively restless look—a sign that he is making an effort to understand the meaning of the words fully, is interested in conversation, or waiting for an important discussion. But if the rotating movements are too fast, this may be a signal of his uncertainty.

Business view: Focused on a triangle formed by a combination of three points—the eyes and the middle. If you look at this triangle most of the time during a business contact, you can create a serious, business-like conversation. This view is also called direct, accompanied by openness, and willingness to communicate, the truthfulness of statements, and free discussion of acute problems. A variety of business views can be attributed to a flattened, centered view. When the students of the discussion partners move from the centers to each other and freeze in this position, the partners seem to see a problem in front of them. Such an opinion arises when discussing a specific, complex, and urgent situation.

Social ("secular") look: Best suited for neutral communication. The gaze of one of the communicators falls below the level of the other's eyes towards him and falls into the eye-mouth triangle.

An intimate gaze occurs when the gaze is shifted downward to other parts of the interlocutor's body. The interlocutors seem to be looking at each other, often without noticing it themselves.

Side view: You can see when the pupils of the eyes are moving right or left at the same time. So they look left or right when the person does not trust the interlocutor, they are critical, negative about a person or information. If the eyes are narrowed, then mistrust is accompanied by aggressive emotions, and if it is open, then the person wants to hide the fear. Often appears in a person who is used to control the situation, to manage it. He carefully observes everything that happens around. Less often, squatting is a message of interest.

Most often, the side blink carries information about contempt for whom it is necessary to communicate it to, for a great reluctance to reveal itself even in the smallest.

Avoiding gaze: Thrown by people out of fear, timidity. And it is also found in those who want to deceive others. This gaze is unpleasant—it is constantly moving from the face, from the hands to the clothes, then to the other parts of the body and again to the face. You never know what this person thinks, even if he agrees with you, he has no faith. Among the deceptive views can be distinguished the thief's gaze (fleeting escapes from the opposite gaze) and the deceiver's stare (eyes that run fast in all directions, eyebrows in the form of thin ropes).

Evaluate the appearance or look at a meeting: So ("from head to toe") only a person who is confident in the situation and can control it, explores another.

A lethargic look: Can be seen in very calm, non-emotional people or any person in a boring, or familiar situation. You may be left with the impression that a person is asleep. This may be the gaze of a lazy, short-sighted person, whose facial features are bulging and has watery eyes, with a gaze that moves slowly from object to object.

Aggressively insulting: Demonstrated by those who like to show their clear superiority, strength, ready to "crush" the other. On such a person—there is contempt or emptiness, no emotions, and the interlocutor is not visible.

Piercing look: It is often found among those who have the authority, and the duty to demand laws, work, reports, instructions, and, also, have the right to accuse.

A controlling gaze: Characteristic of observant people who follow even the smallest actions, movements, and words of others.

Oily look: This is a palpable, unceremonious, hidden look. A wink often accompanies it. A variety of this appearance can be considered the look of a careless person, but the eyelids are blue.

An enchanted species: Can be seen in a person in an elevated state, captivated by the strongest emotional experiences close to ecstasy.

Access is the process of receiving inside information from the interlocutor—photos, sounds, words, sensations that build memories, fantasies, etc.

You can determine your partner's experience, his or her dominant representation system, and his or her type of thinking using "access keys."

Access keys are specific non-verbal behavior that show how information is obtained.

The information you need for human representative systems can be obtained in many different ways and observing eye movement is the easiest.

The access keys are eye movements

The "scanning" models of oculomotor reactions are related

to the internal processes needed to update the mind about memories or to build future experiences.

You can be sure that the person is gaining internal access to the corresponding representative system when you catch any of the oculomotor reactions. You can determine which representative systems they are using if you observe the eye movement of a communication partner.

The hypnologist observes the movements of the partner's eyes and uses key predicates that correspond to the position of the client's eyes. Not only that. The direction of the gaze can tell you whether he is remembering something stored in his memory, some experience that happened in the past or building something new for himself.

People systematically move their eyes in certain directions, depending on what type of thinking is found in them. Eye movements are often combined with purely individual reactions, taking into account the person's actual attitude to the mental images that appeared in front of him (eyes went to the left and pupils narrowed—an unpleasant auditory memory of something).

We will now present the eye movements again that provide the most important information in nonverbal communication. The direction of the gaze is indicated by the object you are observing. If it's "left," it means to his left hand, not yours. Well, and to the right, respectively. You are unlikely to confuse the top and bottom.

1. - The Movement of The Eyes to The Left

Eidetic image (image-memory). When we see it from our experience: "What color is the wallpaper in your room?" And together with the verbal response, you will get a left look, typical of visual memories.

"What color was your friend's suit yesterday?"

2. - Defocusing the eyes

The eyes are out of focus, and their position is fixed, the pupil is slightly dilated. Visual images can be eidetic or projected.

3. - The Movement of The Eyes Up to The Right

The constructed image. Virtual representation of images, events, or objects that we haven't seen before. "What will an orange elephant look like in raspberry spots?"

The auditory recollection of those sounds we have heard before. "How does your phone alarm sound?"

Hearing construction. The auditory representation of sounds we have never heard before. "What does your name sound like if you say the opposite?" "How will your alarm clock ring if you cover it with a metal bucket?"

4. - "Phone position" eye movement down to the left

Internal dialogue closed the auditory presentation. Conversation with yourself, internal conversation. This point of view coincides with the function of speech control when one carefully chooses the words to be uttered. This view can often be seen with the interpreter during the interpretation, with the reporter making a responsible report with the interviewer.

5. - Eyes down to the right

Kinesthetic presentation. The sensation of emotions, tactile sensations, sensation of movement, smell. How do you feel when you feel joy? What do you feel when you run? "Do you remember how mustard plaster burns?"

Interestingly, there are no constructions in kinesthetic—we cannot imagine those sensations that we have not experienced.

How to understand the interlocutor for eye movement

The eyeballs move according to what sensory process is currently going on in mind. In most cases, this movement serves as a fairly reliable indicator of how a person's mind works.

There is even a typical pattern of eyeball movements called a "lie detector": the direction of gaze from the visual structure (right up, right horizontal) to speech control (left down); in the inner experience it corresponds to such a sequence—first imagine, construct how it could be and then say only what corresponds to it, nothing more.

"I believe! These eyes do not lie. After all, how many times has he said it?"

If this is your belief, then this is your main mistake. You underestimate the value of human eyes.

Understand that language can hide the truth, and eyes sometimes cannot see!

Suppose you are asked a sudden question, you don't even flinch, and in one second you take control of yourself and know what you need to tell to hide the truth. You say it very convincingly and not a single fold of your face moves, but, alas, worried by the question, the truth from the bottom of the soul for a moment jumps in the eyes, and it's over. It's been spotted, and you're caught!

I don't know what a husband who is also a father is like, but he will be the best lover if he goes on an inner-kinesthetic experience. His inner experience is connected with kinesthetic—with touches, caresses….

The upward movement of the eyeballs occurs with a predominance of visual processes, and the side, with a predominance of auditory. Looking down is usually associated with kinesthetic sensations or internal dialogue.

The nature of eyeball movements also depends on whether the invocation process is in progress or whether sound or visual images are recreated. For instance, when scrolling through possible scenarios related to something that has never happened to you before.

The pattern of eyeball movement is called the "lie detector"—for example, the direction of gaze from the visual or auditory structure to the control of speech—this in the internal experience corresponds to this sequence.

So, the upper floor is visual, and the middle floor is auditory, the lower is divided between kinesthetics and speech control. It is convenient to use the property on the left to facilitate orientation, which is "more true" than the right.

The oculomotor response patterns have a reasonable neurophysiological rationale. Eye movement up and to the left is the usual way people use to stimulate the dominant hemisphere as a method of accessing visual memory.

The upward movement of the eyes to the right, on the contrary, stimulates the left hemisphere of the brain and gives constructive images. That is, a visual representation of things that one has not seen before.

You can check by asking yourself simple questions.

Ask your partner questions that will trigger memory images, for example:

- What color is the front door of your apartment?
- What does your bedroom look like?

Examples of audio questions:

- Do you remember the song you liked?

Or kinesthetically:

- How do you feel when you dive into the sea?
- How do you feel that you are hungry?

Lack of attention to the access keys often confuses. You often hear complaints:

"My son doesn't listen to me at all. We sit in the same room, I tell him something, and he pretends not to hear me. "

In this case, the dissatisfied mother was busy with her inner images and tried to get a sound response, but she did not notice what was happening "outside," to put it mildly. Namely, those moments when the son perceives the information as indicated by his eyes.

What does a gaze mean, the direction of the gaze, the dilated, and narrowed pupils? Careless acting looks, looking below, left, right, up, down, and blinking often? The look and the direction of the gaze can say a lot about a person's thoughts, feelings, and experiences.

Let's start with the pupils (Look into my eyes, and you will see the truth)

Pupils expand or contract under certain lighting. It all depends on the mood and brightness of the lighting. If a person is emotionally agitated, then his pupils become slightly dilated than in the same light, at rest. The same thing happens when a person looks at something he likes. They don't just say, "my eyes are on fire." A person with dilated pupils looks the most attractive and enchanting.

But if the pupils narrow, then aggression, anger, and irritation increase in a person.

Raised eyebrows (sign, gesture- Hey, hello!)

Eyebrows are raised when we notice a pleasant person next to us, and we want him to notice us. This is nothing more than an expression of interest. People who stay with a stony face and do not raise eyebrows when greeting are considered aggressive, sympathy for them is much less. Know that if you raise your eyebrows, the person will certainly repeat your gesture and maybe even smile back.

Raised eyebrows in women (Gesture, sign - Hold me or obey)

Women with raised eyebrows and large eyes are considered submissive, which is why they are very successful with men. Men want to hug and defend. In men, everything is different; the lower the eyebrows, the narrower the eyes. So, men want to show their authority and seriousness. Recently, however, women have begun to use this view. And if the eyebrows are thick, then they are as aggressive as powerful and able to conquer.

Looking below (Gesture, sign - playing with you)

If a woman's head is slightly tilted and looking down, it is a signal of humility, which men like so much. It gives the woman a look of "childish naivety and purity of soul." Such a look evokes real parental feelings. And if a smile complements all this, then the effect is simply stunning. In a dispute, the interlocutor is likely to take the side of the person who looks cute and obedient from below.

The scenario can be viewed from two sides. If it is complemented by a flirtatious smile and a sparkle in your eyes, then you are interested in the interlocutor. Women use this "hated" look during flirting. But if in addition to the look on his face there is a smile with lowered corners of the lips and frowning eyebrows, then the interlocutor is most likely hostile, and it is better to hide from his field of vision.

Frequent blinking (gesture, sign - stick with eyes)

Usually, a person blinks about 10-20 times a minute. Did your interlocutor start blinking harder? Only in this way, often blinking, his brain wants to "throw" your image from the subconscious. When a person starts blinking stubbornly, closing his eyes for 2-3 seconds, you should know that he is just tired of communicating with you and cannot tell you about it personally due to embarrassment or other reasons. In this case, it is better to find another person to talk to and continue to communicate with.

Running eyes (Gesture, sign, look - Where is the way out...)

Did you notice that your interlocutor's eyes began to flow from one side to the other? No, no! He is not doing gymnastics for the eyes! He is looking for a way to withdraw (or looking for a target if he is a special intelligence agent). He is tired of your conversations, or they are not interesting to him. He might even try to smile with pursed lips in return, imitating interest, but you know, most likely when you turn your back, he will run away.

Social look (See, gesture, sign - Just talking through the eyes)

During normal communication, the interlocutor's eyes "draw" a triangular area that affects the eyes and nose. In this area, we focus on a simple situation that is safe for us. Such a view is not considered aggressive or hostile. This is how communication between people of the same status and age takes place. Easy and simple.

Intimate look (Intimate "conversation" through the eyes)

Thanks to improved peripheral vision, women can discreetly examine a man, keeping their eyes everywhere. But men do not know how to do this, and they carefully examine the object of their adoration. The intimate gaze "outlines" a triangle between the eyes and its tip forms on the chest, and if people are at a distance, it passes from the eyes down to the inguinal area. The look is not hostile, meaning that the person most likely wants something more than communication with you.

Authoritative look (authoritative conversation with eyes)

The authoritative gaze is centered in the triangle between man's eyes and "his mythological third eye" above the eyes along the bridge of the nose. Usually, this view is used by authoritative, confident people. It carries the strength and desire to suppress the interlocutor. People with a mild temper are sometimes advised to use this look to look more serious, complementing it with lowered eyebrows and narrowed eyes. It is with this look that the interlocutor can interrupt an annoying conversation.

He looks up-down, right-left

Where do the eyes of the man sitting opposite look? The eyes are the mirror of the soul! If the eyes are directed up to the left, then the person is most likely trying to remember the image he has seen before or what he has done before. And if down to the right, then we recall the emotions and feelings with which this or that action was performed. If it is directed from the left to the ear, the person remembers the melody or the sound heard, and if he mysteriously looks down to the left, an internal dialogue takes place. Such views do not last long and pass almost instantly, and the main thing is to catch them.

Head straight, head up

The raised head is typical of people who participate in a conversation. This position is neutral, does not bring aggression, or, on the contrary, deep indifference. Small nods can supplement a raised head during a conversation, or a person can rub his chin, thinking about what has been said or heard. In any case, you can be sure that the interlocutor is listening to you (unless he froze with an unblinking look, most likely in a trance in this situation). If the chin is forward and slightly upwards and is accompanied by a kind of downward gaze, then the person is arrogant, and you need to be more careful when talking to him.

Tilt head to the side—a look with a tilt of the head

A sloping head on one side is a symbol of humility. At this point, the person wants to show; he does not pose a threat because he opens his throat. Also, tilting one side shows interest in the conversation. Often, to look more attractive, women bow their heads in the presence of a man. By often showing people a "defenseless" neck, you can bring them closer to you.

The head is lowered forward (Sign of disapproval, the gesture of aggression)

Bulls always set their horns forward when they are aggressive. A bowed head and a look of gloom with eyebrows and dilated nostrils gather signals for others about a person's negative and aggressive mood. That he is ready to tear to pieces anyone who will not be favorable to him or will not be pleasant to him. So, you better wait until one straightens one's head or at least tilts it to the side.

Otherwise, each of your words may have the effect of a "red rag," and you may be "lifted by the horns."

All the above gestures, points of view, and examples can only be used in context and are not an exact indication of one or another decipherment of actions. Remember that you should not judge by just one criterion and interpret actions in your direction. Don't be biased.

CHAPTER 9

BODY LANGUAGE MISTAKES TO AVOID

An old saying goes that a photo is worth a thousand words.

But how much is body language worth?

During a conversation, the words that come out of your mouth are far from the only form of communication.

We all have ways and a posture when speaking that say a lot about what we are feeling at each moment.

Some of them are universal and even easy to understand.

Of course, you need to know what to look for and have mastery over each gesture's meanings.

A simple change of voice, for example, can indicate fear, irritation, or even that the person in front of you is about to cry.

This goes for both personal and professional levels.

Do you want to find out what some of these actions, which are usually involuntary, mean?

Body language and its reading are not an exact science. There are no hard and fast rules for interpreting unspoken signals. Even scientists trained to read people like a book make mistakes, especially when observing experienced players who consciously control their behavior.

Positive Body Language

Positive body language includes proper eye contact, active engagement/listening, and targeted gestures that emphasize the message you are trying to convey. Research shows that people who use positive body language are more confident, competent, and more convincing and have more emotional intelligence.

Here's how it works:

1. Positive body language changes your attitude

It has been discovered that consciously adjusting body language to make it more positive improves your attitude because it has a strong effect on your hormones.

2. Increases testosterone

If we think about testosterone, we typically concentrate on sports and rivalry, but testosterone's value covers much more than athletics. Whether you're a man or a woman, testosterone improves confidence in yourself and makes others see you as being more reliable and positive. Research indicates that positive body language raises 20 percent of the testosterone levels.

3. Reduces cortisol

Cortisol is a stress hormone that interferes with work and creates negative effects on health in the long run. Lowering cortisol levels minimizes stress and allows you to think more clearly, especially in difficult and challenging situations. Research shows that positive body language reduces cortisol levels by 25 percent.

4. It creates a powerful combination

Although a decrease in cortisol or an increase in testosterone is great in itself, the two are a powerful combination commonly seen in people in positions of power. This combination creates self-confidence and clarity of mind that are ideal for dealing with tight deadlines, difficult decisions, and large amounts of work. It is known that people who have naturally high testosterone levels and low cortisol levels manage to work under pressure.

5. Make yourself feel nicer

In a study by Tufts University, subjects viewed audio recordings of doctors communicating with their patients. Only by observing the doctors' body language could the respondents guess which doctors eventually sued their patients. Body language is a huge factor in your perception and can be more important than your voice or even what you say. Learning to use positive body language would make people respect you and have more trust in you.

6. Transfer jurisdiction

Researchers found, in a study carried out at Princeton, that one second of a candidate's footage for senator or governor was enough for people to predict exactly which candidate was elected. Although this does not improve your confidence in the voting process, it does demonstrate that there is a clear basis in body language for the interpretation of competence.

7. Improves your emotional intelligence

Your ability to effectively express your feelings and ideas is essential to your emotional intelligence. Individuals whose body language is negative have a contagious and damaging impact on those around them. Working to enhance your body language affects your emotional intelligence profoundly.

We often think of body language as a result of our attitude or how we feel. That is true, but psychologists have also shown that it is true and vice versa: a change in body language also changes your attitude.

Negative Body Language

Hands close to the mouth: Passing the hand over the lips, placing objects close to the mouth, and touching the chin can indicate the attempt to fail with the truth, as of someone afraid of being caught in the act.

Clenched lips: Compressed and closed lips can denote that you try to avoid saying what you think or not wanting to answer a question that has been asked. In the ride of this action, the closed jaw can also be an acute sign of stress and a message that there is discomfort in being in that situation.

Looking without direction: Looking is, without a doubt, one of the most expressive parts of our body, being possible to perceive when someone is sad or even very happy from it. In the analysis of body language, looking up or right usually indicates a certain confusion (like looking for a mental image while winding up). Upwards or without direction can denote irritation and contempt.

To contract the forehead is a sign seen with certain negativism because a certain doubt, tension and even nervousness can appear.

Crossed arms: This gesture may be one of the ones that most create physical barriers between the communicator and his receiver, and it may show certain irritability or rejection to the moment he is going through.

Body Language Mistakes to Avoid

Body language is one of the most important vehicles to interact with. During a conversation, speech or pitch, you always use facial expressions, body gestures, and hand movements to communicate your message.

Using facial expressions, body gestures, hand movements, and the body language of the legs, you can stream your content with success and show confidence.

If you use this inappropriately or inaccurately, they can become a source of distraction for your audience, and it can conflict with your message.

1. The different hand movements

A very common mistake of people in meetings, conversations, and presentations is certainly the language of the hands.

Hiding your hands, shaking them, or moving them too much demonstrates your nervousness and can give your audience the feeling that you don't believe what you're saying.

Keeping your hands in your pockets is also a gesture that indicates that you are afraid, not knowing where to go or not interested in what you are doing.

If that were not enough, it could still make your interlocutors think that you are unkind to them. Remember that if you don't look confident, people won't buy whatever you are saying.

Instead, try to keep your arms in front of you openly. Use your hands to explain your point of view through concise and calculated movements.

Watch your hand movements; this can testify against you.

2. Crossed arms

Crossing your arms can also give you the impression that you are enthusiastic about the information you are going to give, or something is wrong.

It is a defensive posture that will signal defense and resistance and create a distance between you and your audience.

Instead, keep your arms open and at a distance from your body, almost as if you are giving a big bear hug.

This open gesture is engaging and welcome. It will convey a message of peace and confidence to your audience.

3. Avoiding eye contact

Avoiding eye-to-eye contact with your audience and looking at your watch, your feet, or constantly looking at the presentation screen, will make you sound playful and unprofessional.

Instead, always consider making eye contact with your audience when expressing your ideas.

Moving your head quickly during the presentation will portray that you are personally interested and involved.

4. Bad posture

The position is one of the most important attributes of body language while delivering a presentation.

If you are leaning your back and shoulders in a posture that lets your neck hang, it will defiantly convey a weak message, and your audience can start thinking about your professionalism.

Instead, point in a neutral direction, regardless of whether you are sitting or standing.

Adopting a bad posture will make you feel bad.

5. Doing bad body movements

Walking back and forth by moving your arms quickly will give your posture a totally strange feeling.

Instead, if you need to move in any way in your meeting or presentation, that move must have a purpose. It is also important not to just stand in one place.

Interact with everyone during your presentation so that you can send a positive message to all parties.

6. Watch your legs

During a presentation, the legs are the most difficult members to control because of nervousness or concentration to convey the best ideas and a good image.

Constantly shaking your legs if you are standing will signal to your audience that you are uncomfortable and restless, which is not a good thing. They want to feel that you are giving yourself completely to the meeting.

Instead, make controlled movements for the audience.

When you move during a conversation or presentation, make the audience feel that you have been practicing these movements before—make them believe that you are an experienced expert.

7. Forget to smile

Your face is the most important aspect of creating a good impression. Unless you are breaking bad news, it is appropriate that you are smiling, even during a business meeting.

Start your presentation or greeting with a smile, and as a result, the audience will receive your message more willingly.

Try to keep your smile on during the presentation,

particularly when you want to make people laugh. People will respond to a smile with another smile in return.

The interaction is the key to a remarkable presentation.

Always smile, it will make a great impression on people.

8. Inappropriate use of hand gestures

Hand in the pocket is a body language of neglect and disinterest.

On the other hand, moving your hands during your presentation supports each word with a more powerful meaning.

Whenever you want to make an important point, emphasize your words with hand gestures. Your audience will remember the fact or the information better when you anchor it with a specific gesture.

TEST: Does your boss have emotional intelligence at work?

Keep an eye on his body language and hands.

Try to avoid these bodily gestures to make a professional impression.

For a salesperson, giving the image of professionalism and confidence is much more than just saying the right thing at the right time.

You need to look trustworthy, successful, and you still need to show that you have the credibility to talk about what you do. Companies and people want to partner with successful salespeople and companies!

If you start to observe your behavior, you will see that, even unconsciously, you will end up making some faux pas.

Carefully observing your movements in the middle of a meeting, presentation, and even an informal conversation will make you identify and correct your gestures to make the best impression possible.

Start now and ensure that your image is the image of a great seller in the medium term.

These are eight fatal body language mistakes you should avoid: remember them even when you're alone.

As you have seen, body language is very important. So, pay attention to your facial expressions, leg positioning, posture, and gestures with people.

CHAPTER 10

THE ART OF PERSUASION

Persuasion is the art of convincing anyone of anything!

Yes, it is possible to convince others to do what you want as long as it is good for them.

It is not manipulation, and it is not a way to get other people to fulfill your desires, much less a way to take advantage.

If that is your view of persuasion and looking for a way to control others, this chapter is not for you!

However, if you aim to implement actions beneficial to all parties involved, you will learn how to convince others using the most effective techniques.

Scientists have been studying the reasons behind the SIM for more than 60 years, and one thing is a consensus: convincing someone to do something is not just a reflection of charisma, it is science.

Whether to sell, to capture emails, to ask for help from someone influential in the market, to know what persuasion is and how to use it can bring many points of advantage for you and others.

What is persuasion: The secret weapon to convince people

Persuasion is a communication strategy that uses logical, rational, or symbolic resources to induce someone to accept an idea, an attitude, or action.

Persuasion is not used only in copies, landing pages, or during a sales argument.

It is present in the most diverse situations of our day-to-day activities, such as when we try to convince someone close to making a decision that we think is correct or even when negotiating a discount in a store.

You certainly already influence people around you without even realizing it, either with attitudes or arguments. What you will find here is just one way to enhance your persuasive potential further.

Whether to convince your boss that you deserve a raise, to ask a favor for someone influential in your niche market, or even to make more sales online, knowing what persuasion is and how to apply it can mean the difference between failure and success.

The number 1 rule to convince anyone about anything is as much as possible about the person you want to convince and meeting their biggest objections.

This rule is so important that you should write it down to never forget it. Without it, no technique to increase your persuasion will work.

The right time to start an argument

You can know all about the best words to persuade someone, what body language you need to adapt, and even know what the person wants to hear.

However, if you choose the wrong time to use all of this, there is no point in knowing what persuasion is, you will fail to convince even the most flexible people.

People are more easily persuaded to thank someone, as they feel in debt.

And if anyone wishes to thank you for everything you've done, it may be a perfect idea to add what you already know about convincing. And, of course, to make people thank you for something, you need to send first before you can care about getting it.

Don't use YOUR strengths

Do you consider yourself good at writing? Or do you know how to use the best examples to convince someone of something? Perhaps your strongest point is your charisma.

But do you want to convince someone? Then, don't use your strengths.

Use those of the person you want to persuade!

It sounds strange, but our abilities determine the way we think and act. And different people think differently.

To persuade someone, you need to speak "the person's language." It's no use talking in Portuguese with a Japanese who doesn't know the language, right?

Empathy. This is the key to success in persuading people.

So, put yourself in the hands of your audience, and consider if and what he or she would want to be persuaded of.

It's not what you say that is important, but how you say it.

What is the profile of the person you want to convince?

Empathy is a special ingredient that will lead you to convince people. But to generate empathy, it is necessary to observe and understand the difference between the most common profiles, which are as follows:

1. People who think together vs. individually: Those who like to think alone need more time to decide. And preferably at a time when they are alone. Therefore, an email with several arguments is a good weapon to achieve this profile. Those who like to make group decisions love brainstorming sessions, and this can be a good opportunity to discuss ideas and thus convince a group thinker.

2. Who likes to speak vs. who prefers to listen: This difference between profiles is easy to see. Those who like to listen can easily pay attention to what you are saying, while those who prefer to speak tend to lose concentration. To hold these people's attention, put it in focus every time you speak. Or choose writing, which works well. To encourage listeners to speak and provide important information, ask very specific questions to avoid generic responses.

How to increase our capacity for persuasion

As John Ruskin said, "He who has the truth in his heart must never fear that his tongue lacks the power of persuasion." Probably this is the best option. However, psychology has studied other theories that can be very useful in certain specific situations.

Before continuing, know that by persuasion, we mean the ability to seduce, convince, impress, or fascinate a person.

Some psychological theories to improve persuasion

The term "persuasion" may have had some negative connotations in recent years. We live in a world of global uncertainty and strong consumerism. We are continually bombarded with advertisements that appear to be convincing, whose motives are not necessarily as straightforward or simple as they should be, but far from belonging to worthy causes.

It is therefore important to make the difference between

persuasion and manipulation. The latter lies in honesty, which exists in persuasion but not in manipulation; from a persuasive perspective, the other knows, since this is how it was presented to him, that we are trying to convince him of something. In contrast, from a manipulative perspective, this information tends to be concealed, hidden.

Persuasion is understood as the ability to influence another person honestly, which gives a great advantage to the people who developed it. This is why it is important to know some theories that are valid over time.

The amplification hypothesis

A firm mentality, conveyed with confidence, is very immune to convincing. However, it softens if it is expressed with uncertainty. In this case, arguments based on an emotional basis are very resistant to logic, and vice versa.

So, by carrying this hypothesis promulgated by Clarkson, Tbormala, and Rucker to practice, your possibilities of influence will increase if the attitudes that you project have the same meaning as those of the interlocutor. This is precisely what gives a name to the theory: if you want to persuade someone on a sport-related subject and you both support the same sports team, for example, the power of your arguments will then be amplified.

The manipulation theory

This theory handles four maxims to seduce a person; ensuring that the information is as complete as possible, ensuring the authenticity of this information, its relevance to the subject matter, and presenting it in such a way that it can be fully understood by the other.

This hypothesis, which might sound very poor, is very

rational and fair. As Ruskin said, if you have the facts on your hand, you don't have to think about not being convincing. However, it is necessary to be well prepared and to have great knowledge of the subject, as well as to know how to explain them, to convince someone.

Nonetheless, it is difficult to defend yourself against such a strategy, especially if your interlocutor is skillful with words. It is necessary to observe his nonverbal language, which reflects contradictions between the assurance of his speech and what his gestures say. Having a little idea of the subject, I can point out what the most fragile part of his argument is.

The priming theory

This psychological method of persuasion is commonly used in advertisement. It is focused on the networks of interaction that we need to create in our minds. Indeed, when memory is activated, a concept or a feeling, in turn, allows the activation, for a limited time, of everything associated with this memory. For example, if you are told about the breakfasts of your childhood, it will be much easier afterward to make you buy milk.

The priming must be very subtle; thus, the person being stimulated is not aware of how he is influenced, even if he knows that he is in an influence brand since it is a publicity question. In another case, we would speak of manipulation.

The standard of reciprocity

This is a widely accepted social norm. It's as simple as giving something and waiting for something else in return. It is not a voluntary act but established and accepted by all.

Carrying out this standard can be as simple as saying thank

you. Faced with the offer you make to him, you wait for your interlocutor to send you this courtesy, and reciprocity must be proportional to the type of service rendered.

The principle of scarcity

In a way, all human beings need to control their world. Having free will over what surrounds us is important. This is why when something is scarce, the desire to have it increases.

This psychological technique is also widely used in the advertising world; think of the famous slogans. So, if you consider yourself a victim of this practice, ask yourself if you need the rare good, feeling, or emotion that is offered to you.

All of these psychological theories of persuasion go beyond the mere theoretical field. They have been put into practice and demonstrated to be functional. You have likely used them at some point in your life without even being aware of them.

Method of dark persuasion

How vital is persuasion to a leader? Can success be achieved without the power of persuasion? Studying the world's most influential leaders in various fields shows that knowing how to persuade is a fundamental skill for them.

Belief is a characteristic that allows us to influence others. For this, it is necessary to understand how to listen, have charisma, and credibility.

1. Persuading is not manipulating. Manipulation is coercion by force for someone to do something that is not in their interest. Instead, persuasion is getting people to do things that are also in their interest.

2. Persuade persuasive people. Everyone can be persuaded at a specific time, but that does not mean that it is short-term. To convince, it is necessary to identify the people who are in the right moment to be persuaded and to focus our energy on them.

3. Opportunity. Persuasion depends on context and timing.

4. Interest in being persuaded. It is impossible to convince someone who is not interested in what you are saying. People spend most of their time thinking about money, love, and health, so to be persuasive, it is essential to know how to speak correctly on these issues to attract people's attention.

5. Reciprocity forces. When someone does something for you, you feel compelled to return it. Helping each other to survive is part of human DNA. If we have small gestures with others, then it is easier to ask them for things.

6. Persistence. The person who is willing to insist on a goal becomes more persuasive. The great leaders of history could sustain their efforts and messages to the masses for a long time. It is the example of Abraham Lincoln, who lost eight elections before becoming president of the United States, but who maintained his effort throughout.

7. Congratulate. Congratulations positively affect everyone, and good-feeling people are more likely to trust you. Honestly, congratulating people, even for simple things, is an excellent way to convince them.

8. Set expectations. Much of persuasion goes through the ability to manage the expectations of the other.

9. Don't take anything for granted. Always defend your value, not in fact that your interlocutor does not need what you offer.

10. Create scarcity. Everything that has value is usually scarce. The persuaded must be led to believe that the product we offer is uncommon, even if it is a service.

11. Create urgency. You have to be motivated to make the other person believe that they must act immediately. If he is willing to be persuaded now, we should not let him think about it, for he may not be so receptive in the future.

12. Lean on images. What we see is more powerful than what we hear. You have to perfect the first impression that is given.

13. Tell the truth. Sometimes the most effective way to persuade someone is by saying things that no one else is willing to say. Hard facts are pervasive.

14. Build a good relationship. You have to be open and take relationships to a field in which the interlocutor feels comfortable.

15. Flexibility. The most flexible person is the one in control. Children are convincing because they are willing to go through many stages to get what they want (cry, pout, beg, be charming...).

16. Transfer energy. Some people drain energy from others. Instead, persuasive people know how to transfer their energy to others to motivate them. There are many ways: eye contact, physical contact, laughter ... or merely knowing how to listen.

17. Communicate clearly. If a preteen is not able to understand what we want to explain, it is too complicated. You have to simplify things until highlighting only what is essential.

18. Be prepared. You have to know more about the other person than what the other person knows about you. It is the best way to gain an advantage and be able to carry out more effective persuasion.

19. Keep calm. No one is effective when they are 'on.' In the tensest situations, it is best to remain calm and not show emotions. In conflict situations, people turn to the person who controls their emotions.

20. Be moderate. People are not comfortable in conflict. Try to lower the tension level, be reasonable, and avoid an emotional place based on self-control.

21. Trust. If you believe in what you do, you will always be able to persuade others.

CHAPTER 11

NEURO-LINGUISTIC PROGRAMMING

What is NLP?

NLP, which stands for Neuro-linguistic programming, is a topic that is increasingly mentioned and intrigued by both business circles and those interested in personal growth and development. It can often be found in recent business and management literature and personal development books. Also, there are more and more lectures about different NLP techniques, as well as texts, videos, and audio materials on the Internet.

As a result, more and more people are coming into contact with NLP techniques. As with all the novelties that attract attention, and at the same time offer different ways of thinking, the mention of NLP provokes different reactions. Sometimes it can be heard that it is a matter of manipulating or selling fog, while some will even back down when they come in contact with an NLP expert, fearing the influence of that person. But what exactly is behind the word NLP?

How did NLP come about?

To make it easier to answer the question posed, it is good to go back to the past, to the 1970s, the period when the foundations of what NLP is today were laid. Richard Bandler and John Grinder, two curious enthusiasts, a student of psychology and mathematics and a professor of linguistics, shared an interest in understanding what makes top psychotherapists (of the time) so excellent at communicating and working with people.

They were interested in how they think, how they experience themselves, others, and the world around them in general, and what they specifically do to achieve results that no one else has achieved. Intensively and very systematically studying the work of three amazing people and experts, Fritz Pearls, Milton Erickson and Virginia Satir, they began to notice certain rules and patterns of their action. Which sometimes therapists themselves were not aware of, but did so intuitively, as a result of many years of reflection and experience.

Imitating experts

Understanding how those experts work, Bandler, and Grinder themselves began to apply this through contact with other people and realized that they could achieve similar results. For them, it was the beginning of discovering the path to excellence, which they decided to share with everyone else. Soon, their work began to be influenced by other top experts of the time. They studied human nature (such as Gregory Bateson, British anthropologist, linguist, and systems researcher), which resulted in the further development of NLP, which continues today.

NLP is still evolving

In its 40 years of existence, NLP and its many researchers and creators have maintained a spirit of curiosity, and have continued to study the experiences of top practitioners in various fields of human activity, adding findings from the research and scientific milieu to contribute to a systematic study of human activity. Nature, but also (what is perhaps more important) ways to develop and make the best use of the opportunities we have as a human species.

In addition to psychotherapy, NLP is successfully used in

leadership, business, sports, education, counseling, and other areas where there is interest in developing human resources and achieving excellence.

What is behind the (name) of NLP?

The very name Neuro-Linguistic Programming, coined by Bandler and Grinder to describe the knowledge they wanted to offer the world, conceals three key areas of NLP study:

Neuro - comes from the Greek word neuron (nerve cell) and refers to knowledge about the human brain and how we experience the world around us.

Linguistic - is the Greek word lingua (language) and refers to how our communication (both verbal and nonverbal) affects us and our environment.

Programming - refers to researching and understanding our "mental programs," i.e., the usual ways, habits, and strategies that we use in our actions, which sometimes help us, but also cause us to retaliate in achieving the desired goals and even leads us to unwanted results.

In the first step, NLP lets each individual know himself by getting to know how he experiences the world around him, communicating with him, and achieves (or not) his goals. In the next step, it offers an opportunity to get to know the ways of thinking and acting, which through human history and the successes of other great individuals (yes, NLP was fundamentally created by learning from success, not from mistakes) proved to be a good way to achieve quality communication. So, with others, all to solve the same life equation, the positive result of which we all strive for—a purposeful, fulfilled, and joyful life.

When you get a chance to get to know NLP better, the

question you need to ask yourself is whether you are willing to learn how to live life to the fullest, achieve the desired results, and improve relationships with others.

If the answer is yes (you are ready for positive changes), then know that you are ready to allow all the knowledge and skills that NLP can offer you, bearing in mind that you are the one who will decide whether and how to use it in his life because the most important thing that NLP will always remind you of is that the person who has full responsibility for solving his life equation is just you.

Verbal vs. Non-Verbal Communication

To be a full member of society, communicate with other people, and achieve success, you must have communication tools, receive and transmit information, or communicate. The means of communication that a person uses are numerous and varied, but they can be combined into two groups: verbal and nonverbal.

Verbal communication and its role in human life

Verbal communication is considered to be an exclusively human form of communication. Its main means are words that have meaning and endowed with meaning, as well as messages that consist of words, such as texts or sentences.

Of course, animals also healthily exchange information. However, no matter how diverse, such communication is not speech, and the sounds emitted by animals do not signify objects or actions. They only convey a state, above all, emotionally.

Speech and language: communication and differences

Speech and language are very similar concepts, but they are not identical, although most people find it difficult to distinguish between speech and language. And here everything is very simple. Speech is a process of transmitting information, and language is how that process is carried out.

Language as a product of society

Language is social, and it is the result of long-term development, it originated and formed in society and is closely connected with a certain social environment. There are national languages that originated in the distant past. They have gathered a wealth of information about the history, culture, economy of an ethnos, mentality, way of life, and even its geographical location throughout millennial history. For example, in the Sami language— northern people living in Norway and Finland—there are more than 100 words for snow and ice, and in the Eskimo language, there are at least 500. In Kyrgyzstan, more than ten different words are used for names of different age groups of horses.

There are so-called Sub-languages: slang and dialects. They are formed in separate territorial or socio-professional communities based on the whole country. If dialects are no longer clearly expressed, then slangs are sometimes very strange in their sound and word meaning. These include youth slang, student slang, car enthusiasts, players, IT professionals, copywriters, etc.

Language is standardized both in terms of pronunciation and in terms of word order in a sentence. The rules of grammar and vocabulary are unshakable and must be followed by all native speakers; otherwise, they risk being misunderstood.

Every word has a meaning, that is, a connection with an object, phenomenon, or action. Remember, in S. Maršak's fairy tale "Cat's House," the cat explained to her guests:

351

"This is a chair - they sit on it. This is a table - they eat on it." That is, she expressed the meaning of the terms. True, many words are polysemantic (semantics is the science of meaning). So, the word "chair" can mean more than just a piece of furniture. The words "key," "pencil," "mouse," etc. have several meanings.

In addition to meaning, a word has a different meaning, which is often individual. For example, the word "beauty" is not always praised, and it can have a meaning that is directly opposite to the meaning. Even more different meanings in holistic statements, which often leads to problems in understanding people who seem to speak the same language.

Speech and its features

If the language is social, then it is individual; it reflects the speaker's personality traits: education, social affiliation, temperament, the sphere of interest, emotional state, etc. The speech characteristics of a person enable him to create a full-fledged psychological portrait.

Their speech is filled with emotion. And the words we choose, the construction of sentences, and individual meanings depend on them. And it is closely related to non-verbal means such as intonation, volume, and tone of voice.

Speech functions

Speech can be considered an activity related to human interaction. Because this interaction is diverse, it then performs several functions:

- **Communicative** - a function of transmitting information, which is considered the main one.

It is expressed in the transmission of emotions.

- **Motivation** - influencing other people to encourage them to take any action or prohibition.
- **Significant** - the function of marking, manifested in the naming of objects, phenomena, and actions. The presence of this function is significantly different from the sound communication of animals.

Speech communication has a very high value in human communities, so it is so important that a child masters speech over time. And so, for a time, the mute was considered inferior and mentally retarded. However, as psychologists and linguists have discovered, with the help of verbal means in live interpersonal communication, people do not transmit more than 20% of the information. Is it amazing? But that is the case, 80% comes from nonverbal communication.

Nonverbal means and their types

When it comes to non-verbal means of communication, they primarily resemble gestures. However, gestures are relatively small, and the "youngest" group of non-speech means. Many of them are inherited from animal ancestors and are reflexive, so a person cannot control them.

Expressive reflex reactions

Such reflex reactions include expressive movements — external manifestations of those changes in the human body that accompany various emotional states. The most well-known and most noticeable expressive movements include the following:

- Redness and blanching of the skin, accompanying

feelings of fear, anger or discomfort.
- Tremor - trembling of arms and legs, sometimes lips and vocal cords (fear, strong excitement).
- "Goosebumps" - a feeling associated with the excitation of hair follicles on the body (fear, excitement).
- Change in pupil size: dilatation - anxiety associated with a rush of adrenaline (fear, anger, impatience) and contractions (hostility, contempt, repulsion).
- Galvanic skin reaction (increased sweating) is accompanied by strong excitement, anxiety, often fear.

Because these nonverbal modes are based on natural reflex reactions that a person cannot control, these means of communication are considered to be the most sincere. A simple observation will help you identify the mismatch between a person's words and the feelings he is experiencing.

Olfactory communication tools

The oldest sources of information related to the human condition are olfactory means of communication. These are scents, primarily a person's natural scent. We have lost the ability of animals to be guided by smells, but they still influence the formation of attitudes towards other people, although we often do not notice this. The smell of sweat is traditionally thought to be unpleasant, but this is not always true. For example, the sweat of a person who is in a state of sexual arousal is saturated with pheromones, and its smell can be very appealing to a member of the opposite sex.

In addition to natural, artificial scents that create mood, excite, or relax, there is a certain value in communication.

But the role of odorous agents in communication is perhaps the least studied.

Facial expressions and pantomimes

All the emotions and feelings we experience are reflected in our behavior and the nature of the movement. Just remember how a person's movement changes depending on his mood:

- With a smooth gait, a calm person walks slowly. And someone who confidently experiences a wave of strength, activity, and positive moves, walks widely and gives the green light as he walks. Also, his shoulders are turned—these are the movements of a successful, purposeful person.
- But if the mood is bad and the emotional state is depressed, then we see the gait becoming lethargic, stirring, the arms hanging down next to the body, and the shoulders drooping. Frightened people try to shrink, seem smaller, as if hiding from the world, pulling their heads into their shoulders and trying to make minimal movements.

In addition to dynamic pantomime means, there are also static ones. The position that a person occupies during a conversation can say a lot not only about his mood but also about his relationship with his partner, about the topic of conversation, about the situation as a whole.

Human movements are so informative that there is a whole direction in social psychology that studies body language, and many books are dedicated to it. Pantomime largely depends on the physiological state of the body, the change affected by emotions. Still, these are not reflex movements, and an educated person can learn to control them, show confidence in his absence, or hide fear. It is taught to politicians, actors, business people, and people of other professions, where it is important to influence people. In this sense, nonverbal communication is more effective because people believe words less than movements and gestures.

Even more diverse shades of emotions can be expressed on a person's face because of about 60 facial muscles. They can convey the most complex and clearest emotional states. Expressions can be joyful, upset, scared, cautious, contemptuous, repulsive, arrogant, timid, and so on. It is impossible to enumerate, let alone describe, different facial expressions.

However, as a rule, a person correctly guesses the meaning of mimic movements and can be seriously offended by the partner, even if he did not say anything offensive, but his appearance was eloquent. And children learn to "read" facial expressions from early childhood. I think a lot of people have noticed how a baby starts to cry when they see a mother frowning and blooming in a smile in response to her smile.

A smile is generally unique, standing out among nonverbal means of communication. On the one hand, a smile belongs to innate reflex reactions, many more animals, especially social ones, can laugh: dogs, dolphins, horses. On the other hand, this mimic reaction is highly valued as a means of communication that people have learned to control and even put into service. However, a careful person will still distinguish a sincere smile from a false demonstration of a tooth without caries.

Gesture

These are the most conscious and controlled nonverbal means. They are fully socialized and can even perform the functions of characters. The simplest example of such signs are numbers displayed with fingers. But many other gestures indicate prohibition, invitation, gestures of consent, denial, command, obedience, and so on.

The peculiarity of gestures is that they, like the words of a formal language, belong to a particular society or ethnos. So, they often talk about sign language. Different peoples may have the same sign for different gestures. And the same gesture often has a completely different meaning.

For example, the thumb and forefinger, connected in a ring, in a tradition that came to Europe from the United States, means "okay"—everything is fine. In both Germany and France, this same gesture has an almost opposite meaning—"zero," "empty," "nonsense,"; in Italy, it is "beautiful," "big," and in Japan "money." In some countries, such as Portugal and South Africa, such a gesture is generally considered rude, and in Tunisia and Syria, it poses a threat.

Thus, for normal understanding, it is necessary to study not only the language of the words of another nation but also sign language so as not to get into a mess accidentally.

Nonverbal agents associated with speech

Among the means of communication are those that do not play an independent role and are closely related to speech activity. But they are also called non-verbal means. It is the intonation with which pronunciation is pronounced, raising and lowering the tone, pause, volume, and speed of speech. Such tools also convey information about a person's emotional state. For example, the more excited and upset a person is, the faster and louder his speech becomes, and an indecisive voice and frequent pauses in speech give an indecisive or frightened person. The innocence of speech is very important in communication; sometimes, it is enough to understand what a person who speaks an unknown language wants to communicate. Paleolinguists believe that intonation as a means of communication originated even before the most complex speech.

Considering the main types of nonverbal means, it becomes clear not only how important they are, but also that they permeate all levels of communication literally. In interpersonal communication, they can completely replace words, and then people are told to understand each other without words. It happens that your partner is offended and angry, and you are confused to ask, "Well, what did I say to that, that you were offended?" So, he was not offended by 20% of the information you conveyed in words, but that 80% was shown by non-verbal means: intonation, facial expression, gaze, etc.

Verbal or non-verbal - what it is and what kind of communication is more important

Ancient beeps warned of danger or conveyed important information that a bush with edible berries was growing nearby.

Today, verbal communication is something that not every person can do without—starting with morning coffee for messengers to talking to colleagues at work about the boss's new relationship.

Differences between types of communication

Verbal and nonverbal communication

We learn to express our thoughts with the help of words; in school, they teach reading and writing. But speech and

MANIPULATION, NLP AND BODY LANGUAGE STOICISM

text are not the only possible ways we can convey information. The first in our lives, a natural and easy way to express thoughts, with the help of gestures and body language. Throughout life, we successfully combine these two methods of communication: verbal and nonverbal communication.

What is verbal communication

Verbal communication is the most well-known way for a person to transmit and receive information using oral or written language. Such communication takes place between two or more persons. To reproduce speech, a person has clear diction, a certain vocabulary, and knowledge of the rules of communication.

Vocabulary and syntax play an important role in the process of human communication through verbal communication. The first implies a certain set of words that belong to a certain language. The second dictates the rules of thought formation.

Verbal interaction has two important functions:

Which means. With the help of words, a person can present any description, and have an idea of the information received. The dictionary helps a person to analyze the received information, build connections between the objects about which the information was received, and distribute the degree of significance (most importantly, secondarily).

Communicative. Its task is to convey attitudes towards the information received or reproduced. When we speak, it is expressed through pauses, accents, the intonation of the voice, in the letter - correct spelling, punctuation, and text instructions.

Despite the greater importance of verbal communication in a person's life, it has several disadvantages:

- The inability to articulate one's thought clearly and bring it about.
- The complexity of the perception of another's narrative.
- Misunderstanding of received information.
- Multiple meanings of the same words.
- Language difficulties between bearers of different cultures, religions, ages, etc.

Scientists believe that verbal communication occupies a minimal, in terms of importance, place in human interaction skills. The quantitative utility index is only 15% compared to nonverbal skills. Science has given them 85% importance.

How to explain the term "nonverbal communication."

Nonverbal communication is the interaction between individuals without the use of words, linguistic methods of communication. To convey thoughts, emotions, a person, in this case, actively applies body language: gestures, facial expressions, posture, visual impact. Nonverbal communications can be unconscious, include the above methods of transmitting information and special. Others include language for the hearing impaired, deaf and dumb, and Morse code.

Body language helps a person create a connection between interlocutors, give meaning to words, and express emotions hidden in the text—the peculiarity of such communication insincerity. A person unfamiliar with the psychology of such communication is unable to control their emotions and body language. All non-verbal signs have their character: imaginary, open, insecure, friendly, belligerent, and suspicious.

It is important too! Understanding possible nonverbal cues give a person an advantage over the other person.

With such knowledge, the speaker can attract the attention of the public and adapt to their point of view. Business people and managers in important negotiations, using the language of the opponent's body, decide on his honesty and the correctness of the actions taken.

In conversation, posture, gestures, body language is of the utmost importance. Scientists have discovered that with differences in verbal and visual information, perceived by man, the latter will remain in the subconscious mind. With the help of nonverbal communication, the interlocutor can convince the correctness or subordinate his or her words to doubt.

Elements of the visual relationship include:

- Manner of holding (movement, action in a given situation).
- Emotional overtones (hand movements, facial expressions).
- Body contact (touch, handshake, hugs).
- Eye contact (student change, persistence, duration).
- Movement (walking, place of residence in one place).
- Reactions (response to some events).

Types of verbal and nonverbal communication

Verbal and nonverbal means of communication refer to methods of transmitting the information. Each of them, in turn, has a broad division into species.

Verbal communication involves presenting information

using words, which are divided into the oral presentation and written speech. Each of them has subtypes. Oral speech includes:

Dialogue (exchange of information between one or more persons). Includes:

- Conversation - the exchange of information in the process of simple natural communication.
- Interview - an interactive process for obtaining certain professional information.
- Dispute - verbal exchange of information to clarify the situation, discuss the conflict.
- Discussions - reasoning in front of the audience to get a unified position on the difficult situation.
- Controversy - dispute using various scientific opinions.

Monologue - continuous performance of one person. That includes:

- Report - pre-prepared information based on journalistic, scientific materials.
- Lecture - comprehensive coverage of a particular problem of experts.
- Performance - a small presentation of pre-prepared information on a particular topic.
- A message is a small analytical summary that contains fact-based information.

Written speech is divided into:

- Instant (transfer of textual information immediately after writing, followed by an early response).
- Delayed (response information is received after a

long time or does not arrive at all).

Worth to mention! The tactile form of communication can be distinguished into a special category of verbal communication. Such communication is typical of people without hearing or sight. At the time of information transfer, they use a "handwritten letter."

Psychology studies, both verbal and nonverbal communication, allow the use of specific categories for the correct assessment of communication. As a result of many years of research, there are generally accepted ways of interpreting different forms of information transfer.

Nonverbal communication also has several types of communication. That includes:

- Kinesics - a set of body movements (gestures, postures, facial expressions, looks).
- Tactile acts - ways of touching another person.
- Sensory perception of the interlocutor from sensory organs (smells, tastes, color combinations, thermal sensations).
- Proxemics - communication takes into account the comfort zone (intimate, personal, social or public).
- Chronicle - use of temporary categories in communication.
- Paraverbal communication - transmission of certain rhythms during communication (the rhythm of voice, intonation).

Features of verbal communication

Verbal communication is characteristic only of human culture. Only people can express their thoughts in words. That is the main feature of this relationship. Also, you can mark:

- Diversity of styles (business, conversational,

scientific, artistic and others).

- Exclusivity (words can describe any sign system).
- Ability to talk about a person (culture, level of knowledge, upbringing, character).
- Consolidation of expressions, phrases for certain cultures, social groups (fascism, communism, nihilism, democracy).
- The need for implementation in life (lack of verbal communication skills can be an insurmountable obstacle to personal and professional growth).

Features of nonverbal communication

The main feature of a nonverbal relationship is the complexity of controlling one's body movements, arms, facial expressions, and other important elements of such communication. Among other features of nonverbal communication note:

- Signal duality (body signs, movements that are accepted around the world are imitated, others will vary, depending on the culture of the population).
- Truthfulness (it is impossible to hide all signals that reflect real emotions completely).
- Creating a strong connection between the interlocutor (the whole picture helps people to gather a complete picture of the person, to shape their attitude towards him).
- Strengthening the meaning of words in verbal communication.
- The ability to explain the resulting thought before appropriate verbal descriptions appear.

How verbal and non-verbal communication helps in everyday life

Verbal and nonverbal interaction are integral parts of each other. Only a combination of these forms of communication gives us a complete picture of the information received. To communicate effectively with others, you must have skills in both of these areas.

Verbal and nonverbal communication briefly leave an impression on the person a few minutes after the start of communication. The level of oral and written language will speak to the culture and intellect level of the individual. Gestures and facial expressions will inform you about your emotional state and attitude towards the situation.

Speaking in public is not good enough to prepare a speech. The speaker must have public speaking skills. Certain speech building techniques allow the audience to become interested. But words alone are not enough. The speaker should be able to stay in public, make certain gestures, perform attention-grabbing movements, and entice the intonations of the voice.

Verbal and non-verbal means of business communication are inalienable knowledge of the top management of any company. In many countries, not only company directors but also ordinary managers need to know how a person behaves during ordinary communication, during interviews, and making important decisions.

By using gestures in the conversion process, a person can try to explain things that are difficult to reproduce in words. The interlocutor usually perfectly understands what they wanted to convey. Trying to talk to strangers, without enough vocabulary, people increase the color of their voice and actively gesture during communication. In teaching mathematics, explaining some functions, the lecturer can follow the words with a pattern in the air; for him, it is a way of visualizing words for the audience—a little help in understanding.

Man, resorts to various forms and methods of communication daily. That is our natural need. Verbal and non-verbal means of communication briefly provide an opportunity to form a certain opinion about the interlocutor, speaker, or opponent from the first minutes of communication. It is impossible to isolate any as the most important way of transmitting information. Both types of communication are informative and completely complementary.

Verbal and nonverbal communication

Communication is an integral part of every person's life. Thanks to the exchange of information, the expression of our thoughts, opinions, advice, and feelings, we can normally live in society, set goals for ourselves, and confidently approach their achievement.

Not always in disputes, friendly conversations, and simple exchange of information, interlocutors openly express their thoughts and feelings.

Verbal and non-verbal communication — these two components are inherent in the communication of each of us. Being able to recognize signs of nonverbal communication during a conversation makes it much easier for people to form a correct opinion about their environment.

The essence of verbal communication - what it is and why it is needed

Spoken communication means oral and written language. With their help, we can express our opinions and thoughts, honestly discuss with a companion, argue, share impressions with friends, and talk about what we have seen, heard, read, etc.

When one speaks, the other listens very carefully and responds responsibly. It can be an agreement, anger, a dispute, or just the absorption of new interesting information. Lack of verbal communication makes every person lonely, withdrawn, and isolated from the outside world. People come to compromise through disputes, explanations, and presentations of their thoughts and find a way out of difficult situations.

Proper speech is an important factor in verbal communication, which plays for the benefit of all. How quickly a person knows how to move in conversation, answer questions asked, make new connections, and express thoughts, his place in this world will depend directly. When applying for a job, the boss pays special attention to these factors.

In addition to simple words and sentences, the emotional message plays a particularly important role. By intonation, tone, speed of clarification, you can understand the mood of the interlocutor. Shouting, dissatisfaction, criticism often provoke a reaction in the form of aggression, ignoring the interlocutor. When the boss (friend, parents) chooses the words correctly and speaks calmly, it is easier for the employee to process the received information, find the mistake, and correct it.

Means of verbal communication

The main means of this communication is human speech. Thanks to spoken (written) words, people can convey their words and thoughts and learn new information. In addition to understanding and knowing the words, you need to be able to construct them correctly in a sentence and convey them to the interlocutor.

Such ways of verbal communication include:

- Intonation plays an important role in the communication process and helps to show your attitude about the current situation. For a more pleasant conversation, you need to be smooth and calm. In this case, all the data is more understandable and perceived by the listener.
- Voice quality is another important aspect. Of course, everyone has their tone and voice. But your training and ability to own it is a game for good. After all, there are often people with very loud or quiet voices naturally. This brings inconvenience in conversations because others have to listen or feel uncomfortable because of the noise. Unreliable people usually speak almost in whispers, quickly and swallowing the ending. Ambitious and goal-oriented people express expressions, loudly, and clearly.
- Speech speed is another tool that can say a lot about a person's feelings in a particular situation. The type of temperament also plays a significant role. Melancholic and phlegmatic, compared to a sanguine and choleric person, speak slowly.
- Logical and phrase stress allows each person to highlight the most important details in their story. Our perception of the information we hear depends on putting the stress into words correctly.

What is nonverbal communication?

By ignoring the signs of nonverbal communication, people can make a big mistake. Many listen with their ears, even though the "body language" of the interlocutor is shouting the opposite.

Nonverbal language is expressed simultaneously in several forms, which differ from each other.

1. Chinese include pantomimes, facial expressions, and gestures. Very often, in emotional conversation, a person begins to wave their arms (movements), monkeys (mimicry), or assumes a closed pose with their arms crossed over their chests (pantomimes). Any subtle movements in the conversion process can be a sign of neglect, mistrust, arrogance, affection, or respect.

By learning to notice the little things and understand the mood of the interlocutor, you can avoid quarrels and unnecessary conflicts and wait for the right moment to achieve the goal and a calm mood. After all, very often, a person can see in what mood someone returned from work (or school). It can be a heavy, hunched gait, long silence, unwillingness to answer questions, or closed poses. If you approach a relative (friend) with reproaches and aggression for nothing, it is impossible to avoid an emotional response.

2. Takesika is another form of nonverbal communication. Without knowing its basics, conflicts and misunderstandings often occur between people. Touches are the main component of this type. Handshakes, hugs, pats on the shoulder, and more include taxa. Depending on how exactly these movements take place (distances, compression force, etc.), the mood or attitude of the person towards the interlocutor directly depends.

Very often in public transport at the time of the busiest traffic, people have to gather. In this case, many feel uncomfortable. Strong proximity due to crowds leads to people not intentionally invading each other's private space (range 115 to 45 cm). On a subconscious level, this is considered a danger and causes responses in the form of dissatisfaction, limitations.

3. The components of prosody are volume, intonation, and tilt of the voice. They are more recognizable and understandable signs for most people. Almost everyone knows what a raised voice and sharp intonation mean.

4. Extralinguistics - these are additional reactions during the conversation. These include laughter, sighs, incredible shouts, and pauses in speech.

Extralinguistics and judgment act as a complement to verbal communication. With their help, you can determine the mood and emotional state of the interlocutor.

Building relationships, taking into account the secrets of non-verbal communication:

In the process of communication, verbal and nonverbal types of communication are equally important for a person. Good orientation and understanding of "body language" will allow you to avoid deception, see the true feelings of your opponent, or hide your own. Speakers are specially educated and oriented to the principles of conversation and bilingual communication. Artists, philanthropists, politicians, and other speakers use self-control in all interviews and speeches. It helps not to reveal true thoughts and feelings and to avoid public condemnation.

Taking into account all the nuances of non-verbal communication and the correct recognition of its essence, each person will be able to understand the interlocutors, establish profitable relationships, and achieve their goals. The ability to speak correctly and attract listeners guarantees trust, a desire to cooperate and help.

Establish personal and business relationships or avoid

fraud, deception - all this can be if you correctly recognize the message, which manifests itself on the interlocutor's subconscious level. Sometimes facial expressions, postures, and gestures speak many more words.

Top secrets to help you recognize a person's true emotions in the communication process:

1. Excessively intense gestures indicate emotional arousal. Too fast movements are a sign that the narrator is trying to give his best to the listener. Most often, friends talk similarly about their victories and achievements that have happened in their life situations.

It is important to note that a person's nationality and temperament play a significant role in this factor. It is well known that Portuguese and Italians almost always use gestures in the conversation process. Finns are more reserved.

2. Many of us are used to reading emotions in the face of your interlocutor. Looking at the mimicry of friends, you can notice a lot of useful information.

Eye contact is an important element of any dialogue. How easy it is for people to look into their eyes, and the degree of their connection depends. With discomfort, deception, lies, and hypocrisy, a person always looks away or tries to avoid direct contact. A very long and close look at an unknown person or a stranger is evidence of a negative and aggressive attitude. In the process of communication, each participant in the conversation should be pleasant and simple.

3. Walking enters the pantomime and can say a lot about a person. Looking from the side, you can see the inner state and mood of the person walking. A raised head and a wide stride always testify to trust and a positive attitude.

Shrugging of the shoulders, heavy movements of the legs, and a lowered appearance always speak of the opposite, namely - a bad mood, thoughtfulness, and concern. Being in anger, the gait is usually sudden and fast.

4. The position of the interlocutor is another very important point that can say a lot about the mood of the interlocutor to communicate his attitude towards the narrator, and everything that happens. Everyone knows that arms crossed on your chest, speak of isolation, unwillingness to communicate, or share your opponents' points of view.

These little things play a significant role in the career-building process. After all, if during the discussion (project creation, distribution of duties) staff nod and agree, they are at the same time in a closed position - it is worth doubting their sincerity and desire for support.

By giving the person something to hold, you can push him to open it. One speaks of openness, honesty, and the desire to communicate when his body is turned and the free (not crossed) place of his legs and arms. To remove the discomfort during the promise, which is felt when you first meet, you can listen to a psychologist's advice and reflect on his positions, facial expressions, and gestures. So, you can join the wave of interlocutors and establish contact.

To reflect, that is, to repeat the pose, gestures, and facial expressions of the interlocutor. This way, you can get involved in one wave and facilitate communication.

5. A handshake can also say a lot about a man's relationship. Excessive compression indicates a person's authority and aggression. The barely visible squeezing of the fingers speaks of insecurity.

Win trust and win listeners, make them trust and make

friends - all this is possible if you control your emotions and learn how to use non-verbal communication properly. Very often, the foundation of trust in the missions of sectarian churches, administrators, politicians, and speakers lies in their proper mood. Attitude, intonation, presentation of information, view - all these little things have special meanings in the process of speech, business negotiations, looking for investors, etc.

It can take years to learn how to control your feelings and prove it with nonverbal communication fully.

Why is knowledge of nonverbal communication so important in the modern world?

Often people misunderstand the feelings and intentions of their friends. In addition to body language, inner state or habits are also inherent. Not always a closed attitude indicates a bias towards the interlocutor. It happens that a person is not in the mood to engage in a cheerful discussion and share their thoughts. It all depends on emotions and inner spirit.

Therefore, the ability to notice all the little things and compare them with each other helps to find friends, understand relatives (acquaintances), not rush to conclusions and make the right opinion.

Internal features also play a significant role. Most people have their habits. Some are silent, and others twist their lips into a tube (bite them), raise their eyebrows, and so on. Such habits cannot be attributed to nonverbal communication and equated with personal relationships.

As you begin to learn the secrets of nonverbal communication and compare subconscious signals with spoken phrases, one should pay attention to one's behavior. After introspection, by observing how the body

373

reacts to different phrases, people, and events, each person can understand others more adequately.

Being able to recognize (understand) body language, a person will be able to find true friends and like-minded people, achieve their goals, gain interest among listeners, and see negatively envious people, liars.

What exactly is verbal and nonverbal communication?

Communication is the most difficult process of interaction between people to achieve mutual understanding, gaining a certain experience. Every day a person rotates in society, establishes contacts with colleagues, households, friends. To achieve his goal in communication, a person uses verbal and non-verbal means.

Consider these two groups separately.

Verbal communication: language functions

Verbal communication is the use of words to convey information. The main tool is speech.

In communication, there are different goals: making a message, finding answers, criticizing opinions, encouraging action, reaching an agreement, etc. Depending on them, speech is built—orally or in writing—and implemented a language system.

Language is a set of symbols and means of their interaction that acts as an instrument for expressing feelings and thoughts. The language has the functions:

- Ethnic - the language of different nations has its own, which is their trademark.
- Constructive - adds thought to sentences, sound. When expressed verbally, it becomes clear and distinct. The speaker can evaluate it from the side

- what effect it produces.

- Cognitive - expresses the activity of consciousness. A person gets the most knowledge about the surrounding reality through communication, language.
- Emotional - colors of thought using intonation, timbre, diction features. The function of language works in moments when the speaker is trying to convey a certain emotion.
- Communicative language as the main way of communication. It provides a complete exchange of information between people.
- Contact setting - meeting and maintaining contacts between subjects. Sometimes communication does not carry a specific goal, does not contain useful information, and plays an important role in further relationships. It also serves as a basis for building trust.
- Accumulative - through language, a person collects, and stores acquired knowledge. The subject gets the information, wants to remember it in the future. An effective way is to record the minutes or keep a diary, but the appropriate paper media is not always at hand. Word transmission by mouth is also a good method for assimilating information. Although the book, in which everything is structured and subordinated to a certain goal, the meaning is, of course, the most valuable source of important data.

Speech activity: language forms

Speech activity - a situation in which communication between people takes place through verbal components of language. There are different types:

- A letter is a fixation of the content of a speech on paper or electronic media.
- Speech is the use of language to convey a message.
- Reading - the visual perception of information recorded on paper or computer.
- Listening is the audio perception of information from speech.

Based on the spoken form, communication is oral and written. And if we consider this depending on the number of participants, it can be divided into a mass, interpersonal.

Both literary and non-literary forms of language are different for each nationality, and they determine the nation's social and cultural status. Literary language is exemplary and structured, with stable grammatical norms. It is also presented in two forms: oral and written. The first is a speech that sounds, and the second can be read. In this case, the oral speech appeared earlier, and it was a source that people began to use: non-literary speech - dialects of individual nations and territorial features of oral language.

But the most important thing in the psychology of communication is non-verbal communication. The person unconsciously uses various signs: gestures, facial expressions, intonation, posture, position in space, etc. Let us continue to consider this extensive group.

Nonverbal communication

Nonverbal communication is "body language." One does not use speech, but uses other means that enable him to perform important functions:

- Emphasizing the importance. Without mentioning superfluous words, a person may use a gesture or take a certain attitude that indicates the importance of the moment.

- Contradictory. The speaker says a few words but thinks the exact opposite. For example, a clown on stage is uncomfortable and unhappy in life. The slightest mimicry movements on his face will help you understand that as well as exposing a lie if a person wants to hide behind an insincere smile.
- Sometimes each of us follows enthusiastic words with a gesture or movement, indicating the strong emotionality of this situation.
- Instead of words. The subject uses clear gestures and saves time. For example, shrugging or direction should not require further clarification.
- Repeat and amplify the effect of speech. An oral call is sometimes very emotional, and nonverbal means are designed to emphasize the strength of your statement. Nodding your head with the appropriate answer "Yes" or "No" signifies trust and intransigence.

Types of nonverbal means

A large group of kinesthetic - external manifestations of feelings, emotions of a person during communication. This is:

Gestures and pictures

Interlocutors evaluate each other long before the conversation begins. Posture, gait, gaze can give, in advance, a person's uncertainty or, conversely, self-confidence, with claims to power. Gestures usually emphasize the meaning of speech, give it an emotional nuance, put accents, but their abundance can also spoil the impression, especially at a business meeting. Also, in different nationalities, the same gestures mean opposite phenomena.

Intense gestures determine a person's emotional state. If his movements intersect, there are a lot of them, and then the subject is overly excited, and overly interested in passing his information to the opponent. This can be both a plus and a significant disadvantage depending on the circumstances.

Pose plays no less of a role. If the subject has crossed his arms, he is skeptical and doesn't trust you much. Perhaps closed, unwilling to communicate in principle. If the interlocutor turned his body towards you, did not cross his arms and legs, then, on the contrary, he was open and ready to listen. In psychology, for effective communication, it is recommended to deflect the opponent's attitude to achieve relaxation and trust from him.

Gest

A person's face is the main source of information about his inner state. A dark forehead or smile is a factor that determines further communication with the subject. The eyes reflect the human essence. There are seven types of basic emotions, each of which has its characteristic signs: anger, joy, fear, sadness, longing, surprise, disgust. They are easy to remember, identify, and observe in people to understand the moods of others better.

Pantomime

This may include walking. A closed person or a frustrated person is often scared, lowers his head, does not look into his eyes, but likes to look at his feet. Angry people walk with sharp movements, they hurry, but they are heavy. A confident and cheerful person has an elastic gait or a long stride. It varies depending on the health condition.

There is a part of non-verbal means, taking into account the distance between the speakers—proxemics.

Determines the comfortable distance between the interlocutors. There are several areas of communication:

Intimate - 15-45 cm, here, the person recognizes only those closest to him. The invasion of unknown personalities can be understood as a threat that requires immediate protection.

Personally - 45-120 cm, valid for good friends, colleagues.

Social and public - typical for business negotiations, important events, and speeches from the stands.

Takesika is a communication section dedicated to the role of touch. If it is wrong to apply them, without considering the differences in social status, age, field, you can get into an awkward situation, even causing conflict. Handling is the safest touch—particularly characteristic of men who check their opponents' strength through it. Choose, so to speak, which of them is the most dominant. Sometimes insecurity, or disgust, or flexibility is easily given when a person shakes only one's fingertips.

Voice characteristics

Intonation, volume, tone, the rhythm of the voice can serve as an example of a combination of two types of communication. The same sentence will sound completely different if you alter the above methods. The meaning and effect on the listener depend on it. There may also be pauses, laughter, and sighs, which are colored with additional colors.

It is important to understand that a person unknowingly transmits to his opponent using non-verbal means, more than 70% of the information. The receiving entity must interpret correctly to avoid misunderstandings and quarrels. The observer also appreciates the signals sent to the speaker, and perceives them emotionally, but interpreting all this is not always correct.

Also, a person speaks orally only 80% of what he originally intended to convey. The opponent listens carefully, distinguishes only 60%, and then forgets ten percent of the information. Therefore, it is very important to consider nonverbal cues to at least remember the purpose, the meaning of the recipient's message you wanted to convey.

5 NLP Techniques You Must Master

Correct and timely clues are enough to change the route of your life completely. Well, here you will find as many as five fresh tips.

1. Logical levels of perception

Although this is not a technique, a model of levels of perception, everyone needs to "walk" in it at least several times in life. The fact is that not only firms and society are built at these levels, but also our inner world, and we know that the inside is the outside.

"Walking" through logical levels, you will discover a lot of new things about yourself: who you are, where you are on the life span, whether you are far from the point you want to come to. And if somewhere there was a veil in front of your eyes, then after it will subside, and your life will appear before you in its true form.

These levels are arranged hierarchically, where each higher-level controls the lower ones, making them look like a pyramid. The higher the level, the stronger its influence on our lives and each level has its own "zone of responsibility" and asks the person his questions. It is to these questions that you need to answer yourself.

- **Level number 1. Environment**

<u>Questions:</u> Who am I? What do I look like? What do I have? Where do I live, work, relax? When do I live? What kind of people surround me (with whom I spend time)?

It is this level that we, first of all, begin to redraw when "everything is bad": we buy new clothes, change our hairstyles, go on a trip, meet new people, make repairs, etc. Often such "cosmetic changes" really bring improvement, the main thing here is to treat them with problems at the same level.

- **Level number 2. Behavior**

<u>Questions:</u> What do I do every day? What can I do? What do I want to be able to? What do I want to do?

This is the level of action, and it is on it that it is most useful to set goals for the result. For example: "do English every day for 20 minutes," "call mom," "write a report."

The results at this level determine the results at the first level: we are what we do every day.

- **Level number 3. Abilities**

<u>Questions:</u> What can I do? What do I want to learn?

This is the level of our skills abilities. It rises above the previous two and determines the results on them: we have the results of what we do, but we do what we can. When we learn something new, we begin to do something new, and, accordingly, we begin to receive something new.

As the saying goes, "To have something you never had, you must do something you've never done."

Answer yourself honestly, what skills do you have and what do you want to develop? It can be anything: the ability to get along with people, play the guitar, write code, learn fast.

- **Level number 4. Values and Beliefs**

<u>Questions:</u> What is the most important thing for me in life (what are my values)? What is the world like (what are my beliefs about my values)?

Manipulations at this level are corrected immediately by the three previous levels. This is what we consider the most important, and according to which laws for us, "this is important" works. For example, if one of your values is family, then you subconsciously have a list of unspoken rules about it: "family is the greatest happiness," "the sooner you start a family, the better," "if the family has problems, then everything else does not matter," etc.

Beliefs determine how we achieve our values and whether we achieve them at all. They are like the frame on which the world is built in our head, and the only difference is that for some, it is a frame for the castle, while for others, it is for the hut.

- **Level number 5. Identity**

<u>Questions:</u> Who am I? (better - in different contexts of life: at work, in sex, in the family, etc.)

This is also a matter of conviction, only now not about the world, but oneself. All these "I'm a woman, I should not work so hard!" or "I am a true specialist," "I am a great mom" - issues of identity. Throughout life, a person acquires new diverse identities, which form many results at all previous levels.

We are woven from many identities that "guide" the different contexts of our lives. They are like voices in the head that tell a person who he is and what he can. Answer yourself, who are you?

- **Level 6. Mission**

<u>Questions:</u> Why am I doing what I am doing? For what more?

This is the only level that affects something more than the interests and desires of a person, and they are subject to the interests and desires of the whole world. Here the influence of a person by his actions on the world and people around him is determined; this is the level of interaction between man and the world. Therefore, answering yourself questions of this level, you influence almost everything in your life. Often the answers to this question force people to change their whole path radically.

2. "Well-formulated result"

This technique in NLP is always and everywhere used for setting goals. It's a shame that it is widely known only in narrow circles, because, setting goals for it is the only right option in which your goals are realized by themselves. Sabotage and procrastination leave a person simply rolling toward the goal, like a bowling ball.

Why does it happen? It's just that the "KhSR" technique allows you to neutralize the only personified person and, concurrently, your main enemy—your brain. Special formulations help to reach your limbic system (unconscious) and connect it with the neocortex (consciousness). It is precisely the coordinated work of these two guys that is the key to achieving all goals.

3. "I'm the other way around"

This is also a powerful technique that will enrich your picture of the world with experience, wisdom, and new resources. Having done it, you will feel how much easier it became for you to do what was previously given with a creak, you look at your problems and complex tasks in work or communication from a new angle.

The essence of the technique is as follows: you need to "turn on" your opposite for several hours, and all this time think and act based on it.

For instance. There you are—an active, opportunity person. You like to see life in wide, large strokes, without bothering with the details. You make decisions in your life because you know that your decisions are the best.

And now they say to you: now, dear friend, stay with yourself for several hours with a reflective, thoughtful, slow brake. And do not see opportunities everywhere! Replace strategy with tactics and procedures. Turn on meticulousness. And more, more attention to detail!

Or vice versa: you, all so procedural, thoughtful, doubting, and attentive to details, will transform into an active, large-scale, decisive person who decides to trifle with an internal reference. Perhaps even with signs of a tyrant. Why not? After all, the medal always has two sides.

I warn you, and the first thought will be: "What a horror! How can one live like that?" And then ... Then a new model of behavior spreads heat throughout the body, and you become so unusually good and interesting. And the boundaries of the possible are being pushed.

In both cases, you will learn very, very much.

Often—exactly what you are missing.

4. Creative Walt Disney Strategy

This approach is indispensable for a good result (or at least minimizing losses) for both your business projects and simply multifactor ideas like moving or changing jobs. It gained popularity because it was used each time by Walt Disney and his team to create cartoons. And given their fantastic popularity, this is more than a self-sufficient argument in favor of the method, agree?

The bottom line is to think about a task/project with three roles:

- Dreamer
- Realist
- Critic

Dreamer looks at the idea through the prism of endless possibilities. He describes all the most amazing results, the most daring desires, gives out the most daring and absurd ideas. Imagine that your resources are not limited, and you can realize any of your whims, and start writing down your wildest fantasies, the most beautiful result.

At this stage, it is better to glue the mouth of the cynical part of your personality in advance—she will still have time to speak out. Now let yourself go on a fantasy flight, where your possibilities are endless.

Being in this state of mind, ask yourself the following questions:

- "What do I want?"
- "What is the ideal option?"
- "What benefit will it bring when it is realized?"
- "What opportunities will come with implementation?"

A realist looks at an idea in terms of numbers. He studies the market and all the components that can affect the equation's outcome to sensibly calculate how many resources will be needed to implement the idea. He evaluates expectations and reality to find a compromise.

If the dreamer thought strategically, then the realist's paraphyly is a tactic. It makes a step-by-step route of optimal movement to the plan.

Thinking like a realist, find answers to the following questions:

- "How much time will I need?"
- "How much money will I need?"
- "What knowledge and skills do I need?"
- "Who can help me in achieving and how to persuade them to do this?"

The critic must look at the task with eyes filled with doubt. Here you play the role of the prosecutor, look out for all possible and impossible pitfalls, difficulties that you have to stumble on and assess the height of the barriers you have to jump.

These are the questions you need to answer yourself honestly:

- "What can hinder implementation or slow it down?"
- "What does this project look like for a client? What might he not like about it?"
- "At what stage can something go wrong, and why?"
- "If an idea is realized, what will it rob me of? What will I sacrifice?"
- "Who can be against this idea, and why? How can I get around this resistance?"
- "Is it worth it?"

5. "Change in personal history"

If traumatic events have happened in your life against which complexes or anxiety have grown in you, then this technique is for you. It works great when you need to work on:

- Childhood grievances, unsuccessful experiences (disgraced, failed, offended, etc.)
- The repeated negative situation, "on the same rake."
- Toxic beliefs leading to difficulties ("after 40 there is no life", "you won't earn much money," "not with my happiness," etc.)

Remember, you do not need to work through this technique for injuries associated with the care of loved ones or physical violence (if any) if you have not undergone NLP practice or are not under the supervision of a professional. Take something simpler, preferably from childhood.

The main idea of this technique is this: any negative event injures us only when we do not have enough resources to deal with it. Therefore, to remove the traumatic effect, you need to give yourself these resources in the past.

The bottom line is: You "enter" an unpleasant memory and change it for the better, giving yourself the resources, you need for this past. Resources—this is exactly what you did not have then, to live this situation easily, to get out of it as a winner. Therefore, almost anything will be a resource: support, money, indifference, self-confidence, sense of humor, arrogance, beauty, and so on.

CHAPTER 12

STOICISM FOR LIFE

What's Stoicism?

Stoicism is the ability or the willpower of an individual to control their feelings or emotions. Someone stoic, therefore, stands firm in the face of adversity. For example: "The woman showed stoicism in the face of the tragedy," "You have to have stoicism at the business level if you want to progress," "When I had to be left out of the team, I accepted it with stoicism."

The notion of Stoicism is also used to refer to a philosophical school founded by the Greek Zenon de Citio some three hundred years before Christ. Stoic doctrine promoted the mastery of the passions that generate disturbances, appealing for this to reason and personal virtue.

According to Stoicism, the key to happiness is found in ataraxia: the balance that is achieved when there are no troubles. To achieve ataraxia, the individual must remain oblivious to material vicissitudes and must refrain from making judgments.

Stoicism doubted the existence of sensitive knowledge since perception depends on the subject. Therefore, given the various situations that the same person is going through or the factors that affect the object, it is impossible for there to be an immediate reproduction of a thing.

The Stoic, therefore, intended to live according to reason

and free from passions. Stoicism was invited to dominate the reactions through self-control since Stoicism understood love as a deviation from the rational nature of the human being. So, he fostered a life in tune with natural laws.

One of the current figures of Stoicism is the professor of philosophy, Massimo Pigliucci, born in Italy in 1964, who works in the North American university system called City University of New York. In his book, "How to be Stoic", published by the Ariel publishing house, he offers us a series of tips to take advantage of this current of thought born three centuries before Christ to live better.

According to Pigliucci, there is no single way or group of doctrines to follow to respect the foundations of Stoicism, and this differentiates it from certain religions. Stoics move through life, combining a series of practices and techniques that they find in their own experience, and thus they build their paths individually.

To experience Stoicism in the 21st century, the author offers specific "spiritual exercises" that we can apply in our day-to-day activities:

* **Temperance:** It is a reflection about the fleeting nature of things. This should be practiced with a particular focus on the things that are most precious to you, those that benefit us the most or that we value the most, to understand that everything and everyone ceases to exist sooner or later.

* **Anticipation:** It is good to contemplate the potential consequences of our plans, to avoid being surprised. In this way, we will have more control over stressful situations.

* **Self-control:** We should not be complicit in those who try to hurt us since their provocation can only work if we allow

it. The impulses can lead to our destruction, and we must control them trying to think cold just before taking significant decisions.

* **Solidarity:** Stoicism seeks a harmonious life with our environment, and that is why it proposes to empathize with the pain of others as if it were our own.

* **Observation:** The human being tends to give opinions much more frequently than to observe in silence, which prevents him from enriching himself. It is imperative to find the content before sharing it, to say only things that can serve some purpose, instead of spending saliva and energy covering the silence, one of our most valuable resources.

The quick guide to understanding the Stoics

Stoicism was one of history's most influential doctrines. When we learn that someone is approaching it "with the theory," it's generally because under the Stoics' teachings they face life, and that's because this philosophical movement has some methods to make it simpler for us, if not to solve it. For those who want to get closer to it, here's a short description.

If there is an ideology that has succeeded in dazzling people of all circumstances and ages, it is Stoicism. This branch of thought, whose foundation we owe to Zenón de Citio, would remain at the forefront of philosophical culture for no less than half a millennium (from the 3rd century BC to the 2nd century AD) and would maintain influence throughout the following centuries as history has rarely seen. We are going to review here its most outstanding characteristics that perhaps explain the reason for such success.

One philosophy, two proper names

As we have said, the founder of Stoicism was Zenón de Citio, a disciple of Crates de Tebas. He developed his thinking from the cynical theses of his teacher (hence the precise harmony between both philosophies in various aspects).

However, who made Stoicism a relevant doctrine was Chrysippus of Solos, who directed the Stoa (the Stoic school, located on the painted portico of Athens) from 232 BC. C. to 204 A. C. Thanks to his enormous dialectical talent and his gigantic production—nothing less than 700 works, of which sadly only fragments have reached us—Chrysippus managed not only that Stoicism was a highly relevant philosophy, but that the Stoa arrived to overcome Plato's Academy and Aristotle's Lyceum.

Although there were other renowned philosophers in this school—such as Cleanthes, Panetius, Posidonius, and his most famous disciple, Cicero—we would have to wait for the Roman Empire for the new batch of philosophers of enormous fame to arrive, with Seneca, Epictetus and the emperor philosopher Marco Aurelio.

Man, and his morals, main concern

The center of the Stoics' study is self-explanatory: man. Everything of his philosophy is for man, and more importantly, his morals. At the service of the individual, philosophy, physics, and ethics pose an objective that never seems to lose direction: to teach us to live according to our nature.

The Stoics accept two principles: matter and reason. But in fact, the latter is not something different; we can find it all over the place. According to the Stoics, rationality and Nature are identified, as Nature is the creator of the universe and its substance at the same time. It is because

391

of this that we can assume the world's existence is moral.

Everything, so to speak, is bound by natural law, a universal basis. A union that also embraces man, linking him to the universe, as he is a logical being as well. All of this system shapes an inexorable chain of already-established relationships, triggers, and consequences that we perceive as fate. And stoics are deterministic. They believe the world 's events are pre-established, and we can do very little to change them.

Autarchy: to be happy with self-sufficiency

Like the cynics, the Stoics find that the sage's goal is to ensure that he does not need anything to make life complete. So how does that joy come to be? To live by our moral existence, that is to say, to live virtuously.

Since the sage lives and is correctly decided in harmony with the world, the Stoic ideal is the one Epictetus expressed to us: assistance and resignation. Support it, because your fate will be the same whether or not you like it. It's a divinity-established scheme you can't run from, so we have no choice but to obey it meekly or let it take us away. Giving up, because finding peace will always be easier for us, and with it the desired happiness, if our impulses and appetites do not overpower us. If we have few needs and know how to regulate our emotions, it will be very easy to live happily, hence the value of both laws.

All inside and nothing outside

The point of departure for Stoic ethics is that true happiness depends only upon ourselves. What makes stoic an impregnable character is these ideas. Everything outside matters to him, because all his efforts are to attain goodness, what depends on him, what no one can take from him... Inside. That's the secret to their might.

The Stoic is not afraid of something, no matter how bad things go, as he has achieved ataraxia, the imperturbability of mind. This concept, in the same way, is the ultimate goal that Buddhists seek to attain enlightenment. Due to its existence, the stoic thus continues to live in utter harmony. Neither feelings, nor joy, nor pain or riches has control over a man who accepts his destiny and only cares about living virtuously. The Stoic puts himself above material objects and is fully autonomous, focusing on his inner life.

A sensualist theory

The theory of knowledge of the Stoics starts, like that of Aristotle, the empiricists, or the positivists, from sensible experience. That is to say, of the senses. For the Stoics, it is a process that goes through different stages. In the first place, what comes to us through the senses leaves a representation (an impression, says Zeno) in our reason, which, as we have already said, is the part of "divinity" that we possess and which connects us with the rationality of nature. However, these representations are not yet knowledge. If we simply accepted that as a sample of reality, we would not be before expertise, but before an opinion. For it to become knowledge, that representation must have evidence that invites intelligence to accept it. That consent must be given by hegemonikon, the Self. Understanding comes when the data that the senses offer us pass through the sieve of rationality.

Cosmopolitan

The Stoics, unlike the Cynics, did not despise their peers or society. To the cynic, all those who lived wrongly were only fools, who deserved to be insulted and ridiculed for their stupidity. An architect of it was Diogenes, famous for his rifirrafes with subjects of all fur. However, the cynical acid criticism did not try to correct or serve as an example to his fellow men but was content to belittle them.

The Stoics, for their part, have this critical vision, but they do not share the form. In fact, for them, the idea of community is fundamental. Now, faithful to their thinking and their belief that the fine thread of rationality unites the world, they considered themselves citizens of the world. They did not believe in being here or there for reasons of birth or culture. They were of reason and virtue wherever they reigned.

Four keys to building your resilience

Daily life is peppered with difficulties, small and large obstacles that must be learned to overcome. None of us came into this world with a manual of perfect existence, the one that gives us guidelines for each problem, for each crisis and each difficulty. Therefore, it is essential to develop your resilience. Only then can you face all the adversities that may surprise you in life.

We come into this world like fallen from a strange fireplace called destiny, luck or providence. We are offered a family more or less useful, a society more or less democratic, which grows with certain norms and values, and a social circle in which we create ourselves as we grow.

Continuous growth

As growing people that we are, it is always worth learning from all those trends that come our way, and that can offer us improvement mechanisms. And resilience is one of them, and it is nothing more or less than the ability to face problems and adapt as well as possible to those bumps, to those curves in the form of losses, failures, disappointments, trauma, and even stressful situations.

We must be clear, being resilient does not mean at all, not

feeling discomfort, emotional pain, or difficulty in the face of adversity. Resilience is the ability to take the pain, accept it, and learn from it. At the same time, we manage both our emotions and our responses to cope with adversity in the best possible way.

It is not easy, we know, learning to be resilient is a long process that requires time and a lot of self-knowledge. But once mastered and understood, we will feel more capable and more protected. Let's see then the strengths and some keys to develop your resilience.

1. Insight ability

The first of the keys to building your resilience is understanding yourself. For this, knowing how to listen to yourself and speaking with that inner voice connected with that nervous skein of feelings and emotions will be essential. To achieve this, stop and simply attend to that inner rumor that shapes you as a vulnerable and also strong person.

It is the ideal time to practice mindfulness. This technique will allow you to attend to your thoughts. A fundamental aspect is not to judge any thought that crosses your mind. We just have to watch them and let them go like clouds in the sky. In this way, little by little, we will investigate within ourselves and meet the demons that torment us. So, as we get to know each other, we will be able to face situations much more calmly and deeply.

2. Essential motivation

Adversity can embrace you with its cold and terrible cloak. He will want to take your breath away and plunge you into a lonely corner. But you must not let yourself be defeated.

There are many other things beyond pain, loss, or frustration. Your project, your need to keep going, to hope again for life and yours. We all must have an existential plan, a goal on the horizon for which to continue smiling every morning.

From Buddhist psychology, they defend that adversity should serve as an impulse to learn. Both good and evil can be determined. Therefore, instead of looking at problems as a hindrance in our lives, we see them as a possibility of personal development. Without a doubt, we will be opting for an option that will remarkably enrich us.

3. Emotional self-regulation

It is good that you feel the anger, the pain, the grief, the sadness... it is essential to cry and let off steam. But once we have passed this stage, it is time to get up and regulate these emotions, rationalizing them first towards acceptance and then towards overcoming.

Know your feelings, accept them, and guide them towards an optimal and healing process that manages to strengthen you. Knowing how you feel at each moment is the first step to know yourself deeply. This way, you will develop your resilience.

4. Positive attitude and self-confidence

It is not just a label. It is not that phrase that sells so much and that you find so many times on the walls of your social networks: Maintaining a positive attitude towards life is a necessity. We know that sometimes it is not easy, that darkness devastates us without anyone expecting it, without anyone having prepared for it and that it may be impossible to show a smile in such circumstances.

But rest assured that no dawn could be overcome at dusk,

and what seems so black to you today will gradually lose that intensity if you face it with strength and optimism. And above all, with confidence in yourself.

Being rich depends on your state of mind

How to get rich and live happily achieving financial freedom? Through a model with which to be happy, in addition to reaching our job and economic goals. One of the secrets to making the human being happy depends to a greater extent on his mental state and that of the people around him.

It all starts with the dreams and goals that each person has, depending on age, personal situation, purchasing power, the lifestyle they can lead. Whoever tries to kill our thoughts does so because first, they have stopped believing in theirs. In reality, you should not merely dream of becoming rich: you must do everything possible to improve, learn, and expand as individuals. For this reason, we must define ourselves. We must also bear in mind that we will follow the most appropriate path to achieve the objectives that we set ourselves whenever we are ourselves.

What I have learned in recent years is that success has no secrets. It has a simple recipe, which is made up of determination, continuous training, techniques, and correct psychology. If I have to give a percentage, I would say that psychology represents 80%, because it allows you to see opportunities where there are problems. People overestimate what they can do in 1 year and underestimate what they can do in 5 years. Focusing on what you want is one of the keys to success for people who get results.

It is essential to have a mindset ready to make sacrifices to achieve the proposed goals. Even so, it could be understood that problems with money are not linked to the class to which each person belongs. Paradoxically, those with a lot of money have much bigger problems to solve.

Surely among the goals that make you happy is not to work all day and get home tired, and you do not feel like doing anything else. You may want to have more free time and more money to spend more time with your family and friends, dedicate yourself to a new hobby or fulfill one of those dreams ... who is preventing you from achieving this goal? Although this lifestyle may seem unattainable, it will only be feasible if we become financially free.

Money is only an amplifier that works by increasing what you already are. It will give you more chances, more freedom, more choice, but money alone cannot make you happy. Only an excellent psychological approach to things and people, together with the ability to manage events and moods, will make you happy. You want the results, but the results depend on your actions. And on what do your steps depend? Of the state of mind, you are in. And the ability to locate yourself in a particular state of mind allows you to develop actions that lead you to specific results.

When I first started dealing with money, I underestimated the implications of using the body for managing moods and money in particular. In reality, behind any performance, there are types of breathing and use of the body itself, such that through a specific position and breathing in a certain way, the mind's productive states can be accessed.

It is essential to know what position money occupies in the hierarchical scale of our life. And the correct hierarchical level should be:

1. People
2. Money
3. Things

In this way, those people who put money before other people will not be more productive. Human beings and interpersonal relationships come first than any number. It is having good relationships with people that makes us truly rich. In the second place, we find money. With it, you can buy things, but with words, you can't necessarily buy money. With money, I can buy a car, but with that car, once I am out of the dealership, I cannot get the same amount of money.

How have we learned to walk? Falling, rising and falling again, until we managed to stay on our feet. The same thing happens to someone who wants to get rich. To achieve this, you have to do something that you like and take moments of rest so that in this way, your mental health accompanies your dreams and motivations, with which you will finally achieve that financial freedom that we long for.

The Most Important Stoic Philosophers

The term stoic originates in the term stoicism. Today these terms mean an aversion to all feelings, whether it's excruciating joy, hate or a kind of impassivity passion. The stoicism philosophy, though, is completely new and follows a very new range of concepts.

With time, the philosophy of stoicism developed particularly with the coming of Rome, the original philosophy was rendered in Athens by a Greek philosopher called Zeno of Citium. The more prominent stoic philosophers may be Seneca (the younger) and Marcus Aurelius (Rome's stoic emperor).

The basic teachings of stoicism are that bad emotions come from bad judgment, and the core of stoicism is to overcome these destructive emotions through control. They also say that true happiness is achieved through virtue. Stoics presented the philosophy as a way of life through which you can become a sage.

A sage is someone who has achieved ethical and intellectual perfection. Many philosophers (including Seneca) emphasized the belief that happiness is achieved through virtue. With this being true, a sage would be immune to misfortune since misfortune causes unhappiness, and through virtue, there is no unhappiness. This gives a powerful sense of controlling one's fate.

Stoicism also concerns itself heavily with fate and human free will. They believe in determinism (the idea that all future events are controlled by all past events in philosophy similar to fate), but they also believe in individual free will. This mixture of belief produces both a sense of acceptance of what will be while still trying to change the future for the better.

One of the virtues that stoicism talks about is control. One has to be in control of themselves, and many stoic philosophers talk of how a wicked man is like a dog tied to a cart, and he will go where he will go, but a stoic or virtuous man will go where he chooses. The set of virtues that stoicism talks of are not religious ethics, to say that God laid down a set of rules and will be unhappy if you break these rules. But rather a set of naturalistic ethics. That is even if there is no afterlife, you should still be a good person simply because it is good to be a good person.

Stoicism also puts a lot of importance on the idea of logic. They believe that only through logic and truth can knowledge be attained. Though this seems common logic in today's society, it is important to look back then when the temples told you why a storm had blown in and why the stars had the patterns they had.

One of the greatest lines of stoicism is as follows. Quoted from Marcus Aurelius. "Say to yourself in the early morning: I shall meet today ungrateful, violent, treacherous, envious, uncharitable men. All of these things have come upon them through ignorance of real good and ill... I can neither be harmed by any of them, for no man will involve me in the wrong, nor can I be angry with my kinsman or hate him, for we have come into the world to work together".

Thinking Like a Stoic

There are several ways to understand philosophy. From understanding the three stoic disciplines to building everything on the principle of living according to nature to deriving the stoic principles from his vision of the physical, logical, and ethical foundations.

Thinking about philosophy from different points of view has innumerable advantages, both practical and theoretical.

In this section, we will suggest a simple mnemonic that is related to the first principle: Ignorance of external action. The four Aces: acceptance, conscience, action, and antifragility.

Stoic acceptance

Stoic acceptance is about accepting what is out of your control. Human minds are prone to agonize over the future or the past. We can spend hours ruminating on completely fictitious events. Seneca reminds us to stay in the present. What is out of our hands we can accept.

True happiness is enjoying the present, without anxiously depending on the future. Not to have fun with hopes or fears, but resting satisfied with what we have, which is enough for the one who has nothing.

When we are agitated by what is beyond our control, we are stealing time. We are distracting ourselves from living by our values.

However, it is too easy to desire impossible things. How do you handle this? Marcus reminds us: "When you face someone else's shamelessness, ask yourself this: Is a world without shameless possible? No. Then don't ask the impossible."

Importantly, this does not mean suppressing negative emotions. When we fight negative emotions, they can arise with a vengeance. Instead, we can accept that we will experience negative emotions and direct our attention to what matters.

We can expect things to go wrong in the external and internal world (feelings, emotions, personality, actions, principles, and values). Will it be difficult? The Stoic can accept difficulties and move on.

Stoic Consciousness

Stoic consciousness is based on stoic acceptance. The crucial idea is that it is our mind that causes us suffering. Instead of getting caught, we can take responsibility for our thoughts and actions.

When we lack consciousness, we pay attention to what others think of us, our state, and the external that is in our control. However, these things are not the true cause of our suffering. It is our value judgments that cause us suffering. We would not be held hostage to what others think of us if we did not believe that another person's value judgment is important. Instead, we must focus on what is under our control, our thinking, and our actions. YOU CAN TRAIN YOUR MIND, and THIS IS THE GREAT NEWS.

Epictetus mentions the following, pay attention:

Practice saying to each harsh appearance, "YOU ARE AN APPEARANCE, AND IN NO WAY WHAT YOU SEEM TO BE."

Taking control of our thinking means embracing reality. We are prone to adding value judgments and additional stories to whatever happens to us. This can be helpful, but it often clouds our judgments. We are especially vulnerable when we forget that our thoughts are not reality, that the stories we tell ourselves are often false, and that they retain control over their thoughts.

Stoic action

The previous two themes of Stoicism focused on the mind. Action discipline is about acting in the world. Both disciplines are useless if not combined with the correct action. Marco Aurelio tells us: "Don't waste any more time arguing about what a good man should be, be one."

We have control over our characters. Over time, through small actions, we build habits. It is up to us to act wisely, moderately with courage and justice. We are responsible for our actions. Our actions should never depend on other people.

It can be easy to get distracted with our colleagues, the media, daily circumstances, and forget everything mentioned. This is why acceptance and stoic awareness are so important to the action. What matters is what you do.

Stoic antifragility

Finally, the Stoics were antifragile. Rather than simply being resilient and surviving, the famous Stoics were driven by stressors. This led Nassim Taleb to label the Stoics as "Buddhists with an attitude."

What antifragility does is that it helps us get out of our heads. We are waiting for negative action, instead of asking, "How can I make this go away?" Let us ask, "How can I use this to drive action?" And then we act.

It is important to accept what we cannot change, but it is also important to ingeniously seek the good, whatever the obstacles. Don't lean too much towards the acceptance side.

Each of these aspects of stoicism: acceptance, awareness, action, and anti-fragility are mutually related. A person can go much deeper in a certain aspect.

How to Become a Warrior-Philosopher

Japanese culture is millennial, and throughout its history, it has given great value to the virtues in combat. Unlike what happens in other latitudes, the Japanese fighter must be full of values to be worthy. The word bushido speaks precisely of this and is translated as the warrior's path.

This warrior path, or bushido, talks about a code of ethics that samurai applied. It contains a series of principles, but above all, seven values, which should govern behavior. It is said that members of the ruling class were taught from an early age.

The code name samurai also know the warrior's path. This condenses principles of Buddhism, Confucianism, and other Eastern philosophies. It is still a valuable guide to life. These are the seven virtues and teachings that it exalts.

1. Courage, an indispensable virtue of being free

According to the way of the warrior, only when you have

courage can you be free. It is the courage that allows us to live fully, without the bonds that fear imposes. It takes courage to decide to act, especially to do great things.

Courage is not blind fearlessness. For it to be true courage, it must be accompanied by intelligence and strength. Fear exists, but we must not allow ourselves to be overcome by it. Instead, we should replace it with caution and respect. This is how true courage will emerge.

2. Let courtesy never fail

In the way of the warrior, courtesy is not simply a set of kind gestures or good manners. In reality, it is a virtue closely related to respect for the other, even if he is an enemy.

Courtesy is, above all, respect and consideration for the other, regardless of the circumstances. This means not being cruel or making unnecessary demonstrations of strength or power. It is a virtue that shows character and a lot of inner strength.

3. Compassion must always be present

The strength and power you have must be used for the good of all people. This is indicated by way of the warrior, who also insists on the enormous value of solidarity. This is a forcefully adorning feature.

Compassion is not just a feeling; it must be translated into concrete actions. Whenever someone can be helped, it should be done. And if you don't have the opportunity to help him, you have to find that possibility.

4. Justice above all

The way of the warrior says that justice has no half measures. According to this ancient wisdom, the just comes from defining what is right and differentiating it from what is not. The right is rewarded, and the wrong is punished.

To be fair is always to seek to act in the right way. This should not depend on what others say but on the person himself. Everyone knows in his heart what is fair and what is not. He must only follow that light that emanates from himself.

5. Loyalty is characteristic of strong and noble spirits

What you say or do belongs entirely to you. Therefore, the consequences are also ours. Hence, you must have a great sense of responsibility before acting or expressing yourself.

Loyalty is, above all, loyalty to oneself. Ability to be consistent or coherent. To that extent, it is also a commitment to answer for actions and words. Loyalty only belongs to the strongest and noblest.

6. The word and sincerity

For samurai, the word has immense value. It is not spoken by speaking, nor is it said by saying. So, on the warrior's path, words are equivalent to acts. When something is said, it is as if it was already done.

In this philosophy, the value of a promise is removed. This is not necessary. Suffice it to say that something will be done to commit to doing it. This is only possible for those who are completely honest with themselves and with others.

7. Honor exalts the human being

According to the warrior's path, the greatest virtue of all is an honor. Being honorable means acting upright, regardless of the circumstances. Fulfill duty and adhere to values, regardless of whether others approve this or not.

Honor is associated with self-respect. This implies not allowing yourself to fall into unethical or despicable behaviors. Honor is so important in this philosophy that if you lose, the only way to get it back is by taking your life.

The most interesting thing about the warrior's path is that being such an ancient ethical code, the values it promotes remain valid. The world would be very different if, in each conflict, or each confrontation, we applied those valuable principles of the samurai warriors.

CONCLUSION

How to manipulate and doing mind manipulation is a skill that is innate to each of us. Everybody is born with it. Each individual reacts and interacts with one another. That is how manipulation works in society. It brings people in and out. It is the way we communicate with one another.

How to manipulate is as important as how to communicate and relate to people. When we relate and convey our thoughts to our peers, we lure them into listening to us and understand our own beliefs if not agree to it. We base our success on how people respond to the thinking that we have. If we get favorable responses from people, we will feel satisfied, and that satisfaction builds up our whole being. If we somehow fail to be understood, we often resort to arguments because of our subconscious fights for the manipulative tactics of others. We do not want to be manipulated, but somehow, we tend to forget that every decision and actions that we take are only products of mind manipulation by others.

The saddest part is that we often fail to realize that we need to manipulate to survive and to be successful. If we only aim for survival, we don't need to practice a lot of mind manipulation techniques. But should we settle for less? We want to become more than and larger than ourselves.

The first thing we need to consider is that we need to understand that manipulation is not negative. Somehow, negative connotations impact the way we deal with people. We thought that being frank and direct about telling others our need is a kind of manipulation and, therefore, bad. We thought that when we ask someone to do the things our way it is a kind of manipulation, then we refrain from asking for help. We then fail to realize that we miss the chance to have a new door for an opportunity.

We take pride too much in ourselves about playing fair while the world is not. What we are trying to achieve, though, is not to trick everyone and mean them bad. We like to open our eyes to the opportunities that are just waiting to be unlocked. If we put up a cocktail party because we want to invite and be acquainted with somebody who we know can help us well with our interest, it is a kind of technique that we need.

Mind manipulation is within us. We do not need special psychic power to be able to manipulate people and be successful. We need to know the techniques and skillfully practice it.